The Frontier Republic

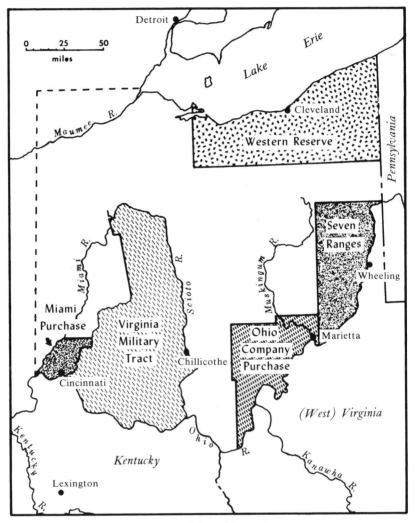

Detroit

Lake Erie

0 25 50
miles

Cleveland

Western Reserve

Pennsylvania

Maumee R.

Miami R.

Scioto R.

Muskingum R.

Seven
Ranges

Wheeling

Miami
Purchase

Virginia
Military
Tract

Ohio
Company
Purchase

Marietta

Chillicothe

Cincinnati

(West) Virginia

Ohio R.

Kentucky

Kanawha R.

Lexington

Kentucky R.

The Ohio Country

Map drawn by Robert L. Brewer.

The Frontier Republic

Ideology and Politics in the Ohio Country, 1780–1825

Andrew R. L. Cayton

The Kent State University Press
Kent and London

Library of Congress Catalog Card Number
ISBN 0-87338-332-X
Manufactured in the United States of America
The paper in this book meets the guidelines for permanence and durability of the
Committee on Production Guidelines for Book Longevity of the Council on Library
Resources.

Library of Congress Cataloging-in-Publication Data

Cayton, Andrew R. L.
    The frontier republic.

    Bibliography: p.
    Includes index.
    1. Ohio—Politics and government—1787–1865. I. Title.
F495.C35   1986   977.1′03   86–4706
ISBN 0-87338-332-X

FOR MARY AND ELIZABETH

Contents

Preface

The most critical period in any revolution is the one that follows the rejection of an ancien régime, the time when people try to make sense of why they have fought and what they have achieved. Conflict invariably characterizes such eras, and post-revolutionary America was no exception. Indeed, Americans in the Early Republic were often seriously at odds with each other.[1]

This situation was inevitable. Once the unity engendered by opposition to a common enemy dissipates, revolutionary movements generally splinter into different groups that compete with each other for the right to shape the values and structures of the new society. Each group justifies its claim to leadership by describing its opponents as base and selfish betrayers of the true revolution. Conflict among factions over the proper interpretations of the meaning of the past and the promise of the future has often undermined the more radical characteristics of revolutions. But in the aftermath of the American Revolution the competition for control of the new nation and the definition of the revolutionary legacy that would shape it was more subtle and the conclusion more synthetic than elsewhere.

In this study of ideological conflict in post-revolutionary America, I have concentrated my attention upon the thoughts and activities of Americans concerned with the development of government and society in what became the first state created out of the Northwest Territory—Ohio. Many Americans in the late eighteenth century were convinced that the new republic would reach its apogee in the West.[2] But they were less united in envisioning the specific character and structures of the society to be established there. Indeed, the settlement of the trans-Appalachian frontier intensified the already pronounced ideological confusion of the Early Republic. If a frontier can be defined as a zone of cultural competition, a region lacking widely accepted political institutions or social norms, a place in which values are in flux and the locus of sovereignty uncertain, then the Ohio Country in the late eighteenth and early nineteenth centuries qualifies on all counts.[3] In fact, the lack of ideological cohesion produced political bickering of the highest (or lowest) order.

But it was neither insignificant nor unproductive bickering. Ultimately, the most impressive thing about the settlement of Ohio was how quickly the frontier period passed, how rapidly men resolved their differences into a relatively stable society fully integrated into the larger Atlantic world. The early history of Ohio is a story of both disintegration and reintegration. Despite the many physical and economic changes that marked the lives of settlers, there was a continuity to the political debates of the Early Republic. Whatever the specific issue, the settlers of Ohio constantly returned to larger questions of sovereignty and the viability of a liberal, democratic society. Like many Americans in the decades that followed the founding of the United States, they were engaged in a generation-long debate over the question of whether a society constructed around autonomous individuals without the guiding influence of any government or institution could long endure.

There were two dominant points of view. The first, which I associate with squatters and the Jeffersonian Republican proponents of statehood for Ohio, emphasized the primacy of local sovereignty and demanded the fullest possible expression of democratic rights. To argue that many Americans in the Early Republic behaved democratically is not to say that they believed in democracy as modern Americans tend to define it—mass participation in choosing a government; rather, it is to say that they exhibited a style of behavior which involved denying the inherent superiority of any person or institution. Having explicitly rejected an ancien régime that rested on patronage and deference, they were eager to establish a world where a relatively open competition of talents among white males would be the primary path to wealth and success. Their foremost concern was with personal independence or liberty.[4]

While such beliefs were powerful and pervasive, an important number of Americans, the Federalists and those who shared their philosophy, were not convinced of either their righteousness or their practicality. Seeking to bring regularity to what they perceived to be a disordered society, they called for strong institutions to arbitrate among and guide the interests of the citizens of a national society marked by increasing pluralism and economic complexity. Their understanding of history and classical republican conceptions of government taught them that the practice of "democratical equality" would eventually degenerate into anarchy and tyranny. Thus, they continually preached the necessity of social interdependence.[5]

In this study, I have tried to analyze the origins, development, and partial resolution of the controversy that arose between these two points of view. I have drawn my evidence primarily from the writings and actions of men involved in what we would call political activities. But I do not intend this book to be an account of party organization and strategy; readers interested in such topics should consult the fine work on early Ohio politics by Jeffrey P. Brown and Donald Ratcliffe.[6] Rather, my concern is with the history of men thinking about the natures of government, society, and the exercise of power. More often than not, the white male settlers of Ohio gave the fullest expression to their ideas in the course of championing a specific cause or person. While the book takes the shape of a narrative of political events, my goal is to elucidate and evaluate the ideological origins and ramifications of those events rather than to tell the story of the events themselves.

From the beginning of settlement in the Ohio Country in the early 1780s, it was clear that there would be no deference to traditional leaders and established authority. Government officials and local gentries charged frontiersmen with abandoning the normal rules of social behavior when they refused to defer to their judgments. But many settlers saw their defiance of authority as an assertion of local and individual prerogatives, their birthrights as freeborn Americans. They explicitly contended that the customs that had governed colonial America—as well as western European society for centuries—were no longer applicable. By becoming champions of individual liberty and local sovereignty, they forced men in positions of power to accommodate, but not to surrender, their notions of social order. In the end, the government and society of nineteenth-century Ohio were the products of a synthesis of conflicting revolutionary visions of the American future.

Readers should be aware of the fact that I have retained original spellings and grammatical constructions in quoting from letters and manuscripts. Only in rare cases have I pointed out errors in the text.

Like all historians, I have contracted a number of debts in the course of preparing this book which I am delighted to acknowledge. The staffs of several libraries and historical societies, especially the Dawes Memorial Library at Marietta College and the Ohio Historical Society, were indispensable in helping me to locate the sources for this study. Subsequently, several historians gave me important comments on bits and pieces of the manuscript; they include Ray White, Mark Fissel, Peter Onuf, Jeffrey P. Brown, Emil Pocock, Lester Cohen, Ronald Shaw, Don Harrison Doyle, Steven Boyd, and my former graduate school colleagues Dan Jones, Paul Gilje, and John Larson. Richard Aquila, Len Hochberg, and Shank Gilkeson offered me both scholarly advice and friendship while I was revising the manuscript for which I am particularly grateful. And the very specific suggestions of the two anonymous readers for the Kent State University Press helped me enormously in preparing the final draft.

This book began life as a discursive and somewhat disjointed dissertation at Brown University. Donald M. Scott's comments and encouragement were very important in pointing the way to major revisions. John L. Thomas was an exemplary first reader of the dissertation; I value his perceptiveness as a critic only slightly less than I value his friendship. Gordon S. Wood directed the dissertation by allowing me to write what I believed I had to write while reminding me that my goal was to persuade an audience of historians. Professor Wood's professional integrity and intellectual creativity made my years at Brown memorable and this book far better than it otherwise would have been.

Finally, I would like to acknowledge the assistance of members of my family. My parents, Robert F. and Vivian P. Cayton, and my grandparents, Lee and Irene Pelley, never faltered in their support (both emotional and financial) of my career. It was my grandfather who inspired my early interest in history and who did the most to nurture it with his enthusiasm for the subject and his confidence in me.

While all of these people have been generous with their time and advice, none bears any responsibility for the final product. But Mary Cayton does. Her duties as a teacher, scholar, mother, and wife keep her very busy. She has not read all of this book and she has no intrinsic interest in the early history of Ohio. But she has always understood why it was important to me. It is true that in many ways this book has absolutely nothing to do with Mary Cayton. But it is also true that in a multitude of more important ways it has everything to do with her.

Muncie, Indiana / Oxford, Ohio
March, 1986

1

Congress *v.* Squatters
1780   1786

From the point in western Pennsylvania where the Allegheny and the Monongahela rivers meet in muddy union to give it birth, the Ohio River flows almost a thousand miles to the south and west. Its course is rarely straight. On a map the river appears like a collapsing staircase, falling haphazardly toward its junction with the Mississippi. Along the way it collects the contributions of a number of lesser streams. From the south come the Kanawha, the Licking, the Cumberland, the Kentucky, and the Tennessee; from the north flow the Muskingum, the Scioto, the Miami, and the Wabash. The drainage area of these rivers, combined with those of the hundreds of creeks and streams that give them strength, makes the effective valley of the Ohio River a large one. Its domain extends at least a hundred miles on either side of its channel. Even today, at regular intervals tamed by dams and crossed by bridges, the river still dominates its valley.

Geographically, there are two parts to the domain of the Ohio—the upper and lower valleys. For the first several hundred miles the river flows through the foothills of the Appalachians, surrounded by small mountains that slide sharply down to the river bed. The rough terrain in what is now West Virginia and eastern Ohio makes farming an unrewarding task. Except for the bottomland beside the river and its tributaries, this region had little to attract anyone besides hunters and semi-subsistence farmers until the Industrial Revolution made the coal and other minerals within its hills valuable.

After the Ohio River passes Cincinnati, however, and traverses a big bend to the south, the land along its northern bank begins to flatten. Away from the river, this development begins some fifty miles to the east. West of the Scioto River, the foothills give away abruptly to great acreage of fertile plains that gradually approach the Ohio as it continues along its course.

In the late eighteenth century, the lands north of the Ohio River attracted the interest of a wide variety of Americans. While all of them had great expectations about exploiting the Ohio Country's natural resources, they found it difficult to forge a consensus about the future of the region. In particular, they could not agree on whether local or national interests should take precedence in the development of the territory. And until they could resolve their differences (as well as those with the Native Americans already living on the lands the Americans coveted), the Ohio Country would remain a frontier, an area without stable economic and social structures or a widely accepted source of political authority.

To many prominent Americans in the 1780s, including George Washington and members of the Confederation Congress, the lands north of the Ohio River were of critical financial and strategic value. The American Revolution had left the national government saddled with a huge debt and few viable means of financing it. Lacking the power to tax under the Articles of Confederation, congressmen saw the sale of public lands as a certain source of revenue, what David Howell of Rhode Island called "a sufficient fund to secure the final payment of the national debt."[1] Just as important, the future Northwest Territory was a potential buffer against the British in Canada and the Spanish west of the Mississippi River. The Ohio Country was one of the most promising bulwarks of the young American republic.

Virginia's March 1784 cession of its claim to the territory north of the Ohio River (in return for a tract of land east of the Scioto River reserved for its revolutionary war veterans) seemed to clear the way for development of the region under congressional control. British claims had ostensibly been extinguished by the Treaty of Paris, negotiations were underway with Indians that would climax in the January 1785 Treaty of Fort McIntosh establishing a boundary at the Cuyahoga River, and Congress had voided all land company claims as part of its agreement with Virginia. Still, some congressmen feared, as James Tilton put it in February 1784, that the territory might "slip out of our hands if not speedily attended to."[2]

Accordingly, in April 1784, Congress passed an ordinance designed to guide the development of the Northwest Territory, as the region would eventually be called. The Ordinance of 1784 provided for the establishment of seven territories with temporary governments that conformed to the laws of the original thirteen states. When Congress was satisfied that an individual territory had twenty thousand free people, it would grant permission to form a permanent government. In the meantime, Congress would govern the region in order to preserve "peace and good order among the settlers." The territories could become states when their population equalled that of the smallest of the original thirteen states and two-thirds of the states agreed to their admission to the Union. As potentially democratic as the Ordinance of 1784 was, it was not an invitation to local self-government. Rather, Congress was trying to protect its western investments by insuring that the evolution of government and society would be guided by its paternal hands.[3]

The national government acted quickly to assert its authority because frontiersmen were threatening to develop the Ohio Country on their own. The land across the Ohio River had attracted residents of western Pennsylvania and Virginia for years. During the American Revolution, many of them began to build temporary settlements along the northern bank of the Ohio and its tributaries. These settlers had no legal right to occupy the land; technically, they were squatters. But their conception of property ownership depended more upon actual possession than legal titles. Further, they had little respect for a distant national authority and felt no obligation to sacrifice their individual interests so that the national debt could be reduced. Their concern was with local custom and individual rights, not the aggrandizement of Congress.

As early as November 1779, Colonel Daniel Brodhead, the American commander at Fort Pitt, reported that people had settled all along the Ohio River and "thirty miles up some of its branches." Two years later, Brodhead's successor at Fort Pitt, General William Irvine, confronted the same problem. Despite the obvious dangers of Indian attacks, Irvine noted "sundry meetings of people at different places for the purpose of concerting plans to migrate into the Indian country, there to establish a government for themselves." In April 1782, advertisements posted on trees announced a meeting at Wheeling "for all who wish to become members of a new state on the Muskingum."[4]

Exactly how many people illegally claimed land in the Ohio Country before 1787 cannot be precisely determined, but army reports clearly establish the number in the thousands. The squatters tended to settle in close units along the Ohio River and in the valleys of its major tributaries. They grew corn, hunted, and lived in crude cabins. While their settlements were not towns, the danger of Indian attack and the necessity of mutual aid kept families close together.

Ordinary settlers hoped to obtain more than land by moving across the Ohio. They also wanted the distribution of land and the organization of society to take place in a competition governed by local rules and customs rather than directed by the national government. Before the end of the American Revolution, several hundred residents of Kentucky asked Congress for permission to move their families across the Ohio, protesting that their land and improvements had been "Engrossed into the hands of a few Interested men." A 1779 Virginia land act had so favored speculators at the expense of ordinary settlers, they claimed, that to remain in Kentucky was to become "Slaves to those Engrossers of Lands and to the Court of Virginia."[5]

Such attitudes led the squatters explicitly to reject any notion that the settlements in the Ohio Country should be directed by Congress. They wanted the process kept as close to the actual participants as possible. Several dozen potential settlers, for example, objected to the Ordinance of 1784 because they erroneously believed that it required that "no man can take out a warrant for less than Eight hundred and fifty acres," an amount "more than many of the people on our frontiers are able to purchase who would be glad to become Adventurers." The petitioners told Congress that they expected "every Indulgence in particular that of Locating of Lands and time allowed us for the payment of the monies for Said Lands." Above all, they wanted the Ohio Country settled without prearrangement or prescription. Let each adventurer, they urged Congress, take out warrants "according to his abilities" and locate the same "in what manner they shall see fit."[6]

For ordinary immigrants into the Northwest Territory, land was more than a commodity to be bought or sold, or a place to be leased from some distant landlord. It was the foundation of a family's independence, status, and future. To own land was to be free of all forms of slavery, whether in the form of semifeudal obligations to landlords or more impersonal debts or taxes.

The protection of the family was crucial to immigrants because it was the one thing that gave order and predictability to their lives. In the highly mobile society of the frontier, most traditional institutions were weak, if they existed at all. Neither governments nor churches exerted the influence that they did in more settled areas. There was nothing besides the family around which to build a sense of community, a sense of belonging to a group. It was thus no accident that "massive westward migration" enabled Americans "to *preserve*" and "to *extend* . . . an agricultural society composed primarily of yeoman freeholding families." Even two centuries later in many parts of Appalachia the family remains the basic social, economic, and political unit. The squatters settled in the Ohio Country because, as a group of them informed Congress, most of them had "no property in Lands." West of the Ohio River they hoped to improve the circumstances of their families by settling the "Vacant Lands" there.[7]

If the family survived migration pretty much intact, other institutions did not. And in the vacuum that resulted power tended to concentrate in the hands of the assertive leaders of larger families. The society of the squatters was by no means egalitarian. Men by the names of John Amberson, William Hogland, Charles Norris, and others dominated the rude settlements. In the highly personal world of the Ohio Country, locations simply took the name of the most important settler. Thus places such as Hogland's Town, Amberson's Bottom, and Norris Town appeared wherever a particular man had earned the respect of his neighbors.

The career of Joseph Ross probably epitomizes the general nature of frontier leadership. Born in New York around 1730, Ross had been captured and raised by Indians. He eventually escaped, only to spend the rest of his life on the fringe of settlement in a kind of perpetual restlessness. Still, if Ross was a rootless man, he had acquired the skills necessary to survive on the frontier; he was an accomplished hunter and Indian fighter who was used to taking care of himself. In 1784, Ross moved his family and some neighbors, who were sometimes referred to as tenants, across the Ohio to an area called Mingo Bottom. There the group erected rudimentary cabins and cleared enough land to grow a few acres of corn. Ross made his claim to the land by cutting the bark of the trees located at the corners with a tomahawk. The middle-aged frontiersman's experience, initiative, and skills made him the natural leader of the small settlement.[8]

Frontier leaders like Ross were too rude, too lacking in visible cultural and financial attributes to be mistaken for gentlemen in the East. They could never have been dominant on the levels of state or national society. But in their local communities they were powerful men. They were mostly older men (in their fifties) who belonged, judging by petition signatures, to large families; their age and experience gave them authority within the family unit, the strongest social institution on the frontier. Such men had often accumulated some capital either in the form of land or slaves. While money mattered little in the Ohio Country in the 1780s, men such as Isaac Williams gained importance by running small, makeshift general stores; there they bartered guns, powder, salt, and other items for land, corn, or furs. By dominating the primitive local economy, they reinforced their position as local leaders. Finally, luck, determination, and personal strength were crucial in securing prominence on the frontier.[9]

Ross, Hogland, and others like them comprised a kind of natural frontier aristocracy. They were not wealthy men; they did not have extensive connections with leading citizens in the East. Society in the Ohio Country in the 1780s was rudimentary. Its leaders were men who had succeeded in defending and advancing their own interests. Because the lines of authority were still being sorted out and because the society was so unstructured, almost everything came down to a personal defense of personal interest. Disagreements were often resolved by personal combats that amounted to little more than a primitive kind of duelling. Men like Ross and Hogland had earned their positions. Congressmen and other prominent Americans, however, perceived the squatters' primitive lifestyle and their contention that they were capable of settling across the Ohio on their own as anarchic. Unless some direction was given to the distribution of western land and to the development of western society by America's enlightened and established leaders, members of Congress and other men of prominence feared that the Ohio Country would be ruined by selfish individualism and social chaos.

West of the Monongahela, magistrate and leading landowner Dorsey Pentecost told the prominent lawyer James Wilson that "Numbers of the more Considerate and Orderly People" were complaining of the infatuation of "the Indigent and Ignorant" for engrossing land in the Ohio Country. "Orderly People," to be sure, did not object to land speculation, just the chaotic manner in which it was being practiced across the Ohio. The squatters believed that Congress would grant them preemption rights, Pentecost reported. But he ardently hoped that they were mistaken. Certainly Congress would not sell the land or grant preemption without discrimination. Pentecost advised Wilson to get Congress to pass "the most Positive Law against any Person taken Possession of One foot of Land without a Legal Title or permit in his hand." Meanwhile, he wanted an immediate proclamation forbidding settlement in the Ohio Country. If such an action was not taken and rigidly enforced, "the people will run into the Country, and one Example will produce another until the Combination will grow so strong that it will become not only Troublesom but impossible to dissolve it, the end of which will be Anarchy and Confusion, and Consequently the destruction of the People."[10]

In 1784, while on a tour of the West to secure his lands, George Washington found a "rage for speculating in, and forestalling of Lands on the North West side of the Ohio." "Scarce a valuable spot, within any tolerable distance" of the Ohio River "is left without a claimant. Men in these times talk with as much facility of fifty, a hundred, or even 500,000 Acres as a Gentleman formerly would do of 1,000 acres." Hundreds of ordinary men had converted what Washington and Pentecost thought of as orderly speculation by gentlemen like themselves into a wild, anarchic land rush. People roam "over the Country on the Indian side of the Ohio," observed the disdainfully jealous Washington, "mark out Lands, Survey, and even settle them."[11]

What was happening on the Ohio frontier was part of the larger revolution in American life in the late eighteenth century. Washington was upset by more than the fact that people were taking up land without legal titles. More ominous for gentlemen with traditional notions of how a society ought to function, the frontiersmen were behaving in ways that struck at the very heart of traditional social relationships. The squatters did not demand political democracy, in the strict sense, but they did begin to take control of their lives, to argue that as human beings they were ultimately as important as gentlemen, and to blur the age-old line between gentle and simple folk.

However the squatter's behavior is defined, it clearly frightened Washington. "To suffer a wide-extended country to be overrun with land-jobbers, speculators, and monopolizers, or even scattered settlers," he asserted in 1783, "is inconsistent with that wisdom and policy which our true interest dictates, or which an enlightened people ought to adopt." Unless Congress acted to establish its authority in the West, Washington feared that the Ohio Country would fall into the hands of "a parcel of banditti, who will bid defiance to all authority."[12]

The illegal settlers northwest of the Ohio were hardly an organized threat to the United States government. But congressmen believed their actions constituted a dangerous challenge to the social order of the young republic. The frontiersmen seemed too selfish, too ignorant, too concerned with immediate gratification. Rash and spontaneous, they were unworthy of being considered citizens of a republic; they were no better than criminals, a collection of lawless "banditti" who put their personal interests above those of the community as a whole. "Feeble, disorderly and dispersed Territories," noted the Congressional Committee on Indian Affairs in September 1783, had a "tendency to produce . . . depravity of manners."[13]

In the same month, Congress issued a proclamation forbidding settlements on lands claimed by Indians "without the express authority and direction of the United States in congress assembled." Virginia's congressional delegates explained that the action was necessary to prevent the region from becoming "profitless." Even more frightening, the land would "become a prey to lawless Banditti and adventurers, who must necessarily have involv'd us in continued Indian wars and perhaps have form'd Establishments not only on dissimilar principles to those which form the basis of our Republican Constitutions, but such as might eventually prove destructive to them."[14] The proclamation proved hardly sufficient to its purpose, and the settlements north of the Ohio remained in place.

Congress, nonetheless, continued to plan the development of the Ohio Country. In 1785, it passed a Land Ordinance providing for the survey and sale of the lands northwest of the Ohio River. Under the leadership of the geographer of the United States, Thomas Hutchins, surveyors from every state arrived in the upper Ohio Valley in the fall of 1785. Over the next year they braved Indian dangers and wilderness obstacles and surveyed the first seven ranges west of the Ohio River. The ranges were about fifty miles wide, and ran south from a line drawn west from the point where the Ohio River crossed the Pennsylvania border. With land recorded on charts, Eastern purchasers could now buy land by number and location. Initials on trees were not required.[15]

A more important group of government representatives on the Ohio frontier included the soldiers under the command of Lieutenant Colonel Josiah Harmar. A Pennsylvania veteran of the American Revolution, Harmar had arrived at Fort McIntosh with three companies in the latter part of 1784. By the summer of 1786, Harmar had approximately six hundred men available for duty. The colonel's major tasks were to protect the surveyors, keep the peace with the Indians, and restrain intruders on the public lands. In the fall of 1785, Harmar established Fort Harmar at the mouth of the Muskingum River to help in accomplishing his duties.[16]

Amidst the influential reports of fertile land and good streams sent back East by soldiers and surveyors were very negative impressions of the intruders on the public lands. Samuel Holden Parsons, an Indian commissioner from Connecticut and later a judge of the Northwest Territory, warned Congressman William S. Johnson in the late fall of 1785 that Congress was acting far too slowly to keep the lands so necessary for paying off the national debt and so attractive to Eastern purchasers. The frontiersmen were unruly beyond any conception, Parsons told Johnson, and the commissioner wanted their irregular behavior to extend no "further than the present settlers." Parsons could only characterize the frontiersmen as "our *own* white Indians of no character who have their own Private Views without Regard to public benefits to Serve."[17]

Throughout the observations of the agents of Congress ran the belief that the hundreds of people squatting on the lands west of the Ohio were the direct antithesis of good citizens. They were selfish, individualistic, unrestrained, and a threat to legitimate authority and good order, not to mention the economic interests of the national government and its leading citizens. Colonel Harmar complained in 1786 that the squatters were "in general averse to Federal measures, and that they could wish to throw every obstacle in the way to impede the surveying of the Western Territory, agreeably to the ordinance of Congress."[18] Winthrop Sargent, a Massachusetts surveyor and later secretary of both the Ohio Company of Associates and the Northwest Territory, believed that only "the Terrors . . . inspired" by the army stood between the "valuable Tracts of Land on the Ohio" and the squatters who would steal them from Congress and deserving veterans of the Revolution. Without "those military Gentlemen . . . a lawless Banditti—powerful and dangerous" would take "the very best Farms in the Country." Despite being "as much enamered with the country as ever," surveyor John Mathews of Massachusetts thought that "the present inhabitance" would forever be fighting the Indians because "the truth is they are both saviges. Tho their are many good people yet the number of worthless fellows" was large enough "to keep them in a broil."[19]

Such fears about the future of the Ohio Valley had come to a head in early 1785. Congressmen agreed that action stronger than a proclamation had to be taken. Therefore, with the signing of the Treaty of Fort McIntosh in January 1785, the Indian commissioners at Fort McIntosh acting under directions from Congress ordered Colonel Harmar to use "such force as he may judge necessary in driving off persons attempting to settle on the lands of the United States."[20]

Confronted by this threat of force, the settlers west of the Ohio organized to protect their interests. In March 1785, the squatter John Amberson initiated a call for elections to choose a convention to write a constitution for the trans-Ohio region. Amberson called for elections to be held at the mouths of the Miami and Scioto rivers, on the Muskingum River, and at the house of a settler named Jonas Menzons. The three hundred families at Muskingum and the three hundred families at the falls of the Hocking together with the fifteen hundred on the Miami and Scioto rivers were to select delegates to meet in a constitutional convention at the mouth of the Scioto on April 10. Amberson justified this action by appealing to the undoubted right of Americans "to pass into every vacant country, and there to form their constitution" as they saw fit. Clearly, the immediate interest of the settlers was to protect their land claims, but the mere fact that these people were organizing to defy their ostensible but remote government and to deny that it spoke for them is significant. There is no record of the convention ever having met, although army officers reported that meetings were held "to comply with the requisitions of the advertisement."[21]

The disagreement between government and squatter over how to dispose of the land in the Ohio Country became violent in the spring of 1785. In early April, Colonel Harmar dispatched Ensign John Armstrong with twenty armed men to evict the illegal settlers. On the morning of April 4, the soldiers encountered the fifty-five-year-old frontiersman Joseph Ross who, with his family and neighbors, had settled at Mingo Bottom in the Northwest Territory the year before.

When Ensign Armstrong informed Ross that Congress wanted him to move back across the Ohio, the settler reacted with angry defiance. He was astounded that anyone would issue such instructions. No matter where the ensign's orders originated, Ross told Armstrong that he was determined "to hold possession" of the land he had so recently claimed. If the army dared to destroy his home and improvements, he would simply rebuild them. Ross and Armstrong's discussion degenerated into a shouting match. When the squatter began to insult Congress directly, the officer had him arrested and sent back to Wheeling under guard. The rest of the settlers were then given a few days to demolish their buildings and to migrate back across the Ohio.

Armstrong continued on with his mission, but he soon found it an impossible task. Despite posted notices, the ensign informed Colonel Harmar in May that people were moving into "the unsettled countries by forties and fifties." From Wheeling to the Miami River "there is scarcely one bottom on the river but has one or more families living thereon."[22] There was little that twenty-one men could do to stop them. In June, Harmar informed Secretary of War Henry Knox that the number of squatters was so immense that he could "sweep them" no further than 120 to 150 miles from Fort McIntosh. While the colonel continued to send out periodic expeditions and erected Fort Harmar in October at the mouth of the Muskingum to help remove the "intruders," his job was overwhelming. "Unless Congress enters into immediate measures," he warned, "it will be impossible to prevent the lands being settled."[23]

In October 1785, Indian Commissioner Richard Butler came across Joseph Ross and his neighbors at Mingo Town and "warned them away." Butler found them conciliatory and obedient, especially when he assured the squatting settlers "that the land would be surveyed and sold to poor and rich, and there would or could be no more of preference given to one than another." But despite this outward deference the important fact was that Ross, more than seven months after his confrontation with Ensign Armstrong, was still at Mingo Town.[24]

Harmar increasingly found his task overwhelming. "Notwithstanding the intruders have been so frequently removed from the public lands," he lamented in July 1786, "several . . . have crossed the river again, and some have ventured to penetrate the country as far as twenty miles from the Ohio." The colonel's periodic expeditions against the squatters had only temporary effects. On one occasion, recalled Levi Munsell, a soldier under

Harmar, one hundred troops burned the cabins and corn of about thirty men near present-day Steubenville. There was little resistance, although the "hunters with their rifles paraded on the bank of the river with every appearance of an intention to defend themselves."[25] But they backed down in the face of the soldiers.

Once the army moved on, the settlers simply returned. Winthrop Sargent found in August 1786 that Menzon's Town had been "destroy'd by the american Troops this Season, in Common with the Habitations, Corn Fields and other Improvements of a number of People up and down the River who had taken Possession of Federal Lands without even the Shadow of Title." Still, Menzon continued to occupy the land he claimed. On flatboats commonly called "Flats," the people "pass and repass themselves and Effects across the River occasionally as the Movement of our Troops may make necessary."[26] Harmar could not keep the Northwest Territory free of settlers. There were simply too many squatters, too many miles, and too few troops.

Thus Congress approached 1787 with little more control over the Ohio Country than it had exercised in 1783. The settlers continually promised to obey congressional "Law and Regulations" only if they were "Consistent with the Rights and privileges of the good people of these states."[27] Clearly, eastern gentlemen could rescue the territory from what appeared to them to be the contentious, individualistic, and anarchic society of the squatters and insure its development as a bastion of the republic only by giving their vision of the American West more specificity and finding more effective ways of implementing it. If the squatters could not be driven off the land, their society would be restructured in ways that would insure that they would behave as the citizens of a model republic should.

2

Planning the Republic:
The Federalists and
the Ohio Country
1786   1788

To survey the limited historiography on Federalist attitudes toward the West is to conclude that, to the extent that they existed at all, they were almost exclusively negative. Federalists, we learn, feared the frontier and disdained its residents as lawless barbarians; they suppressed the Whiskey Rebellion and opposed the Louisiana Purchase. Why? Because the West represented everything the Federalists did not wish to see the United States become. The open, dynamic, democratic, egalitarian frontier of the Early Republic belonged both politically and intellectually to the Jeffersonian Republicans.

To the Jeffersonians, who sought what Drew R. McCoy has termed the development of America through space, the West was the foundation of an "Empire of Liberty." An endless recreation of an agrarian world of independent farmers across the North American continent would allow Americans to preserve the personal independence and public virtue that the Jeffersonian gentry believed was so crucial to the success of republican government. Federalists such as Alexander Hamilton, on the other hand, looked to the East, across the Atlantic to Europe, as a model for the future. More distrusting of human nature, more accepting of inequality and corruption, Hamilton, according to McCoy, saw America's future "not as a virtuous agrarian republic, but as a powerful, economically advanced modern state much like Great Britain." The West apparently had little role to play in a movement "to push the United States as rapidly as possible into a higher stage of development."[1] Or did it?

While disparaging comments about frontiersmen by members of the gentry abound in the late eighteenth century, most of the Federalists' negative assertions about the West in general date from the period after Thomas Jefferson's election as president. In fact, many staunch nationalists had earlier looked to the western frontier as an agreeable scene for social experimentation and the execution of a dynamic plan for development that better fitted Hamilton's vision of the American future than Jefferson's. In the decade between 1785 and 1795, when men of national perspective still believed they could mold America to suit their purposes, some Federalists embraced the West positively as an integral part of America's future. In particular, they focused on the territory northwest of the Ohio River and the efforts to lay the foundations of an America that would expand through time and space simultaneously.[2]

By 1786, many congressmen and other prominent Americans worried that the Ohio Country might prove to be a source of more discord than profit. Doubting the character of most of the people west of the Appalachians, men like George Washington feared that the frontiersmen would fall easy prey to the blandishments of British and Spanish agents and become involved in separatist movements. For almost a decade, residents of the Ohio Valley had demonstrated little inclination to respect the authority of Congress. Clearly, congressmen believed such valuable territory could not be entrusted to people of such dubious character and transient loyalty. The Ohio Country had to be developed cautiously and systematically, in a manner befitting its importance.

During the late 1780s and the 1790s the interaction of the often vague generalities of national leaders and the very specific actions of land company and territorial officials who hoped to make their superiors' suggestions concrete produced an elaborate design for western development. These men shared what recent historians have called a Federalist persuasion. Almost all of them were active supporters of the Constitution of 1787 and the Washington administrations of the 1790s; indeed, some were their leading advocates. More generally and critically, they all shared a dedication to the proposition that a "good, firm energetick" federal or national government was the only "means of preserving the Union of the States and securing the happiness of all parts of this extensive country."[3] They included national leaders such as George Washington, Alexander Hamilton, Timothy Pickering, Oliver Wolcott, and Henry Knox; territorial Governor Arthur St. Clair; territorial Judges Samuel Holden Parsons, James M.

Varnum, and John Cleves Symmes; as well as Rufus Putnam, Benjamin Tupper, Manasseh Cutler, and Winthrop Sargent, all prominent members of the Ohio Company of Associates, an organization of revolutionary war veterans who purchased one and one-half million acres from Congress in 1787 and established the first authorized American settlement in the Northwest at Marietta in April 1788.[4]

The sources of this group's interest in the Ohio Country were many and intertwined, some obvious and well-known. They acted to secure national authority and to control western development partly to prevent the loss of valuable public lands to European governments and squatters. They also wished to preserve and enhance their own personal investments in the Northwest Territory. Land speculation in frontier areas was a major preoccupation of the American gentry in the late eighteenth century and they had long since perfected the notion of controlled development or improvement in order to maintain claims often disputed by frontiersmen and Indians and to insure a handsome return on their investments. Improved land sold in small tracts, and held far more potential profit than large areas of unsurveyed wilderness. Thus in advocating the slow development of the Northwest under national authority, the Ohio Company was following a trail long since blazed by pre-revolutionary war land companies.[5]

Complementing these interests were enlightened concepts about the relationship between environment and human character. In the late eighteenth century, people were believed to be, to a great extent, products of their environment. The power of surroundings to influence character was crucial to eighteenth-century intellectuals who believed history to be a cycle of growth and decay. For by structuring the environment in specific ways, men could potentially accelerate or prolong the clearly defined stages of development through which, they believed, societies inevitably passed. Given these presuppositions, the evident responsibility of American leaders was to bring their nation to the highest possible stage of development and to keep it there as long as possible, even if that required manipulation, or improvement, of physical and social environments.[6]

Benjamin Rush, the scientist and statesman, summarized many of these notions about character and environment in his 1786 description of the typical stages of frontier settlement in Pennsylvania. Often seen as an anticipation of Frederick Jackson Turner's analysis of waves of settlement (with which it does have much in common), Rush's essay is more significant as an example of the close relationship between social and physical structures and human behavior that suffused the mind of western-oriented gentry.[7]

According to Rush, the frontier attracted three kinds of men in succession. The three types could not coexist, for they thrived only under very different circumstances. The first settler quickly acquired the manners of the Indians in whose "neighborhood" he lived, spending much of his time fishing, hunting, drinking, or sleeping "in dirt and rags in his little cabbin." "In his intercourse with the world, he manifests all the arts which characterize the Indians of our country." What eventually forced him to abandon his land was a change in his environment—an increase in population, the arrival of fences, laws, and religion. Either he had to change, accepting civilization, or leave, seeking his former environment in the woods to the West.

Rush's second species of settlers was only slightly more civilized. His world was more complicated, his property more extensive and encumbered with debts, his crops more diverse. But because he lived in a relatively unorganized state, he was lazy, his home bore the "marks of a weak tone of mind," he was "seldom a good member of civil or religious society," he drank, and he possessed "high ideas of liberty," by which Rush meant to imply that he was lacking in republican virtue. The typical Ohio Country squatter would fall within this category.

The final type of settler was by far the most admirable in Rush's eyes. And, not coincidentally, this frontiersman devoted the most attention to improving his property, using manure, building a stone barn, keeping his fences in order, diversifying his crops, and erecting a substantial home with furniture and a large kitchen. Again, the structure of his world directly impinged upon his character and manners. Because he was a substantial property holder, he supported the institutions of social order—government, churches, and schools. Why? Because, according to Rush, "benevolence and public spirit . . . are the natural offspring of affluence and independence." These men alone deserved to be called *"farmers"* for only they were repositories of "republican virtue."

After describing his three frontier types, Rush made the relationship between character and environment explicit. His review of settlement, he claimed, demonstrated "that there are certain regular stages which mark the progress from the savage to civilized life." Whatever qualities people revealed tended to rise "from necessity, and the peculiar state of society in which these people live."[8] Rush's analysis synthesized the intellectual sources of ideas about the frontier. Applying republican and enlightened thought to his observations of western Pennsylvania, Rush's essay reflected commonly held beliefs about the American frontier and the character of its settlers, beliefs that would shape the gentry's vision of the future of the Northwest Territory.

The final source of the Federalists' western design was their public and personal experiences, their interaction with the structures of society in which they had matured. Historians have made much of the New England origins of the Ohio Company associates, territorial officials, and their friends in the national government like Knox, Pickering, and Wolcott. They have ascribed the passion of this group for order and regularity to a Puritan mentality and a traditional fondness for organization in towns. In so doing, scholars have oversimplified the lives, world, and values of these men, for tradition and religion were far less important influences on them than socioeconomic structures that were a long way from the archetypal New England town.[9]

While most were born and raised in New England, they had become men of national, even international, perspectives in the 1770s and 1780s. They tended to be middle-aged in 1787, veterans of the long, bitter struggle that was the American War of Independence. Since most had been officers in the disorganized, poorly supplied, often unruly American army, and a few had been members of the weak, disorganized Congress of the Confederation, not surprisingly in the 1780s they had become staunch advocates of a strong national government. Their perception of social chaos in the aftermath of revolution—rising new men challenging the positions of gentlemen, state legislators acting out of individual interest rather than public interest, Americans defying legal authority in a multitude of incidents, climaxing in Shays's Rebellion—simply reinforced their belief that only a central, overarching authority could preserve America's experiment in republicanism. The founders of the Old Northwest loved regularity and systematic development, and supported governments and other institutions, less because of a Puritan or New England heritage than because of their personal exposure to what they considered to be social disintegration.[10]

These men were heavily involved in the expanding commercial world of the late eighteenth century. Land speculation in distant areas was hardly new to them. They lived in the more commercial cities of New England and New York, the frontiers of American economic development. The Ohio Company itself was a national organization designed to make profits for its individual stockholders through impersonal transactions in the commodity of land. The Scioto Company, another speculative venture created by some of the leading members of the Ohio Company in association with William Duer (an eighteenth-century version of a high-stakes entrepreneur), was designed to and did sell land in the Ohio Country in France.[11] Putting the Scioto Company's shady aspects aside for the moment, it was a worldwide business venture if there ever was one. The Ohio Company associates were clearly parts of an expanding international economy. And they had no desire to see America's commercial growth dissipate on the primitive frontier into a backward slide into the world of the Indian.

Historians have largely seen the Ohio Company, which was organized as a joint-stock corporation by eleven veterans of the American Revolution on March 1, 1786 in Boston, as the climax of a persistent effort by New England officers to obtain payment for their wartime service. Certainly, director Manasseh Cutler and secretary Winthrop Sargent's handling of the purchase of one and one-half million acres from Congress in 1787 and their close association with speculators like Duer and speculations like the Scioto Company tend to confirm that judgment. No one can doubt that the associates were interested in getting land and money. Many of the 594 men involved, such as Alexander Hamilton, had no immediate intention of settling in the West. Because the company seems so much like a speculative venture, its rhetoric has often been dismissed as propaganda designed to gain favors from Congress or to attract settlers to its purchase.[12] One of the five directors of the company, Manasseh Cutler, even found something redeeming about Shays's Rebellion, for example. "These commotions," he told Winthrop Sargent, "will tend to promote our plan and incline well-disposed persons to become adventurers." But it was not merely the force of their rhetoric that the associates believed would convince other people to join. "For," as Cutler himself noted about Massachusetts in 1786, "who would wish to live under a Government subject to such tumults and confusions."[13] Generally believing the assumptions and fears that lay behind much of their exaggerated public prose and anxious private letters, the active participants in the migration were indeed speculators—in the future as well as land.

Many left for the West because of the material and social distress they experienced in the 1780s. Insistent upon describing themselves as "reputable, industrious, well-informed" men with status in society, the members of the Ohio Company assured congressmen that they were "men of very considerable property and respectable characters." If the associates were certain that they were "distinguished for wealth, education, and virtue," they believed other people were threatening that crucial self-image.[14]

Among the first to respond after Lexington and Concord, the future associates had enthusiastically participated in the 1775 siege of Boston. Not only did the American Revolution provide an opportunity to "restore peace, tranquillity . . . Union and liberty" to America, it reinforced at a critical moment the future pioneers' self-image as leaders in personal communities. For the future Ohio Company directors Rufus Putnam and Benjamin Tupper of Massachusetts, James Varnum of Rhode Island, and Samuel Holden Parsons of Connecticut, arrived at Boston as chief officers of local and state militia, indisputable evidence of their social standing and the respect and confidence of their neighbors. Further military service, in the officers' minds at least, only accorded them formal deference within a strictly hierarchical society—the army—in which economic position had less importance than in civilian life.[15]

In the end, fighting for American independence seemed to make economic and social disaster a distinct possibility for many. Sometimes enfeebled and rarely paid, many of those who served their new country spent family fortunes in mere survival. The failure of Congress to pay them, claimed Major General Samuel Holden Parsons, was intensely frustrating to men who "have expended their estates, have hazarded their lives and health, and sacrificed the just expectations of their families for the salvation of their country."[16]

Although their fears were often exaggerated, the difficulties of the future associates did seem to escalate in the 1780s; postwar America seemed unfamiliar and unfair. Parsons, for example, a successful lawyer and a member of the Connecticut legislature before the war, believed himself "nearly impoverished" and in bad health at its end. Despite his election to the state legislature in the 1780s, his fortune consisted of the government securities he received in lieu of pay and his hopes of profiting from "the future disposal of the land" he surveyed in 1786 in a subordinate position. "Insolvent" despite his investment in the Ohio Company, Parsons died in 1789 bewailing "the multiplied troubles which have fallen to my lot."[17]

Unsuccessful mercantile ventures were not infrequent as the former soldiers found it difficult to adjust to a more complex economy. Colonel Ebenezer Sproat, for example, a prewar farmer of substantial means, tried his hand at "mercantile affairs." "Being entirely unacquainted" with trade and having "no taste for his new business . . . in a short time he failed; swallowing up his wife's patrimony, as well as his resources."[18] Officers and their sons bitterly complained of poor opportunities and inequities.

The future associates of the Ohio Company have often been criticized for their seemingly crass pursuit of land, their angry demands for pay from Congress and the states, and their careful attention to the fluctuations in the price of the securities they received in lieu of pay. To an extent, the charge is true; they were frantic for money. But their "grasping" was essentially the pursuit of "a quiet independence" that would accord them a position consonant with the standing they believed they held, or should hold, in society. Commodore Abraham Whipple's approaching "misery and ruin" were incompatible with his election to the Rhode Island legislature in the 1780s. A man worthy of his neighbors' respect hardly mortgaged his farm "for a temporary support," had it sued out of his possession, and faced the prospect of being "turned out into the world . . . destitute of a house or a home," even if he had lost much of his money fighting for his country's independence, and his position as a recognizable community leader.[19]

In 1783, in the midst of growing economic distress, the officers of the continental army organized the Society of the Cincinnati, partly to serve as a lobbying agency to get some sort of payment from Congress, but primarily to perpetuate the formal status they had held as army officers in the socially and economically uncertain postwar society. The medal given to each of its members revealed their longing for order, tranquillity, and respect. The decoration featured the Roman hero, Cincinnatus, in a field, with "his wife standing at the door of their cottage; near it a plough and instruments of husbandry." Three senators were offering Cincinnatus a sword, calling him back to the defense of the Roman republic. Around the edge of the whole ran the inscription, OMNIA RELIQUIT SERVARE REM PUBLICAM. On the reverse was pictured the sun rising over an "open city" with "Fame crowning Cincinnatus" and the legends VIRTUTIS PRAEMIUM and ESTO PERPETUA.[20]

The importance of Cincinnatus as an ideal figure to the participants in the Ohio Company was immense. Of the eleven men who met in Boston in March 1786 to organize the company, six were members of the society, as were four of the company's five directors and its secretary. To the associates, Cincinnatus was a model of ideal behavior in an ideal world—for Cincinnatus, living on the land far away from the tumult and corruption of cities, and sacrificing his happiness so that the republic might survive the chaos of war and enjoy the pleasure and prosperity of peace, made a powerful comparison with their own positions. Cincinnatus was the embodiment of the independent republican. Firm fighters for the American republic in war, the Cincinnati envisioned themselves as its staunchest farmer-citizens in peace. They had had, claimed Mariettan Joseph Barker, "a second education in the Army of the Revolution, where they heard the precept of wisdom and saw the example of Bravery and Fortitude. They had been disciplined to obey, and learned the Advantage of subordination to Law and good order in promoting the prosperity and happiness of themselves and the rest of Mankind."[21] The Cincinnati sternly warned that they would expel any member, "who, by conduct inconsistent with a gentleman and a man of honor, or by opposition to the interests of the community in general, or the society in particular, may render himself unworthy to continue a member."[22]

To their disgust, the officers believed that the war had not only ruined the economic base on which their status rested, it had released anarchic and insubordinate elements. Only symptomatic was the virulent scorn directed at the Cincinnati, as the pretensions and hereditary characteristics of the society raised a storm of protest throughout New England. Mass meetings and memorials condemned the organization as antirepublican and elitist. Shocked at such treatment, Samuel Holden Parsons found the veterans of

Connecticut exposed to "daily Insults" and "contemptuous malignant Neglect." "Without honor," he said, they could no longer live in New England and were seeking homes in New York or farther west.[23] To the veterans, it seemed clear that something had gone wrong in the course of the revolution.

Everywhere they looked in the mid-1780s, the associates of the Ohio Company found ingratitude and growing anarchy in the East making a prospective settlement in the West alluring and idyllic. Ohio Company director Manasseh Cutler summarized the general feeling when he wondered to Winthrop Sargent, the company secretary, in 1786 if "mankind are in a State for enjoying all the natural rights of humanity and are possessed of virtue sufficient for the support of a purely republican government." "Dishonesty, Villainy, and extreme ignorance" were rampant. America, he complained, was "the first nation" to make "a fair experiment of equal liberty in a civil Community," but it seemed to be failing in its calling.[24]

Benjamin Tupper, who believed in 1787 that monarchy was absolutely necessary to save the United States from total chaos, saw, as did many of the associates, a climax to his personal and public discontents in Shays's Rebellion in late 1786. In such a crisis, he cried, "The old Society of the Cincinnati must once more consult and effect the salvation of a distracted country."[25] The Cincinnati did pledge their support of the Massachusetts government, partly because the uprising threatened the value, even the existence, of the securities on which rested the hopes of many to recoup or build fortunes that would secure them an independence. But their personal economic problems symbolized a more general imperiling of the republican experiment in freedom. Not all of the Ohio Company associates merely decried the rebellion. Some, such as Rufus Putnam and Benjamin Tupper, actively joined General Benjamin Lincoln "against the Insurgents," while others sold their farms in utter disgust. Cutler was right when he argued that "These commotions will tend to promote our plan and incline well disposed persons to become adventurers for who would wish to live under a Government subject to such tumults and confusions."[26]

In short, the veterans sought the security of a well-ordered life. In Ohio, Varnum argued, they would find "a safe, an honorable asylum" where equal protection under the law and "the labor of the industrious will find the reward of peace, plenty, and virtuous contentment." When Winthrop Sargent met some old war friends, including Colonel Josiah Harmar, on a surveying trip in the West, they determined, in summarizing the feelings of the associates, that the lands of the Ohio would be a place "where the veteran soldier and Honest Man should find a Retreat from ingratitude." They vowed, once settled, never again to visit the East "but in their children and like Goths and Vandals to deluge a people more vicious and villanous than even the Praetorian Band of Ancient Rome." In the Ohio Country, as one correspondent of Sargent put it, they would be "associated with men you already know, who like yourself, have been ill used, and who when in the new country will know no superiors risen by their villanies above your honest exertions."[27]

In the late 1780s personal financial interests, a desire to strengthen national authority in both East and West, and a passion for social order came together to produce a coherent Federalist vision of the future of the West. Not to be found in a single essay or pamphlet, this design for the West was nonetheless as powerful as the much discussed Jeffersonian "Empire of Liberty." But where Jefferson envisioned an agrarian West—relieving America of excess population, fostering propertied farmers of independent character, and evolving naturally, generally left alone by government—the Ohio Company associates conceived of an "Empire of System," an America expanding through space and time simultaneously, an urban, commercial West fully integrated into the Atlantic world and guided by a superintending national authority.

Specifically, a Federalist West involved interfering with the normal progression of settlement and improving upon it. The founders of the Old Northwest intended to skip the stages described by Rush and proceed immediately to creating the highest possible stage of economic, social, and political existence. To accomplish their goal, they would have to replace the world of the squatter with one of their own making.

What kind of world would that be? In many ways, it would be eastern society, shorn of its flaws and elevated to a higher level of development. Ohio Company Superintendent Rufus Putnam believed that "the western country should in their manners, morrals, religion, and policy, take the eastern states for their modle." The Federalists wanted to fully integrate the Ohio Country into the Atlantic cultural and commercial community. Unlike the squatters, they sought interdependence not independence, urban as much as agrarian development, manufactures as well as farms, social stratification instead of egalitarianism—all overseen by a firm national authority and secured by institutions like churches and schools. Ohio Company director Manasseh Cutler called it "the sublime contemplation of beholding the whole territory of the United States settled by an enlightened people, and continued under one extended government."[28] They demanded the subordination of local to a general interest, the supremacy of law and established procedures. And they expected the gradual coordinated expansion of an urban, commercial society across the American frontier to bring not just trade and cities, but glorious achievements in art, architecture, literature, science, and gentility. The howling American wilderness would become the heart of a great empire, the apex of Atlantic civilization.

The key to the success of this western vision was the easy exchange of goods, ideas, and people between London and Pittsburgh, Boston and Cincinnati. In the late eighteenth century, this meant access to water that could be easily navigated to the sea. The waters of the Ohio Valley were extensive, but they required improvement. Much has been made of the dreams of Washington and others for improved navigation to the West; most discussion has centered on uniting East to West to undermine possible western separatist movements and making western property more valuable. Without denying in the least the importance of those factors in the advocacy of internal improvements, quick and easy communication among very distant areas was also of the utmost importance to the kind of society the Federalist gentry envisioned building.[29]

Indeed, the achievement of that society required abbreviating or eliminating the first stages of settlement described by Rush and the characteristics of localism, individualism, and disorganization associated with them. It presupposed the direct control of the national government under the Constitution of 1787 over the development of western society. If left to individuals like the squatters—people who Rufus Putnam called "privit adventurers who will pay little or no reguard to the laws of the United States or the rights of the natives"—the frontier's future would be lost in a maze of local and selfish interests. Territorial Judge James Varnum believed that one of the greatest obstacles to the success of the Articles of Confederation had been "prejudices too easily imbibed" and "local habits." In forming a new world, territorial Judge Samuel Holden Parsons contended, "the different local prejudices are to be done away and a medium fallen upon which may reconcile all."[30] Only a superintending national authority would possess the disinterestedness to protect such valuable territory from foreign entanglements and to guide it to the highest possible stage of development.

Congress laid the foundations for national authority in the Ohio Country in the Northwest Ordinance of 1787. As early as May 1786, Congressman James Monroe reported that Congress was proposing that the Northwest have "a Colonial Govt. similar to that wh. prevailed in these States previous to the revolution, with this remarkable and important difference," that they should be admitted to the Confederation when their population equalled the smallest of the thirteen states, and when they proved tractable. The assumption, of course, was that men like Joseph Ross and John Amberson would not be organizing the new states. Congressional doubts about the West were so strong, in fact, that Monroe feared that some congressmen would want to increase the requirements for statehood to a level that would keep the frontiersmen out of the Union altogether. Congress could make statehood hard to achieve by making a population equal to one-thirteenth of the number of free Americans a pre-requisite. Such a restrictive policy, Monroe believed, would simply drive the independent frontiersmen into the hands of the British or Spanish.[31]

By 1787 the general sense of Congress was clearly for the adoption of a stronger western policy. With the army unable to evict the squatters in the Ohio Country permanently, with the impact of Shays's Rebellion and a major revision of the general government underway, it seemed necessary and inevitable. Thus, when Washington wrote to James Madison in March 1787, advocating "a thorough reform of the present system" of the general government because of his growing doubts about "public virtue," he natu-rally included his fear that the "Western Settlements without a good and wise management" would be "troublesome."[32]

Such doubts were widespread. Amazed at "The Enterprize" and emigra-tion of his countrymen, John Jay was afraid in the spring of 1787 that "the Western Country will one Day give us Trouble—to govern them will not be easy." Jay worried, moreover, "whether after two or three Generations" the frontiersmen "will be fit to govern themselves . . . for The Progress of Civilization and the Means of Information is very tardy in sparse and sep-arate Settlements." In "such Republiks" as America, wrote the trader Bar-thelemi Tardiveau to Colonel Harmar from the French settlement at Vin-cennes in 1787, "where extensive and far distant frontiers are generally inhabited by a sort of people who are" likely "to mistake the idea of licen-tiousness for that of liberty," an energetic government was requisite. Even Thomas Jefferson worried that the United States would lose the land by delay and by offending the West over the Mississippi question. Because of "the temper of the people" and the international situation, a "separation was possible at every moment." If only the frontiersmen could be retained "til their governments *become* settled and wise, they will remain with us always, and be a precious part of our strength and of our virtue."[33]

In April 1787, Henry Knox, the secretary of war and an associate of the Ohio Company, fervently urged Congress to act. No doubt with his mil-itary friends' plans in mind, Knox argued that "the evils of usurpation and intrusion" were the greatest threats to the security of the United States' lands. "The value of the object—The spirit of adventure—and the sup-posed imbecility of government," he warned, make "the dangers of usurpa-tion on a large scale extremely imminent." Congress had to do something, or the intruders would become large enough to "defy the power of the

United States." Knox, therefore, sought—and got—a resolution authorizing Harmar to act to evict squatters in the Vincennes area. Otherwise, the intruders would easily "wrest all the immense property of the western territory out of the hands of the public."[34]

By the time Manasseh Cutler arrived in New York City in July 1787 for his celebrated negotiation with Congress for the Ohio Company's purchase, the company and Congress were thinking along the same lines. Stronger measures had to be taken to protect the immense property and prospects of the United States, and the elite's special interest in it, from the people on the frontier. There was no conspiracy in the fact that the Ohio Company's purchase and the Ordinance of 1787 were completed in the same month; but it was no coincidence, either, for the interests and goals of both parties were the same. What the Ordinance enunciated as policy, process, and fundamental law, the Ohio Company—by settling land sold by Congress—would carry into reality.

Both expected that a strong territorial government, supported by strong national power embodied in troops and forts, would allow for a coordinated, cautious—or what George Washington called a "regular" and "compact"—settlement of the West.[35] A haphazard dispersal of peoples across an expansive territory would threaten their plans to elevate the tone and character of Western society by eliminating the possibility of controlled, coordinated development. The West should be settled compactly, for with organized, highly developed settlements succeeding each other in a systematic fashion American society would inch its way westward, pausing to replace wilderness with civilization, and refusing to surrender to the disorganizing tendencies inherent on the frontier.

The sale of massive quantities of land to admitted speculators like the Ohio Company and John Cleves Symmes in 1787 might, on first glance, seem to be a contradiction of this policy. But, while the land sales were clearly departures from the form of progressive settlement, they did not violate its spirit. The national government basically entered into an alliance with the Ohio Company and Symmes; if they got land at a cheap price and the promise of individual profit, the government got men who were committed to a certain kind of Western development to act as its agents on the frontier. Much has been made of the advantages the speculators received in the appointments of Symmes and Ohio Company directors James Varnum and Samuel H. Parsons (and later Rufus Putnam) as territorial judges. But what of the benefit to the government that accrued from having men on the frontier whose interests were intertwined with those of the national government, whose financial prospects depended on the ability of the national government to uphold its contractual obligations, and who shared the Federalist vision of the West to the extent that they were willing to become its chief on-the-spot implementers? Both the Symmes and the Ohio Company purchases were more than profitable speculations; they were means of insuring the introduction of order, system, and regularity to the West through what territorial Judge Samuel Holden Parsons called "the systematical mode of settlements." Cutler promised that the Ohio Company "will be a continuation of the old settlements, leaving no vacant lands exposed to be seized by such lawless banditti as usually invest the frontiers of countries distant from the seat of government."[36] The Ohio Country was thus entrusted to gentlemen of the proper persuasion.

In fact, one of the primary arguments used by Manasseh Cutler to obtain the Ohio Company purchase was that it would be a "systematic settlement" of the West by industrious and virtuous men. Congressman Samuel Osgood praised the idea of "System" as surmounting the greatest obstacle to the settlement of the West. But it was Richard Henry Lee who put the matter most succinctly in a letter to Washington on July 15, 1787. The Ordinance "seemed necessary," he argued, "for the security of property among uninformed and perhaps licentious people, as the greater part of those who go there are." To counteract the squatters' pretensions to local control, "a strong-toned government should exist and the rights of property be clearly defined."[37] The Ohio Company purchase, he added, would reduce the public debt and retire public securities. Some congressmen worried about the size of the purchase and the ability of the associates to pay for it. Cutler won most of them over with promises of industrious and systematic settlement and the reminder that the company's purchase would "enhance the value of federal lands and prove an important acquisition to Congress."[38]

Cutler also benefitted from the involvement of himself and other leading Ohio Company associates in the Scioto Company. In return for contracting for the sale of one and one-half million acres to speculators like William Duer and other prominent men, Cutler was able to obtain necessary votes and funds to complete the contract with Congress. But these dealings do not invalidate the idea that the men who wrote the Ordinance and the associates of the Ohio Company were like-minded men. Indeed, they were often the same men. Their ideological connections were as intertwined as their financial ones. They disagreed and compromised over price, quantity, and other matters, but most agreed on underlying assumptions about the settlement of the West.

On April 7, 1788, the superintendent of the Ohio Company, Rufus Putnam, and several dozen men arrived at the confluence of the Ohio and Muskingum rivers and began to improve the land the company had purchased from Congress. They established a town on the east bank of the Muskingum, across from the federal Fort Harmar, and planted crops. By far the most significant event in the first year of settlement was the July arrival of the recently appointed governor of the Northwest Territory, Arthur St. Clair. A resident and magistrate in western Pennsylvania before the Revolution and more recently the president of Congress, St. Clair had accepted the position of governor as a stepping stone to higher office in the young American republic.[39]

Like St. Clair, the founders of Marietta, as they eventually called their community, were firm supporters of the Constitution of the United States, then in the process of ratification by individual states. Obviously, a strong national government would offer them protection from Indians and other nations. But the associates of the Ohio Company went out of their way to praise that "superior wisdom which formed the new plan of a federal government, now rapid in its progress to adoption," to express "unreserved confidence" in St. Clair, and to pledge allegiance to the form of territorial government outlined in the Northwest Ordinance of 1787 for social and ideological as well as defensive reasons.[40]

The members of the Ohio Company above all sought the sanction of the national government as a guarantee of their individual social status. The associates were self-described gentry attempting to establish social and economic hegemony in a fluid, frontier society. Their sole source of legitimacy and authority was the government which had sold them their land and that might appoint them to political offices; only it, they believed, could establish the "regularity, order, and perpetual harmony" that they coveted. The establishment of the local hegemony of the Ohio Company, therefore, was profoundly dependent upon the establishment of the national hegemony of the United States government.

And yet, the reverse was just as true. The authority of the national government in the Northwest Territory was, to a significant degree, dependent upon the local influence of the Ohio Company. The Northwest Ordinance of 1787 attempted to promote the power of the United States by establishing a hierarchical government with power firmly concentrated in the hands of nationally appointed officials. The governor, who virtually had dictatorial powers, and three judges were to govern the Northwest Territory, a vast region that included the present-day states of Ohio, Indiana, Illinois, Michigan, and Wisconsin, until it achieved a population of five thousand free male inhabitants. Local government would be administered by judges of county Courts of General Quarter Sessions, who were to be appointed by the governor alone. The Confederation Congress had chosen leading figures in the Ohio Company to be territorial officials (directors James M.

Varnum and Samuel Holden Parsons were to be territorial judges and company secretary Winthrop Sargent was to be the territorial secretary) because they were men of national orientation and proven loyalties. Staunchly supportive of the new Constitution and personally loyal to their former commander George Washington, they were men whose first allegiance was not to a town, a state, or popular opinion, but to the government of the United States.[41]

St. Clair was therefore happy to receive the proferred allegiance of the associates. He saw Marietta's success in dominating the upper Ohio Valley both economically and culturally as crucial to his efforts to establish the power of the brand-new territorial government. In a July speech to Marietta's assembled residents, the governor took care to emphasize the reciprocal nature of the town-government relationship. Like a patron, the national government appointed prominent members of the Ohio Company to territorial offices in order to solidify its position in the new territory; like clients, the associates in return deferred to the government in order to strengthen their positions in commanding the respect of other settlers.

Reflecting upon "the character of the men under whose immediate influence and example, this particular settlement, which will probably give a tone to all that may succeed it, will be formed," the governor explicitly noted that directors Varnum and Parsons had been appointed territorial judges because they were well-known, "distinguished characters"; thus, "the respect which is due to their station is secured." In other words, they assumed territorial offices because their positions within the company demonstrated that they already commanded the respect of a large number of their fellow citizens. For the same reason, St. Clair would shortly entrust local offices to leading associates.

In Washington County—which the governor created to cover the area from the Pennsylvania border west to the Scioto River, and north from the Ohio River to Lake Erie—St. Clair filled local offices with leading associates of the Ohio Company. The first judges of the Court of General Quarter Sessions were Rufus Putnam and Benjamin Tupper, with Isaac Pearce, Thomas Lord, Return Jonathan Meigs, and Griffen Greene as assistants. The governor also appointed Putnam and Tupper, along with Colonel Archibald Crary, as judges of the Court of Common Pleas. The commission of sheriff was given to Colonel Ebenezer Sproat. In 1790, Putnam resigned as a local judge to become a territorial judge, and was replaced by Joseph Gilman.[42]

The most important of these local bodies was the Court of General Quarter Sessions. Functioning like county commissioners, the justices had broad powers over local life. They supervised local taxation, laid out public highways, established township boundaries, and appointed township officers. In December 1790, the Washington County court created the three townships of Marietta, Belpre (about fifteen miles down the Ohio), and Waterford (about twenty miles up the Muskingum). Again, local officers were leading associates.[43]

With the support of the national government, the founders of Marietta intended to make it a great city that would serve as the hub of the highest level of commercial and cultural exchange. The Ohio Company's painstaking plans for an elaborate city illuminate the urban character of the Federalist plans. Like most western settlers, the associates had high hopes for Marietta. But these men were not just town boosters; they boosted their town as a means to an end—the greater glory of the American empire. Marietta, according to Manasseh Cutler, would "serve as a wide model for the future settlements of all federal lands." The first legal settlement in the Northwest Territory, argued company director James M. Varnum, would be a "bright example" to "add to the felicity of others."[44] The associates would "endeavor to take the lead, and give a Tone to the New States forming in the western quarter." George Washington was particularly pleased that the legitimate settlement of the Northwest Territory would be led by "the Generals Putnam, Varnum, and Parsons, the Colos. Tupper, Sprout, and Sherman. . . . From such beginnings, much may be expected." The plan of Marietta was drawn in Boston in the fall of 1787. The agents of the company reserved 5,760 acres of their purchase at the confluence of the Ohio and Muskingum rivers for a city of 60 rectangular blocks in the general form of 10 blocks wide and 6 deep. All the streets were to be 100 feet wide except for a main one of 150 feet. Of the 60 blocks, the agents appropriated 4 for public use, while the other 56 were to be divided into "house Lots" of 90 by 180 feet.[45]

In the Ohio Country, Rufus Putnam laid out the basic gridiron pattern specified by the agents, but in so doing he took advantage of "the situation of the Ground" and put it to use as a foundation for the orderly city. The most striking feature of the land the Ohio Company bought was a group of ancient Indian mounds, which intrigued the New Englanders. Winthrop Sargent, for example, spent days measuring and preparing descriptions of the mounds. The first thing Cutler went to see when he arrived for his brief visit in the fall of 1788 was the most curious of the ancient monuments, a large cone-shaped mound surrounded by a ten-foot moat. The early Mariettans were obsessed with speculation about the origins of the mounds. Solomon Drowne, interested in attaching some classical virtue to them, suggested that they were not unlike the burial mounds of the ancient Trojans, the ancestors of the Roman republicans. Certainly there had been an elaborate civilization on the spot of the Ohio Company settlement and the Mariettans felt a primitive nobility exuding from its remnants. What the agents resolved about the future of the cone-shaped mound applied for all of "the ancient works." "Every prudent measure," they decided, "ought to be adopted to perpetuate the figure and appearance of so majestic a Monument of Antiquaty." Eventually, they made it the center of their cemetery.[46]

More than merely preserving the mounds, Putnam built the town around them, superimposing the regular plan of the company on the Indian ruins. The larger mounds became the centers of public squares, which were given names associated with the Roman republic. The agents named the land around the burial mound Conus, and reserved blocks called Capitolium and Quadranou focusing on two rectangular mounds. Putnam and the agents established the final of the requisite four public squares at the confluence of the rivers and named it Cecelia. Completing the reminders of ancient Rome, the New Englanders christened their temporary stockade Campus Martius.[47]

The company did not rely altogether on what the land provided to mark their city. They planned a large role, for example, for trees that they would plant. The agents in Boston had ordered rows of mulberry trees placed along both sides of the city streets. Placed ten or fifteen feet from the houses, the trees' duties, according to Cutler, were "to make an agreeable shade, increase the salubrity of the air, and add to the beauty of the streets." The rows of trees would also create natural sidewalks, leaving streets the spacious width of seventy feet. The importance of trees in adding to the beauty and regularity of the city is most clearly reflected in the strict rules for the temporary leasing of the public squares for clearing and other improvements until the danger of Indian attacks had passed. A "Mr. Woodbridge," for instance, was given a lease on the Capitolium in 1791 for eight years on the condition that he "surround the whole with Locust Trees, except at each corner there shall be an Ash" and "that the trees be set out within two years." The elevated mound on the Capitolium, moreover, "with the Ascents leading to the same," were to be "immediately put into Grass and hereafter occupied in no other way."[48]

The names of the city streets were chosen to reinforce a sense of public responsibility among residents of the regular city by perpetuating the fame of its founders and their contemporaries. While the associates gave the streets parallel to the Muskingum River numerical names, the names of members of the Society of the Cincinnati marked the perpendicular avenues. Appropriately, the Mariettans called their main street Washington. Those streets to the south of it they named Knox, Worcestor, Scammel, Tupper,

Cutler, Putnam, Butler, and Greene; to the north were St. Clair, Warren, Montgomery, and Marion. The only break in the ranks was Sacra Via, which ran in two parallel strips from Quadranou west to the Muskingum River just above Washington Street, and preserved part of the noble Indian works.

Indeed, Marietta fulfilled all the requirements necessary for the "perfect harmony" prized in the rhetoric of its builders. The gridiron pattern of the city gave it the desired predictability. The broad avenues and the public squares centered on the Indian mounds united an emphasis on classical order with the elegance of the natural setting. Marietta's plan was not a radical innovation in urban planning. But it was an effort to institutionalize regularity in the physical structure of society. More than a monument of regularity, Marietta was to be a regional economic and cultural center as well. The economic basis of the Federalists' West was agricultural, of course. But from the beginning, they envisioned something more than farms, including manufactures and international commerce. The Ohio Valley, Cutler argued, would soon produce iron, lead, coal, salt, glass, crockery, wines, potash, wood, skins, and other processed goods in abundance. "No country," he contended, "is so well calculated for the establishment of manufactures of various kinds." The Federalist West would not have a colonial economy; it would not simply ship raw materials to the East, but would process plants, meats, and minerals into finished goods.[49]

These products, whether raw or processed, would be sold around the world. James Varnum promised in 1788 that the greatest advantages of the Ohio Country were its "innumerable streams, through a variety of channels communicating with the ocean, and the opening prospect of a prodigious trade and commerce." From the beginning, the Ohio Country attracted merchants like John May and Dudley Woodbridge who tried to establish trans-Appalachian business concerns. The products of the Ohio Country, Putnam believed, would "find their way to the seaports" of Massachusetts, "much to the advantage of her citizens who shall be concerned in the trade."[50] It was no coincidence that, with the conclusion of the Indian wars in 1795, Marietta quickly became a center of oceangoing shipbuilding. Cutler had promised in 1787 that shipbuilding would "be a capital branch of business on the Ohio and its confluent streams." In 1800, the first ship, the square-rigged brig *St. Clair*, was launched with a cargo of flour, wheat, and bacon, which was traded in the West Indies and Philadelphia. In 1803, Marietta became an official port of registry and clearance for ships in foreign trade. By 1808, when the Embargo brought the industry to a halt, the citizens of Marietta had sent approximately 20 ships of 150 to 450 tons to the Gulf of Mexico.[51]

What the town's residents were trying to do was to implement Washington's vision of an Ohio Valley fully integrated into the Atlantic economy. It is here that the canals and roads we traditionally associate with the term internal improvements become important. Such developments would bind West to East and would make land values in the Ohio Valley rise, but they would also substantially affect the character of the economy and society. As soon as West and East became economically interdependent, the Federalists believed local differences would dissipate into a harmony of general interests and shared values; the distinction between West and East would disappear.

It was imperative, the Federalists further believed, to arrive at this happy point as quickly as possible, thereby eliminating the frontier stages of development which fostered the rude, independent, and parochial behavior of the squatters. Thus, from the early 1780s men like Cutler and Putnam as well as Washington were interested in improving communication and transportation between the Ohio Valley and the rest of the world. They discussed portages and canals to link the Ohio and its tributaries with the Great Lakes and the deep rivers of the tidewater; they eagerly anticipated the imminent arrival of the steamboat; they plotted roads through the wilderness, and they moved as quickly as possible to establish commercial links with the outside world by whatever means available.

This nationally controlled, urban vision of the West also involved a different kind of society than we usually associate with the American frontier. Inequality was assumed by the Federalists to be a natural part of civilized existence and they had no intention of leveling society. To the contrary, their city and its hinterland would be dominated by gentlemen property holders who would employ craftsmen, laborers, and domestics. Cutler even urged that European manufacturing companies be invited to the Ohio Country where they could work "under the superintendence of men of property."[52] Western society would thus be complex rather than a simple agrarian paradise, a society built upon the exchange of goods and services and the interdependence of human beings.

The Federalist society in the West would also be marked by the enjoyment of luxury items from around the world, the attainment of high cultural achievements, and the gentility of human relationships. The strong institutions of churches, schools, courts, and government provided for in the Ordinance of 1787 would restrain individualistic excesses and secure social order. Education would "revive the ideas of order, citizenship, and the useful sciences" among frontiersmen whom Cutler claimed were "in danger of losing their habits of government and allegiance to the United States." "Our people," hoped Ohio Company associate Thomas Wallcut, "will be the means of introducing more ambition and better taste to the West." "A communication with all nations," proclaimed associate Solomon Drowne, would allow the introduction of "the most useful and excellent scientific improvements, which are to be found in every kingdom and empire on earth." Indeed, one year of life in "the polished intercourse" of Marietta made Drowne doubt that he lived in a "wilderness" at all. The Federalists had hoped for little more.[53]

The Federalist vision of the West thus involved a rapid improvement of the wilderness into the highest stages of civilization. Americans would not regress into the disorganization, laziness, selfishness, and parochialism so often associated with the frontier, but would progress across space and time into a world of commerce and manufactures, canals and cities, science and order, blending interests in national harmony. The Ohio Country, Thomas Wallcut promised, would become "the garden of the universe, the center of wealth, a place destined to be the heart of a great Empire."[54] The West would be settled without a frontier.

The Federalists' plans for the Ohio Country did not meet with immediate success. In fact, it was their eventual opponents—Jeffersonian Republicans in the new state of Ohio—who actually built the canals, roads, and schools that Washington and Cutler imagined in the 1780s. The national government, moreover, had little to do with these projects. Still, it would be wrong to characterize the Federalists as out of step with the dynamic transformation taking place in the American economy in the Early Republic. They simply overestimated their ability to guide Western development and underestimated the tenacity of frontier conditions. When the Ohio Valley attained a stage of economic and social organization comparable to that in which the Ohio Company originated, even the largely Virginia-born Jeffersonian gentry would echo the sentiments of the early Federalists about the need for system. In the end, internal improvements would be made partly to bind East and West, partly to develop the American economy, and partly to create as equal and as inexpensive an access to world markets as possible. But they were also undertaken partly for a reason the Federalists had sought them: to bring order and system to a society of would-be autonomous individuals by encouraging the highest levels of economic, social, and cultural interdependence and homogeneity.

Whatever their ultimate fate, the plans for the future of the Ohio Valley described in this chapter suggest that some Federalists were, at least for a time, far more than the conservators of traditional economic and social order that historians have often portrayed them to be. Indeed, few people in the early American republic embraced a more creative, more dynamic, or more revolutionary vision of the future of the United States than the associates of the Ohio Company and their allies in the national government.

3

Establishing the Authority of the National Government
1788   1798

One of the most significant things about the settlers of early Marietta, given the prevailing conceptions of a frontier community in the Old Northwest, was their profound respect for national authority. Almost without exception, historians since the days of Frederick Jackson Turner have argued that the Ohio Valley in the Early Republic was what John Barnhart called a "Valley of Democracy," a region whose rapidly expanding population insisted upon the supremacy of local sovereignty and warmly embraced doctrines of social egalitarianism. In the "kinetic setting" of the American frontier, Robert Wiebe argues, westerners felt little respect for distant eastern governments, rejected hierarchy as a mode of social organization, and were unable to develop any "sense of a contained, personally integrated whole." More specifically, Gordon S. Wood has written in a recent major textbook that "it was in the territories of the Old Northwest that American democracy ran its course." There, the "hundreds of commercial communities were so recent and so bustling, the lines of economic authority so tangled and confused, that no clear structures of political authority could be readily transplanted or created." Or, as Stanley Elkins and Eric McKitrick put it in a classic article, the Old Northwest was a region whose "burgeoning capitalism recognize[d] no prior structures, [was] impatient of elites, [and] tolerate[d] few restraints." It was a world of individual opportunity and local autonomy.[1]

Partly as a result of their assumptions about frontier society, historians have tended to disparage the power of the national government in the Northwest Territory and the five states created out of it. They have pointed to vast distances, prolonged Indian conflicts, and the frequent absences and alleged arrogance of territorial officials as its undoing. But, more important, they contended that what Jack Ericson Eblen has called the "fully centralized, nondemocratic form of government" created by the Ordinance of 1787 was, in the words of Randolph Downes, "quite incompatible with frontier conditions." Territorial officials and their supporters, including the associates of the Ohio Company, thus have usually been portrayed as ineffective, stiffnecked, Puritan anachronisms, out of step and out of touch with the dynamic democratic character of frontier society.[2]

This chapter seeks to qualify that perspective through an in-depth study of the relationships between government and society and local and national authority in the town of Marietta. It proceeds from the belief that historians have been so struck by Jeffersonian Republican political triumphs in the Ohio Valley, by the apparently democratic nature of evangelical religion that permeated the trans-Appalachian frontier in the early nineteenth century, and by repeated assertions and descriptions of local prerogatives in a variety of contexts that they have underestimated the achievements of Federalist territorial officials in the 1790s. By treating men like Governor Arthur St. Clair, Secretary Winthrop Sargent, and Ohio Company Superintendent Rufus Putnam as eccentrics or dismissing them as exceptions, historians have failed to come to terms with them.

The town of Marietta was hardly a microcosm of the Northwest Territory. But its citizens had a disproportionate influence with the territorial and national governments as well as being their leading advocates. Far from accepting isolation or demanding local autonomy, the early Mariettans firmly believed that by integrating themselves and the other residents of the Old Northwest into the national patronage system being developed by President George Washington and cabinet secretaries Alexander Hamilton, Henry Knox, Oliver Wolcott, and Timothy Pickering, they could attain their goal of a profitable, stable, and harmonious society.

Ironically, in Marietta, "frontier conditions" like individualism, a scrambled social structure, and the weakness of traditional institutions strengthened more than weakened allegiance to the national government. By 1803, when Ohio became the seventeenth state to be admitted to the American Union, the authority of the government of the United States was secure. Territorial and Marietta Federalists lost office in the same year, but not before they had contributed substantially to the establishment of the rules and contours of power in the Old Northwest.

Although the Ohio Company purchase and the Northwest Ordinance of

1787 were the work of one of the last meetings of the Congress of the Confederation, they became as integral parts of the Federalist program of the 1790s as the Bank of the United States or the suppression of the Whiskey Rebellion—for what they all had in common was a demonstration of the power of the United States under the Constitution of 1787. The foremost task of national officials in the distant Northwest Territory was to show western settlers that "the Government of the United States was not a mere shadow," as St. Clair put it in an August 1789 letter to President Washington. If frontiersmen learned to respect the government of the Constitution, St. Clair believed that they would resist the blandishments of Spanish and British agents, temper their penchant for ignoring the wishes of eastern governments, and become solid citizens of the United States. "Their progeny would [then] grow up in habits of Obedience and Respect—they would learn to reverence the Government; and the Countless multitudes which would be produced in that Region would become the Nerves and Sinews of the Union."[3] With a vertical power structure and the help of the associates of the Ohio Company in administering local government, St. Clair hoped to reverse what he saw as the localist, disintegrating tendencies apparent on the frontier and to attach territorial residents to the government of the United States.

In the first decade of Marietta's existence, local officials appointed by St. Clair sought to become exemplary parts of a system uniting national and local officials. Their efforts were hampered by a number of problems, not the least of which was the omnipresent danger of Indian attack until the Treaty of Greenville was signed in 1795. But they also had to govern a growing, fluctuating body of people who often seemed more attached to individual aggrandizement than to any government, people who seemed to personify the presumptuous ambition and defiance of legal authority that Federalists on both the local and the national levels feared would lead the young United States into anarchy and decline. In the late 1780s, the migration of people down the Ohio River was huge by contemporary standards. Between October 1786 and May 1789, at least 1,019 boats carrying 18,761 people passed Fort Harmar on their way downriver to homes in Kentucky. The number of migrants astonished James Backus, a Connecticut native en route to Marietta in May 1788. People of "every description" were moving through Pittsburgh. Ohio Company associate John May reported that in the spring of 1788, 15,000 people left Redstone, Pennsylvania, for "the Western World." Most of these people settled in Kentucky. Still a Virginia county, Kentucky was safer than the Northwest and had a relatively open method of land disposal. So great was the migration of people to Kentucky that the missionary John Heckewelder remarked in 1792 that the Northwest Territory would soon be purged of its "wicked class, for experience teaches, that as soon as they are made subject to the laws, they leave for Kentucky." Still, Heckewelder estimated 3,220 people were living in the Ohio Country in 1793.[4]

Especially threatening to the authority of the government was its inability to resolve differences with the Indians to the satisfaction of many frontiersmen. The latter were inclined to take matters into their own hands. Kentuckians continued to engage in similar forays. In August 1788, Kentuckian Patrick Brown, calling himself "a major" and claiming authority from the governor of Virginia, led 60 men into the Wabash Valley. According to Major John F. Hamtramck, the American commander at Vincennes, the group attacked the peaceful Piankashaw Indians, killing at least nine of them. A year later, Major John Hardin and 220 Kentuckians gathered opposite Louisville and moved up the Wabash River, killing 12 Wea Indians in reprisal for native attacks.[5] These were only the major manifestations of the escalating hostilities on the Ohio frontier. Such independent actions outraged federal officials because they incited the Indians to further reprisals and threatened the hegemony of the federal government in the Northwest.

National officials had long eschewed war or simple seizure as a means of dealing with the Indians. Even if the land west of the Ohio River was America's by right of conquest, argued Congressional Indian Commissioner Samuel Holden Parsons in 1785, it was more expedient to placate "the Indians by purchasing such tracts as they will sell." Besides, Congress could not afford to undertake a major war against hostile Indians. In any case, according to Secretary of War Henry Knox, there was no need to fight "for an object which may be obtained by a treaty." By purchasing the lands of the Northwest Territory from the Indians, the government could "conform to the modes and customs of the indians in the disposal of their lands, without the least injury to the national dignity." Jonathan Dayton, a leading New Jersey politician and land speculator, believed that settling lands without Indian consent was unjust. Taking land without at least the forms of permission was no better than squatting. "The law of right and wrong is an universal law," asserted Dayton in 1788, "and has its influence amongst the most savage as well as the most polished nations."[6]

Throughout the 1780s, congressional representatives pursued a policy of negotiating with the Indians as part of an overall effort to bring order to the West. After the American Revolution, Congress pressed for a meeting with leading chiefs of the several tribes in the Ohio Valley. In 1784 it appointed Richard Butler, Arthur Lee, and George Rogers Clark as commissioners to treat with the Delaware, Wyandot, and Shawnee tribes. Congress instructed these men to make land purchases, trade, and the establishment of legal boundaries their primary objectives. In late 1784, Butler and Lee met with representatives of the Wyandot, Delaware, Chippewa, and Ottawa tribes, and in January 1785 they signed the Treaty of Fort McIntosh. By this agreement, prisoners taken in the American Revolution were to be exchanged, a boundary line was established at the Cuyahoga River, and whites who settled on lands beyond that regularly established boundary forfeited the protection of the United States. Any person who crossed such boundaries without license was to "be treated in such manner as the Indians think proper."[7]

The Ohio Company associates were strong advocates of peaceful negotiation with the Indians. Rufus Putnam had argued in 1783 that trading factories were a necessary means of establishing permanent peace and mutual understanding between Americans and Indians. "Commerce with these people" would not only be profitable; it would attach "them to our interest." Putnam acted on the assumption that Indians were much like whites. They, "like all other people," he supposed, "forme their attachments where they have their commerce." The exchange of goods would form a strong bond and would lead inevitably to an exchange of ideas; it was, in short, "one grate means of securing the allegince of the natives." Putnam later made it clear that he wanted to purchase land from the Indians "on the principles of Bargains and Sale" in "an experiment of faire dealing."[8]

Like the squatters, the Ohio Company and the government's ultimate goal was to deprive the Indian nations of their land. But leading Americans had no intention of treating the natives in the violent and ad hoc fashion characteristic of the frontiersmen; they were, as Rufus Putnam put it, "people of a different Carracter." Congress intended to negotiate, not engage in expensive and barbarous raids. After all, the Delaware chief Captain Pipe was, according to Colonel Josiah Harmar, "more of a gentleman than the generality of these frontier people" and merited the respect of the government. The success of this conciliatory policy was crucial to the establishment of national authority in the Northwest Territory. The spontaneous behavior associated with attacks on the natives by Kentuckians could not be tolerated. Otherwise, warned Governor St. Clair in January 1788, "the proposed establishments in the country north-west of the Ohio, and the further sale of lands there for the discharge of the public debt" would be impossible. Fearing "that the deep rooted prejudices, and malignity of heart, and conduct, reciprocally entertained and practised on all occasions by the Whites and Savages will ever prevent their being good neighbours," Secretary of War Henry Knox had written in 1787 that "Government must keep them both in awe by a strong hand, and compel them to be moderate and just." Only "a legal coercive power" in the form of more troops and forts would bring peace and "evince to the world the disposition and power of the United States to govern and control their own citizens."[9]

In the 1780s, Colonel Josiah Harmar established Forts Harmar (at the mouth of the Muskingum River), Washington (at Cincinnati), and Knox (at Vincennes) to protect the Indians and the frontiersmen from each other. But, in 1788, the government could muster only 350 troops on the frontier. As a result, Major Hamtramck, the commander at Vincennes, could only observe the expeditions of angry Kentuckians. Colonel Harmar believed that Patrick Brown, the leader of the 1788 raid along the Wabash, deserved "to be hanged" for "setting the sovereign authority of the United States at defiance." "But what could I do?" lamented the undermanned Hamtramck. "I had but nine men fit for duty."[10]

St. Clair, meanwhile, tried to achieve a lasting peace through negotiation. Treaties were, as Knox said, "the only rational foundations of peace." In December 1788 the governor met with several Delaware and Wyandot chiefs at Fort Harmar. Within a month both sides signed a treaty, which confirmed the boundary established by the Treaty of Fort McIntosh in return for six thousand dollars in goods. Trade was also to be improved and white aggressors punished. Nonetheless, despite the friendly atmosphere of the Fort Harmar negotiations, the treaty was of little consequence. The Shawnee and Miami tribes had not attended and remained hostile. The continuing "irregular and unauthorized expeditions" of angry frontiersmen, moreover, meant that the treaty was not considered binding by all Americans and that the federal government could not enforce its will in the West.[11]

By the summer of 1790, however, with white raids increasing and Indian attacks on the Ohio Company and Symmes purchases growing, it was clear to federal officials that they had to act. Otherwise, their authority would never be established on the frontier. Colonel Harmar concluded that the government would have to raise an army to "chastise" the Indians and demonstrate the authority of the United States to white settlers. "All treaties," he argued, "are in vain."[12] The Federalists could not bring peace to the frontier through rational discussion. To deal with the angry natives and to outflank the frontiersmen, federal officials reluctantly went to war in 1790. Accordingly, St. Clair called for Virginia and Pennsylvania militiamen to assemble at Fort Washington in September 1790.

In the fall of 1790, Colonel Harmar led an unsuccessful expedition against the Indians. Congress responded to the failure by authorizing more money and troops for another campaign. But the united natives routed an army under Governor St. Clair in the fall of 1791. The causes of these defeats were many, not the least of which was Indian ingenuity and tenacity. Above all, the Federalists lost because of inadequate resources and poorly trained militia. In fact, the territorial hierarchy had been forced to rely on the Kentucky militia, the very men whose illegal actions they were trying to defuse, for the bulk of their troops. Both campaigns were sabotaged by poor preparation. The defeats were disastrous. St. Clair lost 37 officers and almost 1,000 of his 1,200 troops. The Federalists were not only defeated by the Indians; they were publicly humiliated.

Eventually, the thoroughly trained and well supplied legion of General Anthony Wayne won the Ohio Country for the United States at the Battle of Fallen Timbers in 1794. A year later the Treaty of Greenville established a boundary line east of the Cuyahoga River and approximately 150 miles north of the Ohio River. Peace had come to the Ohio Country and settlement by Americans on a large scale soon followed. But the government's failure to end the war quickly and the military humiliations it had suffered in the early 1790s had not helped the Federalists' efforts to establish the hegemony of the national government in the Northwest Territory.[13]

The prolonged Indian war created a series of hardships and problems for the residents of Marietta. But the associates of the Ohio Company had expected severe challenges to their authority from Indians and frontiersmen. What surprised them was the degree to which such lawless behavior characterized relationships within, as well as without, the company.

By the winter of 1788–89, approximately thirty families and over four hundred people lived in Marietta. Thereafter, Indian dangers reduced the population to a floating group of three to four hundred. While leading associates tended to congregate in Campus Martius, a stockade about a mile above the confluence of the Ohio and Muskingum rivers, many people lived at the Picketed Point, a row of houses and commercial establishments across the Muskingum from Fort Harmar. With a tavern and stores attuned to the needs of river traffic and the soldiers at the fort, the Point developed in miniature many of the tendencies toward raucous individualism and a lack of deference to the national government and its officers that the Ohio Company associates hoped to avoid in their town. Associate Thomas Wallcut was especially upset by Point resident Isaac Mixer, "a man of notoriously vicious character," who kept "a disorderly, riotous, and ill-governed house." Worse, Mixer owned a seven-year-old male slave, "a flagrant trespass upon the rights of humanity; the privileges of American subjects, and the peace and happiness of this jurisdiction, as well as the dignity of the United States."[14]

As a result of such incidents, a group of Marietta leaders adopted a series of bylaws on March 19, 1789, designed to consolidate their authority within the town. Most of the laws established regulations regarding garden rights, sanitation, protection from the Indians, and the clearing of roads. But some dealt with disorderly conduct. The sale of liquor was placed under the control of an appointed Committee of Police; "disorderly Tipling houses or Grogg shops" were to be discouraged; and nothing was to be sold to soldiers without the permission of their officers. All of these regulations were justified by the need for "one uniform System . . . for regulating the interest of the whole."[15] Good citizens would obey them and discountenance those who did not.

Marietta developed a reputation for strictly enforcing community regulations; those who did not like it could and did float on downriver to other settlements. But the passage of local laws to regulate the licentiousness of Virginians and Scotch-Irish—as the Ohio Company associates were wont to refer to anyone who was not a resident of Marietta in good standing, an officer of the national government, or a New Englander—did not solve the most pressing problem in the young community. Much more serious than strangers' challenges to the authority of the federally appointed Marietta leadership were challenges from within the Ohio Company. Despite the rhetorical vision of a virtuous, harmonious town that permeated early Marietta, it was a settlement most distinguished during the first few years of its existence by personal disagreements among its leading citizens.

The fact that the leaders of Marietta squabbled among themselves is not surprising. Both migrations and revolutions are essentially acts of rejection and creation; among the most conspicuous results of both are ideological confusion and social disarray. The lives of the associates of the Ohio Company were thus doubly disrupted, for they had experienced both revolution and migration within quick succession. With traditional rules of social and individual behavior under challenge in America as a whole, the associates found it difficult to reach a consensus on the specifics of what was right, fair, and just, or even on how to deal with each other. Society was scrambled, at least temporarily, and anyone's claim to property or status seemed just as legitimate as anyone else's. In other words, contention and chaos were endemic to the place and time. While the associates railed against the selfishness and unchecked ambitions of other frontiersmen, they fell victim to the same tendencies. The failings they so vehemently condemned in others were not just personal or cultural quirks, but human responses to a very fluid social environment.

In contributing to the development of a national market economy, the associates often found themselves at cross-purposes. They might talk of the advantages of harmony, regularity, deference, and self-sacrifice, they might preach, as Marietta orator Solomon Drowne put it, "that happiness is not the offspring of contention, but of mutual concession and accommodation."[16] But there were few things more common to success in land specu-lation and the marketing of products in the unformed world of the frontier than competition and assertions of individual interests. Like it or not, the associates had to be aggressively self-interested to prosper.

The rancor, jealousy, and suspicions of a frontier boom-town thus char-acterized early Marietta, as the associates scrambled to protect and ad-vance their individual interests and to challenge the interests of others. Take, for example, the unfortunate history of the Scioto Company. The brainchild of speculator William Duer, the Scioto speculation was a disas-trous enterprise from start to finish. In July 1787, when the Ohio Com-pany's negotiations with Congress for the purchase of land in the Ohio Country were not going well, Duer offered to help director Manasseh Cutler obtain the votes necessary to approve the purchase of one and one-half million acres at the price of one dollar per acre and to grant the asso-ciates a one hundred thousand dollar interest-free loan, if Cutler would agree to attach an option for three and one-half million acres to be sold in France as a purely speculative venture. Cutler agreed, Congress approved the sale, and several associates of the Ohio Company (including Rufus Putnam, Samuel Holden Parsons, Winthrop Sargent, and Cutler) received substantial shares in the speculation. "Ye Ohio Company could not have completed their payment without loaning money at ye expence of ye Com-pany," argued Cutler. "We are beholden to ye Scioto company for our purchase."[17] The rest of the story is relatively familiar. Sales in France were slow and those people who did purchase land were rewarded with a misera-ble existence at their settlement at Gallipolis, down the Ohio River from Marietta. The Scioto speculation was a financial failure and an administra-tive fiasco.

It was also a very controversial issue in Marietta in 1788–89. A group of Rhode Island associates, led by director James M. Varnum and Archibald Crary, strenuously objected to the Scioto Company, not because it was immoral or badly handled, but because they had been excluded from it. The Rhode Islanders had joined the Ohio Company in late 1787, too late to share in the potential bounty of the Scioto speculation. But they nonethe-less claimed, at a point when prospects for the speculation were still promis-ing, that their investment in the Ohio Company entitled them to participate in the Scioto Company as well. When Cutler refused to agree, the dissidents denounced "the attempt to deprive us of our rights" as "highly ungener-ous." Calling the Scioto speculation a "Base attempt" on the part of some of the directors (meaning Cutler, Putnam, and Parsons) "to benefit them-selves," they demanded the dismissal of "such persons from Office, who are acting against the interest of the company by favoring this Design."[18]

Cutler felt himself "much injured" by these "representations." He condemned Varnum for "spreading jealousies and discords" among the associates and, after a short visit in the late summer of 1788, left Marietta an angry and bitter man. Back in Massachusetts, Cutler gave up his plans to migrate to the Ohio Valley, fearing that "ye spirit, which has been publickly known to prevail in Rhode island, will be transplanted and prevail" in the Ohio Country. By the "Rhode island" spirit, Cutler clearly meant the reputation of that state's citizens for contentious behavior. Rhode Island was not Cutler's ideal of a "well-regulated society."[19]

But neither was Marietta. Varnum and Crary objected to many things about the way the new town was being run. Rufus Putnam, for instance, offended them with his land distribution policies. In order to insure a rough equality in the division of land in and near Marietta, the associates had drawn for eight-acre lots in Providence, Rhode Island, in 1787. But Putnam, in his capacity as company superintendent, quickly discovered that equality could exist only on paper. Because of the hilly terrain of the Ohio Country, lots necessarily varied in quality. Putnam also wanted to keep the lots close to navigable streams so that agricultural products could be brought to Marietta as easily as possible. While the superintendent strove to keep the eight-acre lots "as nearly equal in quality and situation" as possible, geographical considerations forced him to lay out some of the lots ten miles or more from Marietta. Tracts that were that far from the settlement were considered much less valuable than ones adjacent to the town.[20]

When Varnum and his followers arrived in the early summer of 1788, they strongly protested Putnam's decision to locate the lots along navigable streams rather than "contiguous to the City." Objecting that some of the lots were so far up the Muskingum River that the transportation of produce from them was "impracticable," the new arrivals accused Putnam of disregarding his instructions. The superintendent replied that his actions were necessary given the lay of the land. If some of the first settlers seemed more fortunate than those who had come later, continued Putnam, it was only fair that the original pioneers should receive some special benefits. Putnam's defense further enraged Varnum and his friends and the ensuing conflict according to Putnam, "very much disturbed the peace of the Society."[21]

Eventually, the feuding associates agreed upon a compromise. Three thousand acres of common land were divided into three-acre lots and drawn for in Marietta on July 2, 1788. Unfortunately for the peace of the settlement, the Varnum faction fared no better in the location of these lots than they had with the eight-acre tracts. Again, Putnam reported, Varnum and his friends "raised Some flying Clouds." This time, they proposed "to annihilate the Commons and eight acre lots intirely as now laid out in Sted thereof to lay out a tract (how much they have not Said) in one Square and draw for the Same." By this time, Superintendent Putnam believed the best solution was to give every share in the company a sixty-four acre farm and be done with it. But the Marietta associates voted to reject both Varnum's and Putnam's arguments and to retain the eight-acre lots.[22]

Such squabbles were exceeded in frequency only by their bitterness. Even the deaths of company directors and territorial Judges Varnum and Parsons in January and November of 1789 provided little more than occasions for further spleen-venting. Parsons hoped that the death of the "very unhappy" Varnum would end all animosity. Cutler was almost pleased at the news of his chief critic's death. Varnum's conduct, Cutler confessed, had given him "much uneasiness." Perhaps divine providence had interfered on behalf of the Ohio Company by removing Varnum. "It is a maxim with me, 'that ye Lord be praised for all things,' and in this case," wrote Cutler, "I find no great difficulty in applying it." The news of Parsons's drowning in November similarly pleased the company and territorial secretary, Winthrop Sargent. Parsons's alleged scheme to sell company land to himself at a low price had outraged Sargent. "Alive," the secretary admitted, "I was the Enemy to his low Cunning, and Practices which I considered dishonourable."[23]

And so it went in early Marietta. The associates even fought over the name of the town (chosen to honor Queen Marie Antoinette of France), which some thought "effeminate, exotic," and impossible to "americanize." By the summer of 1789, John May was speaking only to a select few; "The Devill," he declared, "may take the rest." Not even the assurances of Rufus Putnam that "the best people" wanted Manasseh Cutler to return to Marietta could entice the minister to leave Massachusetts.[24] His enthusiasm for the Ohio Country had disappeared in a sea of contention. So bad was the situation that Putnam's nephew argued that "desention" was the greatest obstacle "to the peacable possession of our Beautiful country." Some way had to be found to "keep in equilibrium the . . . tendency of aviric and ambition."[25]

In fact, it was precisely this sort of squabbling among grasping men in a fluid social structure which the Federalists had hoped to avoid in governing the Northwest Territory. By making the national government the ultimate source of legitimate authority, they had hoped to insure stability and to prevent contention. But the Ohio Company associates were beset by the same tendencies toward individual aggrandizement and defiance of authority which they complained of in others. Indeed, it may have been their constant quarreling that made them so insistent about the importance of regularity and harmony.

While Marietta was not always the model of harmony it was supposed to be, personal ambitions and jealousies were also strong challenges to the successful administration of the territorial government. Here, too, the problem was the uncertainty of status and the vagueness of legal boundaries in a frontier society. Territorial officials found it almost impossible to balance their desire for personal fame and fortune with the demands of their jobs.

From the beginning, Samuel Holden Parsons was extremely sensitive about his status as a territorial judge. He wanted Congress to make it clear that he was *primus inter pares* with regard to the other territorial judges, James Varnum and John Cleves Symmes.[26] Salaries were constantly on the minds of territorial officers. They took seriously the contention of presidential secretary William Jackson that they were in the West to gather "a large harvest of honorable fame and private happiness." St. Clair, Sargent, and the judges saw substantial salaries from the federal government as a means to securing in the West that status they felt was slipping away from them in the East. When Secretary of War Henry Knox recommended that Sargent supplement his income through agriculture, the secretary of the Northwest Territory complained that his duties left him too little time to farm. Throughout the decade, Sargent pressed Congress for more money, seeking, in particular, compensation for service as acting governor during St. Clair's extensive absences. With such a large territory to administer, St. Clair also felt his salary "very inadequate" to "support him in the manner that will be expected, and which the Dignity of Government requires." With government salaries remaining small, the territorial officers turned to an elaborate system of fees to provide them with an income suitable to their positions.[27]

Both Sargent and St. Clair worked very hard to maintain strong ties with powerful men in the East. Such connections marked them as important figures and the goal of personal independence did not prohibit obsequious letters. "It will add very much to my Happiness," Sargent promised President George Washington in November 1789, "to contribute to your Excellency's Pleasures." His services were always at Washington's disposal. St. Clair cultivated both Washington and Secretary of the Treasury Alexander Hamilton. Whether or not Hamilton informed him of news in the East, St. Clair would "always find" himself "deeply interested in" the treasury secretary's "Fame and Fortune."[28] And the governor filled letters to Presidents Washington and Adams with expressions of poverty and the petty insults he suffered in the Northwest. Territorial officials sought the favor and recognition of federal officials for more than ambitious reasons. To be legitimized as a man of prominence by those who were above them compensated to some degree for the lack of respect on the part of the ordinary settlers in the West.

Despite all their professions of hard work and devotion to duty, the territorial officials were often negligent in the administration of the Northwest. Whether because of the frustration of trying to bring order to the frontier or because personal interest demanded it, they were frequently out of the territory. In 1798, Sargent noted that Governor St. Clair had spent most of his tenure in the East. Judges John Cleves Symmes and George Turner, appointed in September 1789 to succeed Varnum, were often absent; even Judge Rufus Putnam spent a good deal of time in the East. Judge Turner had to be ordered back to his post several times in the fall of 1792.[29]

Secretary Sargent greatly lamented the impact of the judges' frequent absences "as a very great misfortune to the territory." Their neglect of their duty injured "the reputation and honour" of both the territorial and federal governments. "Private Business" was undermining the establishment of a republican hegemony in the Northwest. But Sargent was not above leaving the territory to press his financial claims with Congress. Nor could he hide his acute embarrassment when he found that he and St. Clair were absent from the territory at the same time when they were both in Philadelphia in February 1794.[30]

Sargent's frequent complaints of official negligence eventually aroused the federal government. How could the authority of the United States be established in the Northwest if the governor and the judges were continually leaving the territory for their own convenience and business? The "long absence" of St. Clair and "some of the judges," President Washington feared, would produce irregularities and encourage "a spirit of riot and disorder, by relaxing the energy of the Laws." Washington was angry that George Turner had to be threatened with legal action to get him to return to the territory. "Such remissness," Washington knew, "not only reflects upon the common rules of propriety, but must implicate me in the shamefulness of their conduct, in suffering it." But even presidential wrath had little impact. When St. Clair called for a legislative meeting of himself and the judges in Cincinnati on September 1, 1793, he had trouble locating Symmes and Turner. When Turner retired in 1797, Sargent argued that his place ought to be filled with someone who would at last "Make the Duties of his office his primary Consideration."[31]

Even when the Federalist officers of the territory could overcome their private interests and coordinate meetings they rarely got along. They were simply too sensitive to every kind of slight, real or imagined. No one was secure in his position and everyone worried about the respect, or lack of it, that he was paid. Although St. Clair and Sargent were usually amicable, there were strains in their relationship. Sargent's frequent service as acting governor in St. Clair's absence occasionally produced a collision between the two men over the boundaries of their respective offices. Winthrop Sargent particularly embodied the tension among the territorial officials over the legitimacy of their positions. So insecure was Sargent that his years as secretary of the Northwest Territory (1789–98) and as governor of the Mississippi Territory (1798–1801) were consumed with petulant protests against all sorts of perceived attacks and reprimands.[32]

Far more serious was the frequent conflict between the executive and the judges in the administration of the Northwest Territory. They especially quarreled in the first years of settlement over their ability to make new laws. St. Clair believed that the territorial legislature of governor and judges could only adopt laws already established in one of the eastern states. Judges Varnum and Parsons argued that territorial officials needed to create laws to meet the special circumstances of a frontier region, provided that they were "conformable" to the laws of the East. Congress, of course, formally upheld St. Clair's interpretation. But, in practice, the territorial legislature often made its own law. Throughout the decade, Congress had to overrule territorial laws because of their innovative character.[33]

There can be no doubt, moreover, that personal interest often lay behind the judges' determination to write new laws. The judges, Governor St. Clair noted in the mid-1790s, were leading characters in the "principal settlements" in the Ohio Country. Even if men like Rufus Putnam and John Cleves Symmes demonstrated "firm character," who could blame the people of the territory for suspecting that they had "but a slender security for the impartiality of their decision?"[34] St. Clair wanted the powers of the judges reduced and the decisions of the territorial legislature subjected to appeal to the federal courts. The national government would serve as an arbiter among the citizens and officials of the Northwest Territory.

If the lack of true judicial disinterestedness threatened the image of law being impartially administered, the constant bickering among territorial officials damaged their credibility with their superiors. In fact, the journal of the executive proceedings of the Northwest Territory thoroughly disgusted Secretary of State Edmund Randolph; it was, he told President Washington in 1794, "very little more than a history of bickerings and discontents, which do not require the attention of the President."[35]

To be sure, some of the contentiousness among the Ohio Company associates and territorial officials was the product of prickly personalities. Winthrop Sargent, for example, appears to have been temperamentally incapable of getting along with anyone. But the incessant squabbling was also the product of a frontier society in which the social structure was scrambled and political authority undefined. Lacking established legal and political institutions, men from the squatters to the territorial judges felt themselves to be on their own and acted accordingly. Still, the disorganization of the frontier did not last forever; it was especially short-lived in the Federalist city of Marietta.

The national government eventually attained the stature intended for it in Marietta because its control of political offices in the town and the territory made it the most powerful arbiter of social status. To a large extent, the initial disputes of the associates were resolved by the deaths of Parsons and Varnum and by the decisions of Cutler and Sargent to live elsewhere. But equally important were the efforts of Superintendent Rufus Putnam to stabilize the social structure of his dissension-ridden town by reviving and strengthening the somewhat dormant reciprocal relationship between Marietta and the national government. Putnam wanted to eliminate the chaos of the early years brought about by the absence of predictable social and political structures. By the mid-1790s, Marietta had acquired a stable sociopolitical system, the national government's authority was secure, and Rufus Putnam had consolidated local power in his hands by making himself the indispensable liaison between the town and the national government.

As it became clear that the establishment of national authority in the West was going to take time and as the political consensus of the early years of Washington's first administration began to collapse, the officers of the United States government welcomed Rufus Putnam as a prominent agent. Hardly born to the status of gentleman, Putnam had made a living in his native Massachusetts as a miller, farmer, surveyor, and sometime soldier, rising to the rank of brigadier general during the Revolution. Fifty years old in 1788, Putnam had migrated to the Ohio Country to secure his financial independence and to establish what he called a "tone" for Western settlement. He had long since passed the litmus test of loyalty to the national government. An active opponent of Shays's Rebellion, Putnam had been an early and firm advocate of the Constitution of 1787. The Ohio Company superintendent, moreover, was a man whose ambition did not exceed his grasp, a man who was comfortable showing as well as receiving deference. In his memoirs, Putnam was proud to point to the "indubitable evidence of the esteam, frindship, and patronage of so great and good a man as General Washington (continued for more than twenty years)" in his appointments as a territorial judge in March 1790 (replacing the deceased Parsons) and as surveyor-general of the United States in October 1796.[36] In Putnam, the national government had a representative on the frontier who happily tied his status to the security of a national hierarchy. Putnam could take orders as well as give them. Politically and socially, Rufus Putnam was a perfect man to represent the United States government in the Ohio Valley.

In keeping with the wishes of his superiors, Putnam devoted much of his thirteen years of federal service to increasing the power and majesty of the United States. He advocated better roads and a regular mail service on the Ohio River as the means of keeping people better informed of their government's policies. In 1791, he urged a more effective prosecution of the Indian war (which was going badly after the defeat of two expeditions) in order to impress frontiersmen with the power of the national government. "Too many," Putnam had told Fisher Ames in 1790, "reguard not the authorety of their own States, nor yet of Congress, more than the Savages themselves." And for the United States to "suffer" squatters and independent expeditions against the Indians "to insult her authorety with impunity" was an outrage. Unless the government acted quickly, it would cost the United States much more than the expense of an Indian war "to reduce" the frontiersmen "to obedience." Instead of "well informed and well disposed Citizens," "Privit adventurers, who will pay little or no reguard to the laws of the United States or the rights of the natives" would, like the squatters of the 1780s, girdle trees and plant corn, and the territorial and national governments would be powerless to prevent them. Putnam had not forgotten that "numbers of these people were driven by the federal Troops at the point of the Bayonet" a decade earlier. If the government could not prove that it could protect its frontier, it would insure that "these people, with others of like principles, will return like a flood and Seize the country to them Selves."[37]

Indeed, Putnam contended in 1794, after General Anthony Wayne's victory at Fallen Timbers, that had the United States acted so strongly earlier, it "would have given a weight and dignity to the Federal Government that would have tended greatly to check the licentiousness and opposition to Government unfeverable in this country"; he believed that the Whiskey Rebellion would never have occurred if people had not had such "a contemptable opinion of the strength of our Government." But now Wayne's victory would assure all people "that the protection of Government will be equally and impartially extended to all."[38] The United States government had no stronger advocate in the 1790s than Rufus Putnam.

But the arrangement between Putnam and the Federalist administrations was clearly reciprocal. For if he advanced and protected their interests on the frontier, they gave him legitimacy and authority within his own community. Cabinet officers called upon Putnam to recommend men for office or to comment upon the character of potential appointees. Since all offices, local and territorial, were appointive, Putnam thus had very real power. Even future Ohio political leaders like Nathaniel Massie and Thomas Worthington wrote to Putnam seeking his patronage.[39] Putnam was clearly the dominant figure in Marietta from the early 1790s until 1803 because, as a territorial judge and then as surveyor-general, he controlled access to a system of patronage that he hoped would preclude a revival of the confusion and conflicts of the early years of settlement. Because power in the town and the territory was apportioned through appointment, Putnam's national connections made him a respected, even feared, arbiter of individual ambitions and claims. No local election ratified his position; his legitimacy came from outside the town.

Like his superiors, Putnam saw political office as something more than a hobby or way to make money; it was a public responsibility to be exercised by gentlemen. Throughout the 1790s, he thus cultivated a coterie of men well disposed toward the national government. Bringing order out of chaos, Putnam saw to it that local offices went to men of demonstrated socioeconomic status and correct principles—merchants such as Benjamin Ives Gilman and Dudley Woodbridge, and lawyers such as Paul Fearing and Return Jonathan Meigs, Jr. He engaged in a system of national patronage appointments and shied away from democratic local elections not because he was some early-day Boss Tweed with a coonskin cap perched precariously on a powdered wig, but because his whole life told him, as it told Hamilton and Washington, St. Clair and Sargent, that stability and prosperity would come to the young American republic only if power were entrusted to the safe and sure hands of men of character in as regular and predictable a fashion as possible.[40]

The system worked well in the 1790s. Putnam secured the postmastership of Marietta for Return Jonathan Meigs, Jr., who was, according to Putnam, "the most popular lawyer in this County[,] of unblemished Carractor." Putnam also played the key role in the appointment of territorial judges. When he gave up his judgeship in 1796 to become surveyor-general of the United States, Putnam was asked by Secretary of State Timothy Pickering to recommend a replacement. Putnam replied that he knew of no one with "any pretence" outside Marietta, and nominated Joseph Gilman, Return Jonathan Meigs, Jr., and Dudley Woodbridge. Gilman, Putnam's first choice, got the position. Two years later, the "gentlemen" of Marietta, under Putnam's direction, recommended Meigs to replace the retiring George Turner; Meigs, too, got the job.[41] Most of the men Putnam chose for offices were much younger than he was, a situation that allowed him to act as an older and wiser figure while preparing ambitious, younger men for a steady rise to power in a stable, predictable sociopolitical structure.

The importance of the system of patronage in keeping Marietta a well-ordered town is best seen in Putnam's reaction to challenges to it. Seeking to avoid a return to the social confusion of 1788–90, he was adamant about appointments being made through established channels. In 1798, Putnam went out of his way when recommending men for a vacant territorial judgeship to denounce the self-appointed candidacy of one Matthew Backus. The young man had had the presumption "to offer himself as a candidate," deliberately circumventing the established system of patronage. Putnam objected to Backus because he "was considered by all clases of people" in a "contemptable light as a lawyer." But it was not his legal skills, or lack thereof, that worried Putnam and "other Gentlemen." Backus not only did not have a patron, he did not have the character or the social status necessary to hold the office, that which President Washington called in another context "celebrity of character." An untrained man like Putnam, who had taught himself to read and write (albeit poorly), could be a judge in the Federalist scheme of things because he was a reliable public figure. But Backus was simply an upstart, an example of the "new" men who so disturbed the Federalists; for him to succeed, or even to be seriously considered, was to invite anarchy and to disturb the social equilibrium maintained by the patronage system. Backus's pretensions were reminiscent of and threatened a return to the open scramble of the first years of the settlement. Thus Backus, who had little chance of getting the appointment without the support of Putnam, nonetheless gave "great uneasiness to every person who has a due regard for the honor of government[,] the dignity of the Courts of Law[,] or intrest of the people."[42] The appointment of Matthew Backus as a territorial judge was a dangerous notion because it would drive a fatal wedge between social and political positions and undermine the power of national representatives such as Putnam.

The challenges of men like Backus were easily deflected in Marietta where the authority of the nationally appointed gentry was relatively secure. Within the Ohio Company settlement, the Federalists had been very successful in creating a stable, predictable society. But Marietta was not the entire Northwest Territory. Elsewhere—particularly in the Scioto and Miami valleys—many people were settling the Ohio Country with a spirit of localism and individualism reminiscent of the squatters of the 1780s.

Representatives of national and local authority had been at odds north of the Ohio River for more than a decade by 1798. In the next five years, the debate became more heated and explicit. Indeed, no issue divided the settlers of the Ohio Country between 1798 and 1803 (when Ohio became a state) more profoundly than the question of the proper source of political authority both in the Northwest Territory and the American republic as a whole.

4

An Alliance of Local Interests
1790   1798

The most successful of the early settlers of the Northwest Territory tended to be those men who arrived in the region with some capital and influential connections. Pioneers such as Rufus Putnam, John Cleves Symmes, and Nathaniel Massie of the Scioto Valley were able to consolidate large land holdings and to exert considerable power over local economic development. But many people who migrated to the river valleys of the Ohio Country in the 1790s bought their land from large-scale speculators only to find that often their titles were disputed by other claimants. Having come to the Northwest Territory "to provide for our families: and in Some hopes of getting a Piece of Land to live on," immigrants were as "Much Disappointed in getting Land" in the Ohio Country as they had been in other places.[1]

The best solution to the problems of such settlers would have been the ordered, regular development of the West called for by Governor St. Clair and the Ohio Company associates. Ironically, the territorial government's very insistence upon legal proprieties and national authority offended people seeking quick resolutions of tangled land disputes. By the late 1790s, many citizens of the territory saw St. Clair as a major obstacle to the fulfillment of their expectations about life in the Ohio Country. If the people of the Northwest Territory could only replace "a government so illy adapted to the genius and feelings of Americans," wrote a newspaper correspondent calling himself "A Friend to the People" in September 1801, "it will be like opening the flood gate to a mill."[2]

The young, largely Southern-born gentry who were gobbling up land in the Scioto Valley were happy to lead a movement against St. Clair. Men like Nathaniel Massie, Thomas Worthington, and Edward Tiffin found the ideological assumptions that underlay the territorial government frustrating. Increasingly dominant economically in their local area, they were unable to achieve commensurate political influence because of the centralized nature of the territorial government. In the late 1790s, Massie, Tiffin, and Worthington began to quarrel with Governor St. Clair over the authority to locate county seats and to appoint local officials. In the first few years of the nineteenth century these petty conflicts grew into a struggle over the locus of power in the Ohio Country: Did agents of the national government, appointed without the consent of the people they governed, or locally elected officials have supreme authority in the Ohio Country?

If Rufus Putnam and Arthur St. Clair were essentially nation boosters, Massie and Worthington were regional and state boosters. The latter's advocacy of local sovereignty against what they viewed as overpowerful national authority was part of a larger movement in American politics associated with Jeffersonian Republicanism. Just as Thomas Jefferson feared the efforts of Federalists on the national level to consolidate power in the federal government as threats to the liberty of Americans, so too did Thomas Worthington see in Arthur St. Clair an obstacle to the full economic and social development of the Ohio Country.[3]

The Northwest Territory's fledgling Jeffersonian Republicans shared the Federalists' belief in the necessity of a correspondence between economic and political structures and thus gladly received appointments to local offices from St. Clair as evidence of their standing in their communities. But they did not share the Federalists' passion for the gradual development of the West under the paternal guidance of the national government. They were in a hurry; they were not worried about "new" men like Matthew Backus; they did not want to defer to or to depend upon the wishes of a distant national authority. Like the squatters of the 1780s, they believed that the key to prosperity and happiness was leaving people free to control their own destinies.

After the 1795 Treaty of Greenville reduced the immediate threat of Indian attacks, the population of the Ohio Country grew dramatically. The Miami Valley was especially attractive to new settlers. Well watered and easily reached, the fertile plains above Cincinnati were a farmer's paradise. By 1801, some fifteen thousand people lived scattered throughout the region. While some resided in small villages, most bought land and took up farming. In the late 1790s, a Cincinnati newspaper reported a small land rush in the Miami Valley. Land that had sold for only two or three shillings per acre at the height of the Indian war now brought better than three pounds.[4]

But the most dramatic demographic explosion in the Northwest Territory occurred in the area just west of the Scioto River. Hundreds of thousands of acres there were legally reserved to Virginia's revolutionary war veterans by a congressional act of 1791. The Virginia Military Tract was a part of the territory not subject to prior survey and distribution by the national government or one of its agents. All one needed to acquire land was a warrant issued in lieu of pay to soldiers by the state of Virginia during the American Revolution. When the warrant was located within the district and registered with the Virginia land office, the owner received legal title to the land.[5] The Scioto Valley attracted almost twelve thousand settlers in the late 1790s. Even regular, autumnal fevers "did not deter immigration," recalled James B. Finley, one of the early pioneers. "A desire to possess the rich lands overcame all fear of sickness, and the living tide rolled on heedless of death."[6]

The central figure in the settlement of the Scioto Valley was Nathaniel Massie, the first in a series of men who came from Maryland, Virginia, and Kentucky to settle the Ohio Country with advantages that would make them economically and politically powerful. Founder of Chillicothe and several other Ohio towns, surveyor and eventual owner of 75,825 acres in the Virginia Military Tract, Massie was, according to his grandson, "by far the wealthiest, most popular and influential" man in the early Scioto Valley.[7] He and his friends dominated the locating of warrants in the Virginia Military District. They built large mansions on huge estates around Chillicothe. Expecting to govern, they were as much a self-perceived elite as the Ohio Company associates. But their conception of the relationship between leaders and ordinary citizens was very different from that of the territorial Federalists. Massie and his colleagues expected to be freely entrusted with power because they believed in the ability of the populace to recognize and reward obvious talents. Their material accomplishments made them worthy of office; popular elections simply confirmed their eminence.

Nathaniel Massie was hardly a typical settler. His father had served as a justice of the peace and a captain of militia in Goochland County, Virginia. In 1783, Nathaniel Massie, Sr., gave his twenty-year-old son what few emigrants to the West had—lands already located in Kentucky, some money, and letters of introduction to prominent men in the West.[8]

In Kentucky, Massie became a leading surveyor. By locating and identifying lands for Eastern clients, the young man reaped a "considerable profit," sometimes receiving one-half of the land surveyed for his services. As a clerk for Colonel Richard C. Anderson, principal surveyor of the Virginia Military lands, and then as a deputy surveyor, Massie became experienced in accumulating land and developed connections with Eastern speculators and Western land agents. By 1786, Massie was beginning to diversify his interests; he briefly entered into a fur and salt trade partnership with James Wilkinson, one of the more enterprising and influential citizens of Kentucky.[9]

As early as 1788, Massie crossed the Ohio River to investigate the land in the Scioto Valley. Ignoring his father's warning "to drop venturing so much," Massie made annual trips into the newly created Virginia Military Tract in the early 1790s. Defying Indians and the wilderness, Massie surveyed, located, and entered land throughout the region. Between 1791 and 1801, he surveyed over 700 tracts of land containing more than 750,000 acres.[10]

Massie also travelled to the East to buy land warrants and to engage clients. Unlike the associates of the Ohio Company, he sought fortune on his own. In 1795, while on a visit to Philadelphia, he engaged a broker to purchase warrants for him. "I have some prospect of making a purchase of One thousand acres of land on the Ohio," Massie told a correspondent. These warrants, giving the right to a specific quantity of unlocated land, were the keys to Nathaniel Massie's success. Once located, the warrant "stands appropriated, and may remain in that situation or longer as a person may think proper or may be removed and relocated at pleasure."[11] As in the rudimentary land system of the squatters, Massie's business was highly individualistic. He had no contract with Congress.

To make his lands more profitable, Massie established towns in the Scioto Valley. In 1796, he started a settlement about fifty miles up the Scioto from the Ohio River. Originally called Massieville, the name was changed to Chillicothe (an Indian word for town). Soon ringed by the estates of prominent landowners, Chillicothe quickly became the dominant metropolis of south-central Ohio. Massie's friend Thomas Worthington was "much astonished" at the speed with which the town grew. In May 1797 he noted that "new arrivals every day" added strength to the 150 families who already inhabited Chillicothe.[12]

Massie actively patronized some men by giving them the benefits of his influence and knowledge. William Hutchinson's pioneering 1927 study of land ownership in the Virginia Military District revealed that of the 3,900,000 acres available in the region, seventy-five men or partnerships received deeds for 3,320,247 acres with twenty-two men alone claiming 1,035,408 acres. Most of these men were somehow connected with Massie. Among the large holders were Richard C. Anderson (23,421 acres), the surveyor of the Virginia Military District, Kentucky Senator John Brown (24,962 acres), and Massie assistants Duncan McArthur (90,947 acres) and John Beasley (12,195 acres). Thomas Worthington, the leading figure in Ohio politics between 1800 and 1820, owned 18,273 acres.[13]

Worthington, who was born in Virginia in July, 1773, had inherited 1,466 acres in the Shenandoah Valley from his father. After a year at sea in 1791, Worthington continued his father's interest in speculation in Pennsylvania lands. In 1795, he bought some Virginia military warrants and went to the Northwest Territory to locate them. Impressed with the fertility of the Scioto Valley, Worthington determined to settle his family there. He applied for a job as a surveyor and contracted, in the summer of 1797, with Duncan McArthur for the location of 7,500 acres at the usual one-fifth commission. By that time, Thomas Worthington and Nathaniel Massie were business acquaintances and correspondents; the latter began to stop at Worthington's home on his trips to the East for more land warrants. In July 1797 Massie obtained Worthington's appointment as "a Major of the militia and a Judge of the court of common pleas" in the newly created county of Adams.[14]

Worthington was only one of many men to benefit from association with Nathaniel Massie. Edward Tiffin, Worthington's brother-in-law—eventually to be the first Ohio governor and later United States senator—shared in his relative's good fortune. Born in Carlisle, England, in June 1776, Tiffin had come to Berkeley County, Virginia, in 1784. There he studied medicine and in 1789 married Mary Worthington. Tiffin, who was ordained a deacon in the Methodist church in 1792, had a strong distaste for slavery. Consequently, he freed his inherited slaves and moved west with his wife's brother in 1798, conveniently preceded by a letter of recommendation from George Washington to Arthur St. Clair.[15]

Other men rose to prominence in the Scioto Valley through more direct connections with Nathaniel Massie. Duncan McArthur, one of the largest landowners in the Virginia Military Tract and later a governor of Ohio, began his career as a chain bearer for Massie in 1793. The son of a Scotch-Irish family, McArthur was born in Dutchess County, New York, in 1772; eight years later his family moved to western Pennsylvania. At the age of eighteen, McArthur served in Josiah Harmar's disastrous campaign and lived as a hunter and Indian scout. After accompanying Massie on several expeditions, he became an assistant surveyor in 1796. With the end of the Indian war, McArthur settled in the Virginia Military District and quickly prospered. Appointed a militia captain in 1798, McArthur obtained "a competent estate in lands, free from incumbrance, on which he could live in a state of independence." Another one of Massie's deputy surveyors, Joseph Kerr, later a United States senator, came to the Scioto Valley from Chambersburg, Pennsylvania. A member of the first Court of General Quarter Sessions in Manchester, Ohio, Kerr settled in Ross County in 1801 and built "a showplace" home on land he purchased from Massie. Charles Willing Byrd came to the Northwest Territory in October 1799 with the advantage of being Nathaniel Massie's brother-in-law. Born at Westover in Charles County, Virginia, in 1770, Byrd had migrated to Kentucky in 1794, and moved to Cincinnati five years later with an appointment as secretary of the Northwest Territory (succeeding Winthrop Sargent).[16]

These men dominated life in the Scioto Valley as much as the Ohio Company associates set the tone of society in the lower Muskingum Valley. Like the New England veterans, these young, ambitious Southerners were heavily involved in land speculation. But in contrast to the highly organized Ohio Company, land speculation (as well as settlement) in the Virginia Military Tract was, by design, a highly individualistic, competitive business. Like the squatters in the 1780s, men simply took as much land as they could obtain warrants to cover. Unlike the squatters' procedures, such activity was usually registered in Virginia land offices. Capital and connections were also crucial to success.

The ultimate goal of these men was obviously individual profit. But obtaining and locating warrants would not make the land profitable; that could be achieved only through reselling tracts at higher prices than were paid for the warrants. Throughout their careers, the Scioto Valley gentry had to compete with the sales of federal lands. As Massie realized, the price of the military lands would in "a great measure" be determined by the price of congressional lands. The federal Land Acts of 1796 and 1800 helped speculators like Massie by setting a price of two dollars per acre for land. This price was so high that land in the Virginia Military Tract appeared more favorable to purchasers "than the terms proposed by Congress." Massie and Worthington also tried to encourage settlers by selling and leasing land in smaller tracts than those offered by the government. Not only did this allow more people to obtain land, it also, noted speculator James Ross approvingly, increased "the chances of selling, and from the number of purchasers more money will probably be received in hand." "The Value of the unsold tracts" would also be enhanced.[17]

Both territorial Federalists and the future territorial Republicans envisioned the Ohio Country as a harmonious society led by aristocrats. But unlike the Federalists, the Scioto Valley landowners neither preached the virtues of stability and controlled development nor feared the dangers of an open, unrestrained, expanding society. They believed that social harmony and economic progress were thoroughly compatible, that private interest and public harmony existed in a symbiotic relationship. The Scioto gentry did not fear unplanned change; on the contrary, they embraced it as the surest path to natural order.

With an optimism about human nature that the territorial Federalists would find naive, the future Republicans argued that the pursuit of private profit was dangerous only when perverted by institutions like the territorial or national governments. In fact, they believed that individual boosterism contributed to the prosperity of society in general. This faith in what amounted to a laissez faire approach to Western development was a natural outgrowth of the economic interests of the founders of the Scioto Valley. They settled as individuals without the organization of a joint-stock company after the Federalists were in control of the territory's political institutions. It was to the advantage of the future Republicans to demand an end to the paternalistic government of Arthur St. Clair.

The Scioto gentry did not expect the Ohio Country to be an open, egalitarian paradise. But their ideas about social structures and political power were more fluid than the rigid, hierarchical notions of the Ohio Company associates and territorial officials. No issues were more revealing of their ambivalence about the relationship between an individual and society than their attitudes toward slavery and religion.

Many Southerners migrated to the Northwest Territory because of their distaste for the institution of slavery. But the widespread opposition to slavery was hardly indicative of feelings of racial equality. In fact, the antislavery attitudes of men like Thomas Worthington and Edward Tiffin were largely an outgrowth of their beliefs in the sanctity of human choice and their opposition to institutions that restrained individuals.

In 1796, a relative of Nathaniel Massie confirmed that among the many people leaving Virginia in search of a "Garden Spot" in the West, those "who have an aversion to Slavery go your way—and these are the most valuable Class of Citizens." Thomas Worthington admitted in 1802 that "the prohibition of slavery in the territory [by the Northwest Ordinance of 1787], was one cause of my removal to it." Slavery was not just unfair to blacks; it was dangerous to whites. It was a curse, Worthington asserted, that would bring "into the country a class of people who will, on principles of justice, consider those who deprive them of their liberty as the worst of enemies."[18]

The problem in the minds of these men was not that blacks were exploited, but that they were coerced into labor. If blacks freely chose to work in return for room and board, the dangers and immorality of slavery could be avoided. As Colonel R. K. Meade of Maryland told Arthur St. Clair in 1789, his slaves would be "freed by a remove to your quarter," but they would not stop working for him. Kentucky emigrant James Finley's father gave his fourteen slaves their freedom when he decided to move across the Ohio River in 1796, but he linked their emancipation with an "offer of removing with him to the new country" and the promise of "support for one year after their arrival." Rather than face a wilderness without any means of support, all but two of the blacks chose to accompany Finley. Thomas Worthington also emancipated his slaves in Virginia in 1798, but his daughter later recalled that most migrated with the family to Chillicothe. Worthington paid them "the current wages." Some occasionally wandered off, but they always returned "to bewail their dear bought" freedom, "which deprived them of the protection so needful to their existence."[19]

Territorial officials did little about the existence of a kind of de facto slavery in the Northwest Territory. Charles Willing Byrd, Winthrop Sargent's successor as territorial secretary, was happy to overlook the law when necessary. When "an Indentured Servant" of Byrd's brother-in-law, Nathaniel Massie, arrived in Cincinnati "in pursuit of his freedom," Byrd employed "Spy's to watch over" the man. The servant, who was called Abraham, claimed that Massie had threatened "to sell him if he did not sign the indenture, and by other menaces he was compelled to subscribe it, and that as it was an involuntary act, he ought to be emancipated by the Judiciary." Byrd disagreed, and imprisoned Abraham until Massie sent someone to retrieve him. In the meantime, the unhappy servant was hired out to so many people for menial chores that he became anxious to return to Massie.[20]

The commitment of the Scioto gentry to antislavery was real, but limited. They opposed an institution that coerced people against their will but did not object to exploiting blacks who "chose" to work for them. In their minds, there was a critical difference between involuntary and voluntary servitude. But for men like Abraham, freedom was a theoretical situation and the choice to labor or not was moot.

The ambivalent attitudes of the Scioto gentry toward personal independence were also revealed in their religious beliefs. Many were strong Methodists. Edward Tiffin was an ordained deacon of the Methodist Episcopal Church, and preached frequently in the Chillicothe area. Worthington had been converted to Methodism in the early 1790s. Both men welcomed Bishop Francis Asbury to their homes on his occasional visits to the Ohio Country.[21] Another leading Chillicothe citizen, Thomas Scott, a native of Maryland, secretary of the 1802 Ohio Constitutional Convention, secretary of the Ohio Senate until 1809, a member of the Ohio legislature, and chief judge of the Ohio Supreme Court from 1810 to 1815, was an elder who preached the Methodist faith before studying law. And the minister of the Chillicothe Methodist church in the early nineteenth century was John Collins, printer and editor of the pro-Worthington *Scioto Gazette*.[22]

To be sure, Methodists in the Northwest Territory were "like angel's visits, few and far between." But the religion was strong in the Scioto Valley. Despite some opposition and ridicule, the Scioto circuit of the church had 472 members by 1805 and Bishop Asbury was preaching to thousands by 1808. "God," the bishop believed, would "yet do great things" in Chillicothe.[23]

Many of the Scioto gentry found Methodism attractive because of its emphasis upon an individual's relationship with God. They disliked the institutional restraints and doctrine of the Congregationalism and Presbyterianism that flourished in Marietta. Worthington and Tiffin were opposed to anything that kept men from reaching their full potential or that obstructed a man's right to choose. Methodism also had strong egalitarian overtones. "I expect," wrote John Sale, the presiding elder of the Ohio District, that "this State will be as the Garden of God and it is pleasing to me to live in a Country where there is so much of an Equality and a Man is not thought to be great here because he possesses a little more of this Worlds rubbish than his neighbour." In this "Land of *Liberty*," men would "wait on themselves."[24]

The Scioto gentry's religious and antislavery beliefs reveal a desire for an open society of autonomous individuals. They defined freedom as the right to choose and assumed that most people would make their choices on the basis of self-interest. Slavery was dangerous and sinful, but servitude was acceptable if men freely chose the condition as necessary to their well-being. Religion should release, not restrict, people. Massie, Worthington, and Tiffin wanted the Ohio Country to be a haven of individual independence, a place without institutional or unnatural restraints on individuals. Society, they believed, worked best when men were left alone to follow their true interests, which they alone could define. Given the success of Massie and his colleagues in accumulating land and wealth in the Scioto Valley, it is little wonder that they advocated a laissez faire conceptualization of society in general.

In the late 1790s, only one institution threatened the independent world the Scioto gentry was trying to create. The territorial government persisted in intruding into what Massie and Worthington considered to be local matters. Arthur St. Clair fundamentally distrusted the ideas that underlay the

Virginians' trust in an open society. He symbolized the superintending institutional control that they despised. Inevitably, the two views of the world came into conflict, making the long-smoldering tension between national and local authority in the Ohio Country explicit.

Arthur St. Clair and Nathaniel Massie never got along. In the summer of 1795, the governor wanted to prosecute the surveyor for allegedly attacking some innocent Indians, but he lacked hard evidence.[25] Still such hostility did not keep St. Clair from appointing Massie and his friends to prominent local offices in the Scioto Valley counties of Ross and Adams; given their economic position, he really had no choice. The appointments were in keeping with the Federalists' insistence upon a correspondence between social and political authority. But the Scioto Valley gentry saw no advantage in loyalty to the territorial patronage system. They trusted their neighbors to recognize their talents and reward them accordingly; their loyalty was to their locality and not to the nationally appointed territorial hierarchy.

The latent antagonism between St. Clair and Massie became overt in 1798. The issue was the location of the county seat of Adams County. Massie wanted the honor for Manchester, a town he had founded, while the governor insisted that it be established at Adamsville. Massie vehemently objected to St. Clair's proclamation declaring Adamsville the official seat of local government. And the justices of the peace defied the governor by agreeing to build the courthouse at Manchester.[26]

That action astonished St. Clair. He called it "contrary to every principle of good order" and "a most unwarrantable assumption of power and contempt of authority." The governor promised to listen to all reasonable requests. But, he argued, county seats "should not be subject to wanton change"; to do so was to foster instability. Finally, St. Clair accused the Adams County justices of putting private interest above that of "the public at large."[27]

Thomas Worthington bristled at this charge. Far from "a wish to create disorder," as St. Clair claimed, or an act of "contempt to the executive," the decision to fix the site of the county at Manchester was an exercise of the rights of local officials. After all, they knew the needs of the county's citizens better than the governor. Worthington also resented St. Clair's insinuation that he stood to benefit from the erection of the courthouse at Manchester. (Of course, the same could not be said for Nathaniel Massie.)[28]

A compromise temporarily resolved the dispute. In September 1798, Governor St. Clair moved the county seat to the mouth of Brush Creek and the new town of Washington. But the issue would not die. Congress eventually reluctantly sided with Massie, but Arthur St. Clair would not budge from his position. The governor's stubbornness was not simply the product of an inflexible or arrogant personality. To allow Massie to determine the seat of Adams County was to forfeit all the efforts of the Federalist hierarchy to increase the power of the national government in the Northwest Territory. In the second session of the territorial legislature in 1799, St. Clair vetoed an act making Manchester the county seat. It would be at Washington. "The removal of seats of justice on light suggestions tends to introduce amongst the people a spirit of discontent, love of innovation, and of cabal and intrigue, destructive of public tranquility, and a preference of private interests to every other consideration," argued the governor in a firm statement of the Federalist position. St. Clair was defending his notion of a West evolving slowly under the firm control of national officials; he was not about to surrender any of his power to local officials.[29]

Massie, Worthington, Tiffin, and others in the Scioto Valley strongly rejected the governor's assertions that the pursuit of their private economic interests would hurt anyone or impede the development of the region. Their experience in claiming land had led them to believe precisely the opposite. From their point of view the true disrupter of order was the territorial government. The Federalists' insistence on restrained development and national control seemed absurd; society, they believed, worked far more harmoniously if men were left alone to decide what their best interests were, if power was in the hands of locally elected officials and not in those of arbitrary officials appointed by a distant national government.

Many settlers in the Miami Valley were coming to the same conclusion in the late 1790s. Hundreds of immigrants to that region had bought land from the speculator John Cleves Symmes, and thereby had become caught in a web of legal and economic difficulties created by Symmes's greed and congressional negligence.

A native of New Jersey, Symmes had purchased several hundred thousand acres from Congress in 1788 and simultaneously secured an appointment as one of the first three judges of the Northwest Territory. Sympathetic to the Federalist vision of the West in the beginning, Symmes quickly proved to be more interested in making money through the rapid resale of his land. The exact boundaries of his purchase remained unclear, a situation that the eager Symmes exploited by selling land outside of the legal limits of his purchase. The judge further complicated matters by failing to meet his installment payments to Congress. Thanks to the effective lobbying of his friends Elias Boudinot and Jonathan Dayton, Congress extended Symmes's purchase to cover his illegal sales. In

1794, the judge received a final patent for 311,682 acres extending northward from the Ohio River between the Little and Great Miami rivers.[30]

Symmes had not learned his lesson, however. He continued to sell land beyond the limits of his patent. "As an American," he told friends in an echo of the claims of squatters, he had "the right of Adam to the soil . . . founded in prior occupancy."[31] Such assertions did little for the settlers who paid Symmes for land only to find their titles declared invalid by the territorial government. Under the federal Land Act of 1796, they were asked to pay two dollars per acre for the land they had already purchased from Symmes. The government, of course, did not recognize their transactions with Symmes and argued that their land was still the property of the United States. A 1797 congressional act granting preemption rights offered settlers little relief because it required full payment within two years.[32]

Governor St. Clair's efforts to protect the interests of the government outraged Symmes and brought the two into open conflict along lines similar to those of the Massie-St. Clair dispute. Again, the underlying issue was local versus national control of territorial society and development. Judge Symmes's quarrels with St. Clair and Secretary Winthrop Sargent and his anger at the federal government's insistence on the original boundaries of his purchase led him to an increasingly strident defense of local and popular rights against the governor's "acts of tyranny" and his "arbitrary conduct."[33]

The "Migrating Multitudes," as the Symmes purchasers called themselves, were just as outraged at their predicament. "There are great numbers sate [*sic*] down upon verbal contracts," St. Clair informed Secretary of State Timothy Pickering. Having paid cash to Symmes, which "he positively refuses to return," and unable to make payments to the government, many people in the Miami Valley found themselves squeezed between Symmes's determination to hold the land he claimed and the government's determination to enforce its rights.[34] The owners of the disputed land really had only two options. They could support Symmes against the government or join the government against Symmes. In other words, they could appeal to either local or national authority.

While some men chose the latter course, most found their futures too tightly linked to the judge to defy him. Without legal titles, some 400 purchasers of land from Symmes argued in 1799 that they bore "the expences of a free people" while they enjoyed "none of their priviledges." Although the government required them to pay taxes, Governor St. Clair refused to allow them to vote for representatives to the territorial assembly because of the property qualifications established by the Ordinance of 1787. "You stand in respect to the right of voting," St. Clair told them, "precisely on the same ground as those who had sat down on the public lands that are not claimed."[35] Deserted by the territorial government, the settlers had little choice but to throw their lots in with Symmes.

The settlers finally got some relief in March 1801 when Congress created a commission to hear the Symmes claims. Secretary of the Treasury Albert Gallatin appointed William Goforth and John Reilly of Columbia (a settlement near Cincinnati) as commissioners, but the process of resolving and confirming the tangled land titles was a long and tedious process.[36]

If anyone deserved to be castigated for the land problems in the Miami Valley, it was John Cleves Symmes. But most farmers found their interest and those of the judge too overlapping to attack him. And Symmes courted popular support and encouraged people to see him as a fellow victim and as the only man who could set things right. Governor St. Clair, on the other hand, attracted the wrath of settlers because of his obstinate refusal to curry public favor. Indeed, he persisted in denying that purchasers of land which Symmes did not legally own were even citizens of the territory. To do so was, in St. Clair's mind, tantamount to abandoning the Northwest Territory to irregular procedures and local autonomy—the very things Congress had hoped his government would prevent.

The governor's paramount loyalty was to the government of the United States and its best interests. But Symmes, and the settlers who had purchased land from him, saw St. Clair as an obstacle to profitable and peaceful development of the Miami Valley. It is not surprising, therefore, that they became staunch supporters of a statehood movement in the Ohio Country. The creation of a state would put more power into local hands and free the Americans north of the Ohio River to handle their problems as they saw fit. Statehood, to many residents of the Miami Valley, was not just a right; it was an "absolute necessity."[37]

Discontent with the territorial government also appeared in the 1790s in Cincinnati—the emerging metropolis of the Miami Valley. From the beginning of settlement at Losantiville (as the town was originally called) in late 1788, the tradition of local self-government was strong in Cincinnati. The early citizens had enacted their own code of laws and elected local officials without the approval of the territorial hierarchy. In early 1790, Governor St. Clair paid his first visit to the Symmes Purchase and promptly renamed Losantiville after the Society of the Cincinnati. He also made the settlement the seat of the newly created Hamilton County. But St. Clair was in a hurry to get to the French settlements in the Wabash and Illinois countries and establish American authority there. Therefore, he spent only three days in Cincinnati and relied heavily on John Cleves

Symmes in appointing local officials. The justices of the peace for Hamilton County included William McMillan (already popularly elected), William Wells, and William Goforth.[38]

Ironically, Colonel Josiah Harmar's decision to build Fort Washington at the site of Cincinnati in 1789 weakened the Federalists' hold on the village. Because of the strategic location of Cincinnati, Fort Washington quickly became the center of military operations in the Northwest Territory. It was from this fort that the disastrous expeditions of Harmar and St. Clair originated. As the military center of the Ohio Valley, Cincinnati was also its financial center. Because specie was almost nonexistent in the West, the certificates distributed by the army in payment for goods were valuable forms of liquid capital. As a result, Cincinnati attracted many people interested in making money quickly. While only a little town of several hundred people and makeshift cabins surrounding Fort Washington, Cincinnati had a disproportionately large number of taverns, warehouses, and trading posts. Its population also was heterogeneous and transient, ranging from women following the army to peaceful Indians seeking to exchange furs for goods.[39]

Given the isolation of the soldiers and the nature of their dangerous and demoralizing duty, it is little wonder that the atmosphere in this frontier town was what the Federalists called irregular. Soldiers found amusement and relaxation in heavy drinking, gambling, and petty quarrels. The Moravian missionary John Heckewelder believed the village in 1792 to be "overrun with merchants" and "teeming with idlers" who were "a people resembling Sodom." Jacob Burnet, the Federalist lawyer, remembered that the army set the character of the entire town; idleness predominated and almost all of the lawyers were "confirmed sots." Territorial laws against gambling, profanity, and drunkenness were almost impossible to enforce.[40]

Throughout the Indian war, the territorial government attempted to control the quantity and quality of Cincinnati's tradesmen by requiring all tavernkeepers and shopkeepers to be licensed by territorial officials. To obtain a license, the storeowner, who often combined trade with tavernkeeping, had to pay a sixteen dollar fee. This measure not only raised money for the government, it was an effort to force tavernkeepers to keep "orderly houses."[41] Above all, of course, it was an assertion of territorial, or national, authority over business activities in the Ohio Country.

Many Cincinnatians quite correctly saw the fee as a deliberate attempt to restrain the natural economic development of their town and an infringement of local authority. In the first issue of the *Centinel of the North-Western Territory,* a newspaper begun in 1793, a writer using the pseudonym "Manlius" denounced the sixteen dollar fee. He argued that the territorial hierarchy was protecting the interests of landholders and singling out tradesmen as "less virtuous" and "less useful" citizens. Manlius preferred a land tax to a fee on tradesmen because it would force "the great land-holders . . . to sell their great tracts in small parcels to such people as will make immediate settlements."[42]

Within a month, Manlius's economic arguments had given way to political and ideological ones. The fee, he believed, was inappropriate in a free republic. Manlius denied the power of an appointed governor and three judges to tax a free people. "The history of the American revolution fully proves to us," he proclaimed, that "the universal language of every American" forbids taking away "their money without their consent" as "the highest species of oppression."[43] The attack on the fee had become an assertion of local and democratic rights.

Increasingly in the 1790s, residents of Cincinnati came to see the Federalist territorial officials as would-be aristocrats. "We thank thee, O Lord," wrote one citizen sarcastically of the territorial government, for "men endowed with wisdom, who, like Tiberius Cesar, tax us without our own consent." He apologized for disagreeing with "thine anointed in sundry instances" and for throwing "contempt on thy servants. . . . Our nobles, O Lord," he continued with an obvious reference to the Scioto Company, "have imported the . . . precious gold and silver of Babylonian France; . . . our elders promised them land, yes, the fertile plains of Gallipolis." The writer ended by hoping that God would assist territorial officials in preventing "all those who are enemies to the divine right of princes, priests, and nobles from entering our territory."[44]

By 1793, territorial Secretary Winthrop Sargent was convinced that the cause of much of the hostility toward territorial officials was the willingness of local officials to accommodate popular wishes rather than uphold authority. As acting governor (in the absence of St. Clair), Sargent declared that in numerous instances "the great invaluable blessing of Trial by Juries" had been "perverted to a Curse in Hamilton County." Since "licentiousness" was the leading characteristic of so many of Cincinnati's citizens, "the magistrate who shall dare to enforce the Laws which are adopted will of Course become the Object of their highest Displeasure." Out of fear, leading citizens like William McMillan were neglecting their duty to restrain "the very great Disorders" in local taverns. Sargent believed that the local justices of the peace would "go with the multitude even to do Evil."[45]

In order to preserve the authority of the national government and its territorial representatives, Sargent used his powers as acting governor in 1793 to supersede the 1790 appointments of McMillan, Wells, and Goforth as Hamilton County justices of the peace with new commissions. The original appointments were made with tenure to last during good behavior; the new ones restricted the justices' tenures to the governor's pleasure. Sargent was attempting to make the justices more dependent upon their territorial superiors than they were on the people of the Cincinnati area; his action was an effort to replace growing local and popular authority with that of the territorial government. The justices appealed Sargent's decision to St. Clair, who endorsed the action of the secretary. Reluctantly, McMillan, Wells, and Goforth bowed to St. Clair's argument that since he, as governor, held his office only during the pleasure of Congress, he could not legitimately issue commissions for local officials to serve during good behavior. In August 1793 the justices accepted their new commissions.[46]

Despite this demonstration of territorial over local authority, St. Clair and Sargent could not control the behavior of Cincinnati's residents. A good example was a 1794 incident involving some peaceful Christian Indians. The trading areas around Fort Washington attracted a stream of Indians in the 1790s. But the white population of Cincinnati, involved in a long and frustrating war, often failed to discriminate between peaceful and warlike Indians. What Sargent called the "rooted aversion of the frontier people" toward Indians produced an atmosphere of tension and suspicion around Fort Washington.[47]

The suspicions gave way to violence in September 1794. Acting on a rumor that a group of fifty-five Christian Indians were preparing to carry off a white child, a crowd attacked the Indians, "badly" wounding and intimidating them. Despite the natives' admitted loyalty to the British, Acting Governor Winthrop Sargent felt obligated to protect them. Sargent clearly saw the attack on the Indians as an act of defiance against the authority of the territorial government. The Indians, he noted, were "under the protection of the Laws of the Land and our national dignity" is "interested in most amply affording it to them." Accordingly, the acting governor placed a guard around the Indians' camp.[48]

This action did not resolve the issue. On the night of September 9, while Sargent was with the Indians, his house was broken into and "two Rifle Balls" were fired near his bed. The Indians left Cincinnati the next morning. But Sargent was even more determined to assert his authority in the town. He demanded an investigation by local magistrates and the suppression of the "disorderly Taverns and Tippling houses which are amongst the principal Causes of the Disturbances at Cincinnati." The Hamilton County justices did hold a court of inquiry and a grand jury issued two bills of indictment. One man was quickly acquitted, however, because the principal witness against him did not appear in court and the other could not be found to stand trial, even though Sargent knew he "was parading the Town in Insult of the Laws." All in all, claimed the acting governor, there was "a too General Disposition" to ignore the whole affair.[49]

If the trial had been a test of territorial authority, the government had clearly failed. Without the patronage system that worked so well in Marietta to bind local officials to the national government, the territorial hierarchy had little influence in Cincinnati. Local magistrates simply saw the source of their power as the people they represented, not the territorial government which had appointed them. If forced to choose between Winthrop Sargent and popular opinion, they chose the latter. In February 1795, a Hamilton County grand jury even indicted Sargent for "usurpation" of the governor's authority while St. Clair was out of the territory. By the late 1790s, many people in Cincinnati were ready to agree with Sargent's initial impression that the inhabitants of Marietta and Cincinnati "seem never to have been intended to live under the same government."[50]

After a decade of territorial government, a wide variety of settlers in the Ohio Country—land magnates in the Scioto Valley, farmers without legal titles in the Miami Valley, territorial Judge John Cleves Symmes, and many residents of Cincinnati—were coming to the conclusion that the form of government created by the Northwest Ordinance of 1787 was "inadequate to the wants of the people."[51] They all strongly objected to the interference of territorial officials in local affairs, particularly officials whose foremost loyalty was to the national government and not to the people of the Scioto or Miami valleys. Indeed, perhaps it was time for the residents of the Northwest Territory to "participate in those inestimable blessings and advantages which flow from a Government chosen by the people."[52] However disparate the natures of their interests, many people were increasingly finding unity in the democratic rhetoric they employed to defend them.

5

"The Only Proper Judges of Their Own Interests"
1798　　　　　　　　　*1803*

The election of Thomas Jefferson to the presidency in 1801 marked a profound shift in the direction of American government. It ended Federalist efforts to restructure the United States through the power of a strong central government and it put power into the hands of a new generation of leaders in individual states. The creation of the state of Ohio was part of this larger national transformation.[1]

In almost every instance, the characteristics of Ohio's Jeffersonian Republicans sharply diverged from those of the territorial Federalists. The former were younger and in a hurry. They delighted in calling territorial Federalists "an old train of Sycophants" who would "forsake" Governor Arthur St. Clair "when they find the loaves and fishes no longer at his disposal." Hearkening back to the origins of the American Revolution, the Jeffersonians compared territorial patronage to corruption in the British House of Commons, just as Thomas Jefferson compared Alexander Hamilton to Sir Robert Walpole. They called for frequent elections instead of appointments, for an independent legislature, for a dimunition in the power of the executive, and for the elevation of local over national sovereignty. Thomas Worthington actively worked for St. Clair's dismissal from office because he believed the governor was trying "to attach to himself a party."[2]

The pejorative connotations aside, this charge reveals that Ohio Jeffersonians knew precisely with what they were dealing. St. Clair, like Hamilton on the national level and Rufus Putnam on the local level, indeed was trying to create a court party. He was trying to restrain local autonomy and to promote stability through the appointment of men who were loyal to the United States government. He opposed statehood for Ohio because he believed that the territory was populated by "A multitude of indigent and ignorant people" who were "ill qualified to form a constitution and government for themselves"; more important, "They are too far removed from the seat of government to be much impressed with the power of the United States." Only "Time" would allow "the cultivation of a disposition favorable to the General Government." Secretary Winthrop Sargent agreed that statehood should be delayed "until the majority of the Inhabitants be of such Characters and property as may insure national Dependence and national Confidence." These two men, so often characterized by historians as arrogant, incompetent, and/or anachronistic, were simply doing their duty as they saw it. If statehood involved the triumph of local prerogatives and demagogues, then it was the responsibility of the territorial hierarchy to oppose it.[3]

The Jeffersonians, on the other hand, hoped that the creation of the state of Ohio would replace a national system of patronage with an open competition of talents in local elections. They deeply resented St. Clair's control over appointments to local offices. They believed that the governor was an aristocratic fool blind to the natural merits of men, a cantankerous anachronism who rewarded only those men who did his bidding. St. Clair even appointed his own son to the office of attorney general of the Northwest Territory. The territorial administration, the young Chillicothe lawyer Michael Baldwin claimed in 1802, was "aristocratic in its principles, and oppressive and partial in its administration." In his opinion, territorial officials were not fit to govern, especially not fit to judge who should exercise leadership in the Ohio Country. Rather, Baldwin contended, echoing the proclamation of squatter John Amberson in 1785, "all power" ought to flow "from the people," for they were "fully competent to govern themselves" and were "the only proper judges of their own interests and their own concerns."[4] In invoking the rhetoric of popular sovereignty to attack the territorial government, Baldwin was rejecting the moral and social leadership of the Federalists and seeking confirmation of his self-image as a man of merit in the opinion of the populace. Like all Jeffersonian Republicans, he was making the people, in a collective sense, the source of his authority as a social and political leader.

Fundamentally, the split between territorial Federalists and Jeffersonians was not a question of aristocrats versus democrats, or New England

Puritan organicism versus frontier individualism, but a question of where to locate the locus of power and what made the exercise of power legitimate. Should political authority be sanctioned from above by the national government's patronage of men loyal to it and committed to a restrained development of the Ohio Valley? Or should a man's eminence in his community be sanctioned from below, through popular elections? The Jeffersonian Republicans in the Ohio Country welcomed the flourishing of the social scramble that had characterized early Marietta as a triumph of human freedom, allowing status and positions to go to men who earned them through the natural workings of elections rather than to be awarded through an artificial system of patronage.

Ironically, the implementation of the second stage of territorial government in 1799 proved in some ways to be more restrictive than the first stage. While it allowed for the election of a territorial assembly, it also strengthened the power of the executive. The governor and the three territorial judges, acting as equals, previously had enacted the laws of the territory. But with the meeting of the elected legislature, St. Clair acquired the power of absolute veto over all laws and the right to call and prorogue the assembly as he saw fit.

Opponents of the governor, moreover, could not always manage a majority in the legislature. Property qualifications for voting and holding office precluded a truly popular government. The outlying parts of the territory (including the area encompassed by the present-day states of Indiana, Illinois, and Michigan) were generally less interested in local autonomy than in the maintenance of federal protection from the Indians and from European nations. The Ohio Company settlements, of course, were strongly Federalist. The Republican opposition was just as strong in the Scioto Valley counties of Ross and Adams where Worthington, Tiffin, Massie, and their allies were consistently elected to the assembly. The crucial, disputed area was Cincinnati. Because of the divisions within the capital of the territory, the votes of the Hamilton County delegates were subject to a variety of local pressures.[5]

The first meeting of the territorial assembly in Cincinnati in September 1799 began peacefully. After electing Edward Tiffin as speaker, the representatives promised full cooperation with Governor St. Clair.[6] It was soon evident, however, that the harmony of the assembly was superficial. There was a sharp contest over the election of the territory's nonvoting delegate to the Congress of the United States. The opponents of St. Clair managed to elect William Henry Harrison, the son-in-law of John Cleves Symmes, over the Federalist candidate Arthur St. Clair, Jr. They also passed laws that angered the governor by challenging his authority, particularly one that named Manchester the seat of Adams County. At the close of the session, St. Clair predictably vetoed that act as well as ten others.[7]

The governor's vetoes did not silence his critics. Thomas Worthington was "more dissatisfied at our present Government" than ever before. Within six months of the adjournment of the 1799 session, Worthington and others determined to "exhibit charges" of executive tyranny and malfeasance against St. Clair. The governor and his opponents were involved in an overt power struggle. Would authority in the Northwest Territory be exercised by local or territorial officials—by men whose authority was popularly derived or those who were appointed by the federal government?[8]

In early 1800, Worthington travelled to Washington, where congressional delegate Harrison was already presenting a case against St. Clair. Worthington and Harrison persuaded Congress to create the Indiana Territory west of a line running north from the mouth of the Kentucky River. Their goal in pressing for this legislation was to limit the Northwest Territory to an area centered on the Scioto River (essentially the lands that would become the state of Ohio). Worthington and his allies believed that the citizens of the consolidated territory, with its capital at Chillicothe, would soon apply for admission to the Union and thereby escape the arbitrary government of St. Clair.[9]

But the governor's opponents were moving too quickly. The October 1800 elections to the territorial legislature revealed resentment, particularly in Cincinnati, at the opposition's precipitous action. Cincinnatians were angry about losing the capital of the territory to Chillicothe, and their anger was skillfully exploited by St. Clair's opponents. The future Republicans remained strong in the Scioto Valley. But the governor's partisans made enough gains to dominate the new legislature.[10]

The assembly met in November 1800 in a two-story log house in Chillicothe; members discussed territorial business on the first floor and drank, gambled, and played billiards on the second floor. Despite the reelection of Edward Tiffin as speaker, the legislature strongly protested the movement of the capital from Cincinnati to Chillicothe. Congress's decision, they declared, was arbitrary and a usurpation of the powers of the territorial legislature. They also chose Paul Fearing, a Marietta lawyer and friend of Rufus Putnam, to serve a two-year term as congressional delegate. Worse still for Worthington, the assembly praised Arthur St. Clair and denounced the charges that had made his "administration unpopular among the good people of this Territory."[11]

The revival of St. Clair's fortunes dismayed but did not disillusion the governor's opponents; they assumed that its source was his power to influence men's judgments through patronage. The governor had become a kind of evil genius in the minds of Massie, Worthington, and Tiffin. Once the "old aristocratic sinner" was "out of the way," contended St. Clair's old foe John Cleves Symmes, "we should all be honest and wise enough to make good republicans."[12] Indeed, the governor's opponents found it difficult to understand how any honest man could support St. Clair. Using the pseudonym "A Countryman," one writer argued in the *Cincinnati Western Spy* that the executive's wide appointive powers made territorial officials "no better than mere tools, in the hands of the governor." True, appointments were generally given "to the most popular men in the county." But once their ambitions were whetted, their obsequious behavior made "the governor almost absolute—the legislature become mere cyphers and makeweights."[13]

So certain was the opposition that patronage was all that unified St. Clair's partisans that they could not credit supporters of the governor and the Northwest Ordinance of 1787 with rationality. When Congress reappointed St. Clair in 1801, Senator John Brown of Kentucky assured Thomas Worthington that the new Republican Congress had had little choice in the face of "numerous and very respectable" petitions in favor of the governor. Worthington angrily replied that all honest, independent men wanted St. Clair replaced. "More than the 'few,' " he claimed, were "interested in endeavouring to curb a tyrant." Worthington protested that St. Clair's supporters were the same kind of people who opposed Thomas Jefferson in the presidential election of 1800 against "the most decided wishes of the people." Yet the Republican victory on the national level had insured the triumph of "truth . . . over error, reason over sophistry, and the majesty of the People over a corrupt faction." If "British influence" had given way to "virtue and reason" in the nation as a whole, Worthington remained convinced that the same thing could happen in the territory.[14]

While the Republicans portrayed St. Clair as a tyrant and his supporters as corrupt office seekers who deliberately kept honest, able men out of office, the Federalists blamed Worthington, Symmes, Massie, and their allies for all of the difficulties facing the citizens of the territory. From St. Clair's perspective, his opponents were "ambitious, designing, and envious men" who were leading the gullible people of the territory to certain ruin. By defaming "the character of their magistrates," these demagogues were destroying the confidence in officials so necessary for the maintenance of an orderly, stable society.[15] Such behavior was, in the eyes of the Federalist hierarchy, almost treasonable, for it totally disrupted the implementation of their vision of a West developed carefully and cautiously under national control. Even appointed officials needed the trust of the people they governed. "As confidence . . . is the basis and support of a republican government," wrote the St. Clairsville lawyer Charles Hammond, "any attempt to destroy the confidence of the people or to alienate their affections from their first magistrate, should be warmly opposed by every friend to *order* and *good government.*"[16]

St. Clair believed that his opponents were upstarts who sought nothing more than personal aggrandizement. They epitomized all the evils that the Federalists had hoped to prevent in the West. Like the squatters of the 1780s, Worthington and Massie were "persons with private views" who would "only use the people as means to accomplish them." Their triumph would lead to a state government that St. Clair feared would "be democratic in form and oligarchic in its execution, and more troublesome and more opposed to the measures of the United States than even Kentucky." They were, said Hammond in a succinct summary of the territorial hierarchy's attitude toward their challengers, "persons opposed to all law and government, except such as are calculated to promote them in their basic designs."[17]

Just as the Republicans believed that St. Clair governed by corruption, the governor believed the source of his critics' power was economic influence. Because most of the land in the territory had originally been held "by a few individuals in large quantities" and then sold in small parcels on credit, "the greatest part of the people are their [Massie and Symmes, for example] debtors." With specie so scarce in the Ohio Valley, people were happy to vote for "a certain candidate" in return for a delay in paying a debt. In this way, " a few persons" (again, read Massie and Symmes) could control the legislature and "serve their interests in preference to those of the whole people." Thus, in November 1800, St. Clair sought a law to prevent bribery, threats, and treating with food and drink from influencing elections. All violators were to be disqualified from serving in the territorial legislature for at least two years. More significantly, St. Clair asked for the replacement of viva voce voting procedures with ballots.[18]

While St. Clair made little progress in reforming electoral procedures, he received strong support from the Ohio Company settlement of Marietta. A town meeting on January 4, 1801, resolved that statehood was an improper measure. The citizens reaffirmed the Federalist vision of the West: quiet growth under paternalistic, national guidance "free from the storms of party and the agitations of intrigue." They continued to believe that a stable social system was the prerequisite of statehood. As long as the people of the territory remained "a mixed mass of people, scattered over an immense wilderness," with scarcely one "connecting principle," statehood was impossible.[19]

In the late fall of 1801, the Federalists sought to consolidate their position. For some time Governor St. Clair had been advocating the further division of the Northwest Territory into two districts separated at the Scioto River. Such a division would slow the momentum for statehood by making the requisite population of sixty thousand more difficult to achieve; it would also strengthen the Federalists politically by splitting the Scioto Valley in half. The two new districts would have their capitals at Marietta and Cincinnati while Chillicothe would sink into obscurity. In December 1801, St. Clair convinced the strongly Federalist legislature to pass an act dividing the territory at the Scioto.[20] William Rufus Putnam, a delegate to the territorial legislature and the son of the Ohio Company superintendent, explicitly supported the Division Act in order "to delay a state government" as long as possible.[21]

The immediate result of the act was to provoke violence in Chillicothe where the assembly was meeting. On December 23, the young lawyer Michael Baldwin and several other men outraged by the Division Act decided to burn St. Clair in effigy before the tavern in which the governor was staying. On the evening of December 24, the same men, who had been drinking heavily, decided "to abuse some of the Members at their quarters." Baldwin, Stephen Cissna, and Reuben Adams went into St. Clair's tavern claiming that they "had an equal right to" enter it.[22]

Inside the public house, Baldwin and his friends quarreled with a pro-St. Clair delegate from the Michigan region. The representative drew his knife in his anger, but was restrained by his friends. Other Federalist legislators began to load their arms. Hearing the scuffle, St. Clair, who was upstairs writing, came downstairs, demanded order, and sent for the magistrate and sheriff. But Baldwin remained "violent" and, according to St. Clair, was restrained from "mischief" only by the sudden arrival of Thomas Worthington, who threatened to put Baldwin "to death with his own hands" if he did not control himself and his friends. The angry Worthington managed to cool the crowd and prevent further violence.[23]

In the succeeding days, St. Clair attempted to get local officials to prosecute Baldwin and his friends. But local officials refused to cooperate. Justice of the Peace Samuel Finley resigned his commission rather than prosecute anyone, and a legislative committee dismissed the events as the results of intoxication. "I should have merited the contempt of every honest man," Finley told St. Clair, "had I ventured to deprive so many citizens of a liberty they are constitutionally entitled to."[24] Once again, local officials, forced to choose between the wishes of the man who appointed them to office and the people of the community, chose the authority of the latter. Not surprisingly, Marietta resident Dudley Woodbridge found the Chillicothe incident reminding him "of Shays and those times."[25]

Republican leaders glossed over the Christmas 1801 tensions. Worthington was certain that the Division Act was such an obviously arbitrary act that the people of the territory would reject St. Clair's leadership. He still believed that "the great body of the people" would want to overthrow "the present arbitrary government, better suited for an English or Spanish colony than for citizens of the United States," if they could simply be convinced of the danger.[26]

But if Worthington turned to the people as the source of his legitimacy in attacking the territorial government, he devoted most of his energies to convincing the national government to make a state out of the territory east of the Great Miami River. He and Michael Baldwin travelled to Washington in early 1802 as the deputized agents of citizens of Ross and Adams counties favoring statehood. From all over the Ohio Country, Worthington and Baldwin received petitions against the Division Act and for statehood. Many citizens of Adams, Clermont, and Hamilton counties proudly joined the residents of Ross in seeking to "shake off the Iron fetters of aristocracy" and in seeing the day when "they shall be governed by a constitution formed by true republicans chosen by the people free from the controls of an arbitrary chief."[27]

Worthington assured Nathaniel Massie that St. Clair's blatant grab for power in the Division Act had awakened the people of the Ohio Country to the tyranny they had suffered under the Ordinance of 1787. At last they realized that statehood would bring a release of energies and the triumph of local, popular autonomy. The territorial government had "made every effort to destroy the prosperity of our country," Worthington told Massie. Denying that the object of the statehood movement was their "own aggrandizement," the two Virginians felt secure in the knowledge that they were only trying "to give the people a government of their own choice and free them from the clutches of a tyrant and his accomplices. . . . Have we not uniformly advocated their rights and thereby drawn upon us the persecution of their oppressors?"[28]

Armed with petitions and full of confidence, Worthington lobbied hard in Washington for a repeal of the Division Act, the creation of a state in the Ohio Country, and the ouster of St. Clair. He bombarded President Jefferson with charges against the governor. According to Worthington, the "unworthy" St. Clair had brought only "ferment and confusion" to the territory. His motives were "his own pecuniary interests" and the gratification of "his ambitions and tyrannical disposition." Among other things, Governor St. Clair had vetoed laws, "wantonly usurped" the power to erect counties, appointed "his favorites to the most lucrative offices," tried "to make the judiciary department dependent on his will," and collected "arbitrary" and illegal fees. Through the practice of patronage and a consistent disregard for popular wishes, St. Clair had proven himself an opponent of "a republican form of government."[29]

It would be easy to dismiss the quarrel between the governor and his critics, as some historians have done, as a personal squabble among men more interested in self-promotion than ideas about government and society. President Jefferson even looked upon the St. Clair-Worthington dispute as a clash of personalities and refused to dismiss the governor. But the territorial Republicans' obsession with the destruction of the territorial governor ran much deeper than the bitterness produced by a conflict of personal interests. Attacking St. Clair and his "tools" as obstacles to the open and rapid development of the West united a coalition of people— urban traders, large landholders, and small farmers—otherwise naturally divided by economic and regional differences. They all shared the belief that statehood would place power in the hands of the people in their local regions and leave them free to promote their individual and group interests as they saw fit. To men who wanted to develop the Ohio Country quickly, St. Clair *was* a tyrant precisely because he sought to limit local authority and to improve the West in a deliberate fashion.

Angered by Jefferson's vote of confidence in St. Clair, Worthington redoubled his efforts to get Congress to create a state in the Ohio Country. In the spring of 1802, Worthington's lobbying and the interest of national Republicans in adding a state to the Union which promised to be firmly Jeffersonian combined to overturn the Division Act and to create the state of Ohio. In April, President Jefferson signed the Enabling Act, which allowed the citizens of the region east of the mouth of the Great Miami River to begin the steps that would make Ohio the seventeenth state in the American Union.[30]

The news of the repeal of the Division Act was the cause of great celebration in Chillicothe. It was hard, reported the former Justice of the Peace Samuel Finley, to "describe the ecstatic emotion excited in the minds of our inhabitants." There was nothing to be seen "but smiling countenances— nothing was to be heard but congratulatory salutations. At night the town was illuminated—The bells would have been rung if we had had them . . . [and] many a conduit . . . ran with grog."[31] The passage of the Enabling Act produced similar scenes throughout the Ohio Country. Thomas Worthington, Nathaniel Massie, Edward Tiffin, John Cleves Symmes, and hundreds of farmers and tradesmen at last had realized their fondest wish; they could now begin anew—this time on their own terms.

In October 1802, leading Republicans were overwhelmingly elected as delegates to a convention called to write a constitution for the new state.

The people of Ross County (Chillicothe) chose Edward Tiffin, Thomas Worthington, Michael Baldwin, and John Grubb as their representatives. In Hamilton County (Cincinnati), eight of ten men on the Republican ticket—including William Goforth, Charles Willing Byrd, and John Smith—were chosen; among the defeated were longtime supporters of St. Clair such as the lawyer Jacob Burnet.[32]

In fact, of the thirty-five men elected to serve in the constitutional convention, twenty-eight were allies of Massie and Worthington. Only Benjamin Ives Gilman, Rufus Putnam, and Ephraim Cutler of Washington County and a handful of scattered Federalist delegates from Jefferson and Hamilton counties were chosen to oppose the Scioto Valley gentry. When the convention met in Chillicothe on November 1, 1802, it chose Edward Tiffin as its president and proceeded to write a constitution that was a radical departure from the Ordinance of 1787.[33]

Led by Worthington and Baldwin, the delegates entrusted power in the new state almost absolutely to the legislature. In this and other ways, the new constitution bore striking resemblances to the state constitutions of the 1770s. The state general assembly was to consist of a senate and a house of representatives. Following the advice of North Carolina Congressman Nathaniel Macon, who reminded Worthington that a strong executive in a free country led to "violent parties," and their own bitter experience with St. Clair, the members of the convention made the office of state governor extremely weak. He would have no veto power and all of his appointments were to be subject to legislative approval; the executive would also be chosen every two years. Thus, the delegates strove not only to "say the natural rights of government are in the hands of its constituents, but to guard them there with such republican strength, that all the inveterate rage and subtle craft of arbitrary power and aristocratic despotism, will ever be able to invade."[34]

The legislature was also given strong control over the judiciary branch. The assembly would elect a supreme court of three judges to serve seven-year terms during their good behavior. This court was required to meet one term in each county once a year and one time at the state capital. The constitution thus made the Ohio Supreme Court largely "a county court: with original jurisdiction in all cases brought before courts of common pleas." The assembly would also elect the judges of three common pleas circuits. The people of local townships would choose their own justices of the peace.[35]

By the end of the convention, the Republican leaders were very happy men. They had written a constitution that reversed the flow of power as it had existed under the Ordinance of 1787. Sovereignty now rested with people in local areas and their biennially elected representatives in the legislature; the executive and appointed officials had been made subject to the will of the people they governed. Through the legislature the people would rule—or more precisely, the natural leaders of society, chosen independently by their neighbors, would see that the new state ran smoothly. So strong was the Republican faith in the harmony of interests among themselves and the citizens of Ohio that they did not submit the constitution to the people for approval.[36]

While Thomas Worthington took the document off to Washington for congressional approval, Ohio Republicans spent the winter of 1802–3 congratulating themselves on a job well done and looking forward to the harmony and prosperity of statehood. They honestly believed that the days of acrimony were gone forever. The first state elections did not shake that confidence. In January 1803 the white adult males of Ohio chose Edward Tiffin as their first governor, with only minimal opposition from Benjamin Ives Gilman of Marietta. Jeremiah Morrow of the Miami Valley was elected to the United States House of Representatives. Within six months, Nathaniel Massie had been chosen president of the Ohio Senate and Michael Baldwin speaker of the house; and the assembly had dispatched Thomas Worthington and John Smith of Cincinnati to the United States Senate. Free of St. Clair's obstructionism and patronage system, leading Republicans at last felt their talents were being amply rewarded.[37]

On March 1, 1803, when Edward Tiffin assumed office as governor of the state of Ohio, he presided over a government based on principles similar to those espoused by squatters in the 1780s against the Congress of the Confederation. Power, both the squatters and the Republicans said, belonged to the people on the local level. It was the undoubted right of Americans, John Amberson had written in a proclamation nailed to trees in the Ohio Valley in 1785, "to pass into every vacant country, and there to form their constitution." Eighteen years later, Republican leaders believed they had finally exercised that right. "The people," Michael Baldwin argued in 1802 in a summary of the position of opponents of the territorial government, "are fully competent to govern themselves" and "are the best and only proper judges of their own interests and their own concerns."[38]

Not even the Ohio Company settlement at Marietta could escape the democratic revolution. In 1801, the first serious challenge to Rufus Putnam's carefully constructed hegemony arrived in the form of a protest against parts of the Marietta remonstrance against statehood led by territorial Judge Return Jonathan Meigs, Jr., Judge Griffen Greene, and tavernkeeper and former soldier Joseph Buell. Meigs and Greene had received offices under Putnam but by 1801 were cultivating opposition to Putnam and his circle of gentlemen and working for statehood in close cooperation with Worthington. Why men who had received the patronage of Putnam should suddenly have "turned Democrat" has been a matter of much speculation by local historians. Some have pointed to their ambitions, to personal quarrels, to the cultivation of Meigs by Worthington, and to slights from St. Clair.[39]

But the major cause of Meigs and Greene's abandonment of Putnam and the Federalist hierarchy can be found in the timing of their shift—after the election of 1800 had made it clear that the Federalists would no longer have control of what future Senator John Smith called "the loaves and fishes" of patronage. The change in national governments, far more than any local issue, robbed Rufus Putnam of his power and his authority. To be sure, the first state elections in Marietta were swept by Jeffersonian Republicans. But the eclipse of Putnam, and the transfer of power in the town, is better evidenced by the rapid turnover in appointed offices. The new state government made Meigs, Greene, and Joseph Buell judges of the Washington County Court of Common Pleas. Through the influence of Worthington, Griffen Greene was appointed Marietta postmaster by the Jefferson administration, replacing David Putnam. In May 1802, Greene was also made collector of revenues. Meigs's father later received an appointment as an Indian commissioner, and Meigs himself would eventually become a judge of the Louisiana Territory, a governor of Ohio, and postmaster general of the United States under President James Madison.[40]

The final blow to the Marietta Federalists was the September 1803 replacement of Rufus Putnam as surveyor general of the United States. With his dismissal from national office, Putnam retired from active politics. Yet he noted proudly in his memoirs that he was happy to join others removed from office "for adherence to those correct principles and measures in the pursuence of which our country rose from a State of weakness, disgrace and poverty, to Strength, Honor and Credit."[41]

In fact, despite their political defeats and the self-congratulation of the Republicans, men like Putnam and St. Clair had accomplished a great deal in fifteen years of territorial government. By the early 1800s, the major prerequisite for a change in political power in the Northwest Territory as a whole, let alone the town of Marietta, was a change in the national government. The most critical event in the shift of power from Federalists to Republicans in the Ohio Country was the election of Thomas Jefferson as president of the United States, for it was control of the national system of patronage that was the preeminent source of power in the Ohio Valley. What had made St. Clair and Putnam powerful under the Federalists would make Worthington powerful under the Jeffersonian Republicans.

Ohio's Republicans really did have more faith in popular government than the Federalists. But, in the end, it was an act of the United States Congress, not an election, that enabled Ohio to become a state in 1803; the procedures established by the Northwest Ordinance of 1787 had been observed.

While Putnam and St. Clair lost office (the governor was finally dismissed by Jefferson in late 1802 for a strong attack on the new state constitution), they did not do so before they had helped to create enduring political and social structures that the Jeffersonian Republicans, despite their intense commitments to local sovereignty and popular elections, would find easier to master and to reform than to replace. The Federalists may have lost the political wars, but they had defined to a significant degree the contours of power in the Old Northwest. And given the utter impotence of that government when Putnam and St. Clair arrived on the Ohio frontier in 1788, that was indeed a substantial achievement.

6

Catalines and Contentiousness
1803   1807

The jubilation produced by the creation of the state of Ohio was, not surprisingly, short-lived. Because the statehood movement had been an alliance of peoples united by little more than the desire to replace national with local sovereignty, it was a coalition that naturally collapsed with the removal of the despised territorial government. Indeed, political conflicts in the decade after 1803 were even more intense and more bitter than the struggles of the preceding decade.

Historians have explained this post-1803 disintegration of harmony in a variety of significant ways. They have focused on rivalries between cities like Chillicothe and Cincinnati, competition between different economic interests, and the revival of Federalist fortunes during the Embargo and the War of 1812. More often, scholars have pointed to personal squabbles, arguing that Ohio's founding fathers simply fell into an inevitable scramble for a limited number of offices.

All of these explanations have merit. But just as important in producing strong political dissension in early Ohio were the difficulties the new state's leaders faced in trying to deal with important ideological questions about the nature of their society and the exercise of power within it. The Ohio statehood movement, which ostensibly resolved the issue of sovereignty on the side of the people in local jurisdictions, actually exacerbated the conflicts over the nature of society and the role of government which had dogged the settlers of the Ohio Country since the confrontations between Congress and squatters in the 1780s.

The state of Ohio had been created by men who offered two alternative visions of social and political organization. On the one hand, they emphasized personal independence and the popular origins of government. They encouraged white males to think in terms of equal opportunity in politics and the economy while upholding the sanctity of individual rights. On the other hand, the means they had employed to achieve statehood seemed to put a premium on interdependence and organization.

To defeat Governor St. Clair, Thomas Worthington had found he had to do more than preach the virtues of personal and local autonomy. He had had to build an alternative system of patronage. Worthington's correspondence is replete with letters from loyal lieutenants such as Philemon Beecher of Lancaster and Return Jonathan Meigs of Marietta apprising him of political sentiment and activities in their areas. These men deferred to Worthington partly because of their shared hostility to St. Clair and partly because they saw in Worthington a man with important connections at the real seat of power in the republic—Washington, D.C. Many local leaders had tied their ambitions for national and state offices to Worthington. Their recognition of Worthington's eminence, in turn, gave him influence in the nation's capital, for he went to Washington in 1802 as the head of a potentially powerful political organization linking local leaders throughout the Ohio Country. Jeffersonian Republican leaders on the national level expected Ohio to be on their side in national elections; Thomas Worthington could organize and secure it.[1]

In short, Worthington became a Jeffersonian Republican version of Rufus Putnam. Many men in Ohio deferred to him because he had influence with the national government while national leaders consulted with him because he had strong support in Ohio. Benjamin Tupper of Marietta, in applying for a position with the federal government in 1804, told Worthington "your General influence is greater than that of any other person in the State of Ohio." Men like Tupper sought appointments to courts, post offices, and revenue positions. And as long as Worthington received letters from federal officials asking him to recommend men for offices, his power was immense. "I pray you to fill" the document appointing a local postmaster "with the name of a suitable character," wrote Postmaster General George Granger in a typical letter to Worthington in 1805, and forward it to whomever "you may select."[2]

There was one very important difference between Worthington and Rufus Putnam. The Federalist leader of Marietta had served only one master;

he saw himself as the agent of the national government first and foremost and he made few concessions to popular opinion. But Worthington had risen to power on a platform that denounced the territorial government for ignoring the wishes of the people and denying men an equal opportunity to compete for offices and resources. In the end, the statehood movement led by Worthington created two sources of authority—the white males residing in the state and the government of the United States—which were, as the history of the Northwest Territory had made clear, not always compatible.

Patronage and political organization presupposed patience, a willingness to work through a system, and the frequent subordination of personal interest to the good of the whole. But many male Ohioans were committed to an ideology of individual autonomy and popular sovereignty. Far from resolving the conflict over the source of power in the Ohio Country, the most important consequence of statehood was to intensify it. Worthington and his allies, the Regular Republicans of Ohio, as they called themselves, would have no more success in bringing order to Ohio politics than the territorial Federalists had had. But their difficulties proved to be more traumatic because the Jeffersonian Republicans were genuinely perplexed by the fact that there was more contention than harmony in their new state. With the approval of the national government, Ohio's founding fathers had created a state dedicated to democratic principles. Precisely how those principles would be defined in practice nobody knew in 1803.

No sooner was Arthur St. Clair replaced by Edward Tiffin than the leaders of the statehood movement found themselves under attack as an aristocracy. Among the leaders of the challenge to Regular Republicans like Governor Tiffin and Senator Worthington were Elias Langham and Michael Baldwin of the Scioto Valley. Langham and Worthington were once friends (they came from the same region of Virginia) but they had fallen out in the 1790s. The former was, according to a mutual friend, too much of a man of the people for the ascetic Worthington. Langham "could take a drink of grog and smoke a pipe, and kicking up a fight and make it up again." In the early 1800s, Langham and Worthington were perpetual foes, the former denouncing the latter as a violent aristocrat. William Creighton, Jr., the first Ohio secretary of state, described Langham as "the great author of bustle and confusion" among the people.[3]

Michael Baldwin was the personification of the tension between personal independence and political organization inherent in the beliefs of Ohio's Jeffersonian Republicans. The Connecticut-born Baldwin, like countless other young men, had turned his attention in the 1790s to the opportunities for financial and social advancement available in the Northwest Territory. He came to Chillicothe in 1799 with letters of introduction, offering "the fullest assurance of his qualifications, morals, and good disposition" to Nathaniel Massie and Thomas Worthington.[4] Within two years, Baldwin had become one of the more prominent citizens of Chillicothe. To some extent, his success was a reflection of his talents. But it was also the result of the patronage of Massie and Worthington. Baldwin's acceptance into the circle of the Scioto Valley gentry was important to him; it gave him confidence and validated his ambitions.

But Baldwin also received validation from the lower as well as the upper levels of the social structure. And it was this dual popularity and dual responsibility that eventually destroyed his ambitions. By 1801, he was firmly opposed to deference and patronage as they were practiced by territorial officials, but he was also torn between the increasingly divergent views of the Chillicothe gentry and the Chillicothe populace as to the proper forms of social relationships. He could downplay this conflict only so long; eventually, he would have to choose between them. Unfortunately for Baldwin's career, he chose the wrong side.

In the early 1800s, Baldwin was very popular with a segment of Chillicothe's population known as the "Bloodhounds." Historians have described them as a "band of cursing, quarreling, fighting rowdies" which was "obnoxious to the law-abiding element of Chillicothe." Harmon Blennerhassett, the Irish emigré involved in the Burr Conspiracy, denounced them as "the rabble" among whom Baldwin was "a giant of influence." These pejorative labels reveal more about the nature of the emerging culture of Ohio than they do about the group itself; while there is little concrete information about the Bloodhounds, it is likely that they were mainly artisans and transient laborers. Baldwin had a hard core of approximately six hundred supporters in elections, almost all of them in Chillicothe.[5]

In any case, Baldwin was clearly the leader of the group, a position he earned partly through intellectual ability, but largely through excelling at the Bloodhounds' favorite activities—drinking, gambling, and defying anything that smacked of authority. Refusing to defer to anyone, the young lawyer often found himself jailed for contempt of court and just as often his Bloodhounds quickly set him free.[6]

The fact that subsequent historians have found such behavior either amusing or antisocial testifies only to the triumph of a different set of values—a different cultural context—than the kind held by Michael Baldwin. By the standards of the late nineteenth and twentieth centuries, his behavior may have been eccentric; but in the earlier part of the nineteenth century he was acting in a relatively acceptable fashion. Baldwin saw himself as part of a local community. In the traditional society of the eighteenth century, drinking, gambling, and participation in extralegal crowd activities (such as the abortive December 1801 mobbing of Governor St. Clair) were norms rather than anomalies.[7]

In this sense, Baldwin's cavalier handling of his debts, his contempt for jails and governors, suggest the actions of a man who put greater emphasis upon his standing in the opinion of the Bloodhounds than he did upon institutions, officials, or the law. An undisciplined man who loved to drink and talk, he sought to prove himself worthy of his friends' respect by gambling, drinking, and entertaining. He enjoyed being a public man, concerned more with the impact he had on society than with the accumulation of money or a steady rise to political prominence.

Baldwin's friendship with Thomas Worthington ended with the near riot of December 1801. Worthington refused to cooperate with St. Clair's futile attempt to prosecute Baldwin. And Worthington and Baldwin continued to work together for the removal of St. Clair, travelling to Washington together in the late winter of 1802. But the two men were no longer friends. In April 1802, Baldwin tried to conciliate Worthington by promising to forget the "little sparring" between them. Yet, in the same letter, the young lawyer announced his intention "to stand on my own legs" by running as a candidate for the Ohio constitutional convention.[8] Baldwin would be polite, but he would not allow Worthington to dominate him.

Baldwin played an important role in writing the new constitution and in January 1803 he ran for the Ohio House of Representatives. Without the support of Worthington or his allies, he managed to win a seat. Gubernatorial candidate Edward Tiffin was disgusted by Baldwin's candidacy. The young man was "like the wind," Tiffin complained, "and beats round to every point of the compass in as short a period." He was "too bad to talk about; he publickly has said he will use means to accomplish his purposes foul as well as fair—he is an infamous young man."[9]

Baldwin, Elias Langham, and other "very noisey and very ignorant" members made the first meeting of the Ohio General Assembly a frustrating experience for Worthington and Tiffin. After electing Langham to be speaker of the house of representatives, the members devoted themselves, according to the clerk of the house, to "Wasting time and Spending the Money of their Constituents in playing Cross questions and Silly Answers."[10] Dissidents successfully stopped a measure to compensate Worthington ally Return Jonathan Meigs for service as a judge with Speaker Langham casting the deciding ballot.

Worthington and other Regular Republicans were flabbergasted by the assembly's behavior. Duncan McArthur lamented that while the senate was "chiefly composed of men of business . . . the lower House is filled with———heads: Bills chiefly originate in the Senate, and are almost as generally lost in the House of Representatives." "We have no news here," Governor Tiffin wrote to Senator Worthington, "excepting low, cunning, trifling, intrigueing conduct of a few restless, ambitious Spirits in our Legislature aided by kindred spirits out of doors, such as M. Baldwin" (who had been appointed United States Attorney for Ohio through the influence of his brother, Abraham Baldwin of Georgia). The Regular Republicans' only consolation was their hope that the behavior of men like Langham and Baldwin would convince a majority of their constituents of their incompetence.[11]

In the fall of 1804, half of their hopes came true. Baldwin won a seat in the Ohio House, but Langham was defeated in his attempt to win a seat in the United States Congress by the incumbent Jeremiah Morrow. Governor Tiffin was quick to admonish the new assembly to behave more decorously than its predecessors. Let "not the rude breath of fame be able, while you are together . . . to tarnish the purity of those morals, which adorn your characters in private life," he warned. Instead, "let a dignified simplicity, and a spirit of amity, conciliation and mutual forbearance be breathed through all your deliberations."[12] Although the members elected Michael Baldwin as their temporary speaker, Tiffin believed that they were "Harmonizing more than heretofore."[13]

Despite the apparent calm of the current general assembly, Ohio's leading Republicans were deeply affected by what they perceived to be the contentiousness of politics in the new state. Ohio, remarked Governor Tiffin in December 1806, was "fruitful in producing Men who [are] self-accomplished for every public station." The fact that there were "very many" men like Baldwin and Langham, who "think themselves equal and perhaps superior to either of us" was disconcerting to Tiffin and Worthington. Others involved in the statehood movement were just as confused by the petty quarrels over offices and resolutions which seemed to dominate legislative meetings. After all, Republicans had sought an independent state on the assumption, as Senator John Smith put it, "that discordant passions will subside and that harmony will be restored."[14] What had gone wrong? Why was there such contention? And, most troubling of all, why did men like Baldwin and Langham meet with even fleeting success in popular elections?

What Tiffin and Worthington objected to most about Baldwin was his style of behavior. Baldwin had all too clearly hitched the wagon of his ambition to the Bloodhounds rather than the gentry. He practiced "violence in politicks"; he had no patience, no respect for institutions and procedures. Baldwin was too spontaneous, too responsive to the wishes of the people, changing his mind to answer their every whim. His behavior was demagogic, Worthington believed; he told people what they wanted to hear. He did not lead; he followed. Tiffin's ideal statesman was a man who was "never . . . awed by the frowns or allured by the smiles of any Man, or set of Men." The Chillicothe gentry wanted a more democratic government than that advocated by Arthur St. Clair, but they did not want an anarchy of egalitarian individualism. "The Sovereign People," wrote Secretary of State William Creighton, could not be trusted. Too many of them did not like their new state constitution, he joked, "because it had no pictures in it."[15]

Whatever the extent of Baldwin's popularity in Chillicothe, Thomas Worthington was fed up with him. The senator, like his allies, wanted a glorious future for Ohio. They were generally deeply religious men with strong senses of personal dignity. They wanted a free society but an orderly one—a democratic government organized and led by a natural aristocracy. They wanted a civilized society, a world of stability, gentility, and manners. Ohio was to be the home of rational, educated, solid, dependable men. The key to maintaining this new society was, in their view, self-discipline; social order would follow from individual order, would come from within rather than without. The citizens of Ohio would not be coerced into order, as the Republicans believed the Federalists had tried to do, but would learn to restrain and refine their energies and desires in order to live in prosperous and orderly harmony. Worthington, Tiffin, and others like them tried to make their lives models of exemplary self-restraint and gentility. They dressed well, they lived in nice homes, they dealt with each other and with the world in a calm and rational fashion.

Michael Baldwin symbolized everything they did not want the citizens of Ohio to become. He lacked sensibility, meaning he acted without regard for the consequences of his actions on others. He was wild, out of control, impulsive, impatient, self-indulgent, careless about time and money, and too eager to follow rather than to guide popular wishes. Where Worthington sought to deal with St. Clair in a legal, institutional fashion, insisting on the proper procedures, Baldwin was direct and violent. Where Worthington concerned himself with building an impressive estate and establishing a solid economic foundation for his family and his community, Baldwin entertained himself and his friends by wasting his money on drinking and gambling. Where Worthington occupied himself with planning the material and social progress of Ohio, Baldwin practiced immediate gratification. More specifically, by continuing to behave in a public manner—by acting to please the Bloodhounds rather than his conscience, by advocating his own candidacies, by calling for "frequent elections, freedom of speech, universal suffrage"[16] rather than government by men of proven talents, by participating in mob activities—Baldwin was violating the basic rules of behavior which Worthington wished to establish in Ohio.

When Baldwin was elected to the speakership of the Ohio House of Representatives, Worthington explained this aberration as the result of the younger man's "real character not being known." Worthington, of course, knew Baldwin to be "the most finished villain," a man who was "quarrelsom, yet a coward—Arbitrary and tryannical yet a sycophant" without "the smallest spark of sensibility." "If I could attribute to him one virtue," Worthington confided to his diary, "it would give me pleasure." The senator was not merely angry. He sincerely believed that Baldwin was a vicious, depraved human being, who, like St. Clair before him, intended to cause mischief for others and pursue his interest to the detriment of everyone else.[17]

The existence of men like Baldwin and Langham made it imperative that true or Regular Republicans expose their deceptions to the public. On July 4, 1803, Matthew Nimmo, a merchant and leading Republican in Cincinnati, warned that despite the "happy . . . political situation . . . there are certain men who are daily vomiting injudicious and invidious remarks on the constitution" of Ohio. "You will find many," Nimmo told his audience, "who assume the garb of professed friendship to liberty to suit their ambitious views." As a result, the citizens of a republican state had to be incessantly on their guard.[18]

Not fully trusting Baldwin and Langham and others like them to trip over themselves or the voters to see through their duplicity, Regular Republicans began to press for more organization and discipline within their ranks. Newspapers started to publish exposés of candidates who were not allies of Worthington and Tiffin. More important, writers like "A Republican" urged the "connecting [of] energies by a systematical organization." Republican societies in each township should meet and elect two delegates to a county convention that would nominate regular candidates and correspond with other societies. Then, "there will be a *union* and not a division of the same interest."[19] The answer to the potential anarchy personified by Baldwin was organization and interdependence.

Such calls, however, had little immediate impact. The legislative meetings of 1804–5 and 1805–6 were more harmonious than their predecessors, but their members still squabbled over what Tiffin considered to be petty matters. Patronage questions occupied much of their time. In the fall of 1805, Elias Langham was reelected to the house. In the same year, Baldwin and "a partey" of "Bad men" made an unsuccessful effort to remove State Auditor Thomas Gibson (a Worthington supporter) from office.[20]

The failure of calls for greater organization and discipline to halt the tide of individualism and egalitarianism was most vividly laid bare in the congressional election of 1806. James Pritchard, an ambitious legislator and Worthington's longtime contact in Jefferson County, announced his candidacy for the seat. He assured Senator Worthington that he had no antipathy toward the incumbent, Jeremiah Morrow of the Miami Valley. But Pritchard felt that it was time for that "rotation in office [which] is agreeable to the Principles of our forming of our Government." After years of service to the cause, Pritchard wanted his reward. "Others," after all, had "given as Much aid to the Promotion of the Cause as Mr. Morrow."[21] Other candidates from the eastern part of the state also came forward, as did Elias Langham. But with the unexpected though welcome support of Michael Baldwin, Pritchard frightened off the others. He and Morrow were the only two candidates.[22]

Worthington and his allies united somewhat unenthusiastically behind the incumbent. Their support for Morrow rested more on a dislike of Pritchard (and Baldwin) than a fondness for the congressman. Worthington was outraged that Pritchard had "come forward on his own." His behavior was the worst example of the growing tendency of Ohio's male population to overestimate their abilities and to threaten the harmony of society by seeking places for which they were ill-qualified. To Worthington, democracy had become "the wretched practice of self-trumpeting candidates for popular suffrage."[23] The distractions, frauds, and lies associated with popular elections were perverting government.

To be sure, James Pritchard was an ambitious individual. But he was doing little more than taking the rhetoric of the statehood campaign at face value. Ohio had been freed of the territorial yoke to allow for an open and equitable competition among white males for power and influence. Now Pritchard's supporters began to attack Worthington and other Regular Republicans as closet Federalists. They denounced Morrow as a disgraceful representative, "the complete tool of the ambitious and designing." Only "*federalists*, land jobbers and speculators" supported him. Repeatedly, correspondents of the *Cincinnati Western Spy* charged Morrow with serving the interests of a corrupt aristocracy and ignoring the wishes of ordinary people.[24]

Worthington and his Regular Republican allies replied that Pritchard was that most dangerous of creatures in a democratic society, a demagogue. The challenger and his supporters were trying "to establish an aristocracy, and plan matters so, that the common people may not have the trouble of thinking for themselves." Would the people of Ohio be "independent enough to think for themselves?" Or would they "be duped and led by those dictators who are paid for thinking for them?"[25]

Despite the fact that Republican organization helped Morrow to a resounding victory in the battle for Ohio's congressional seat, the bitter campaign of 1806 revealed the failure of statehood to resolve the questions of political and social organization that had reverberated in the Ohio Country for two decades. What exactly did a democratic society entail? Did it mean absolutely equal access to the electoral process for any white male who thought himself capable and complete faith in the judgment of the people, as Baldwin asserted and Pritchard implied? Or did it mean individual presumption and collective anarchy taken to such a degree that only strong political organization and discipline could counteract them, as Worthington and other Regular Republicans were beginning to fear?

The growing apprehensions of Ohio's Republican gentry were brought to a head by the crisis provoked by the Burr Conspiracy of 1806–7. Whatever the intentions of Aaron Burr in the Ohio Valley, his activities ended in failure. Whether Burr's goal was a secession movement or an invasion of Spanish territories or simply personal aggrandizement, the uncertain enterprise evaporated. In fact, the only real crisis occurred near Marietta in early December 1806. The Ohio militia seized supplies intended for the conspirators in Marietta while the Virginia militia looted the island estate of Burr supporter Harmon Blennerhassett.[26]

The troops were acting under the orders of Ohio Governor Edward Tiffin. In late November, Secretary of War Henry Dearborn instructed Tiffin to send two hundred men to Marietta to prevent Burr's use of boats allegedly being constructed for him there. The governor took the initiative and induced the recently convened general assembly to pass an act giving him extraordinary emergency powers. Tiffin dispatched the militia to Marietta and commissioned the merchant and leading Republican Matthew Nimmo as his agent in Cincinnati. The times called for energetic efforts, Tiffin told Nimmo, and the legislature had granted him "uncommon powers to counteract any hostile efforts." Nimmo took precautions against a flotilla of boats passing Cincinnati, where a near hysteria had developed. But nothing happened. The seizure of fifteen boats and approximately two hundred barrels of provisions at Marietta effectively ended any threat.[27]

Tiffin acted quickly partly out of a desire to gain "great credit with the general Government and the Eastern States."[28] Smashing an alleged conspiracy against the peace and security of the republic was an excellent opportunity for Ohio Republicans to prove their loyalty to national leaders like President Jefferson. But Tiffin's actions were also the products of a deep-seated fear of Aaron Burr and a profound anxiety about the popular response to him.

As rumors of a potential conspiracy had circulated throughout Ohio earlier in 1806, Regular Republicans had filled the newspapers with warnings about and denunciations of "this modern Cataline." The warm reception the former vice-president had received in southern Ohio in the spring and summer of 1805, when he was everywhere preceded by "the trumpett of fame," had worried men like Tiffin and Worthington. Why was Burr so popular, so successful in attracting popular approbation? Was it a "magical operation" or was it simply a tribute to "the frailty of man?"[29]

Regular Republicans tried to explain the motives of the supporters of Burr to the public and to themselves. A writer named "Sydney" in the *Western Spy* believed that "Disappointment, ambition and avarice" had stimulated Burr and his allies to insidious actions. Skillful and intelligent, they had devised their schemes with "Disingeniousness and subtlety." "A few men of desperate fortune and character," another writer called "Regulus" warned Ohioans, were trying to convince them that "we are a miserable, oppressed people," dominated by a tyrannical East. Regular Republicans, at first putting their faith in the good sense of the citizens of Ohio and the efficacy of rational discussion, believed that there was little to fear from such depraved men. "The honest and enlightened part of the community" would see to it that "the uninformed and ignorant" would understand "the dark and insidious designs of the aspiring and ambitious demagogues who wish to ensnare the people into schemes formed for their own aggrandizement at the expence of their safety, liberty, and happiness."[30]

For Ohio's leading Republicans, the Burr Conspiracy was the supreme test of the capacity of ordinary people to govern themselves. If the people rejected the wily and intelligent Burr, they would stand firm against all ambitious demagogues. "The inhabitants of the Western country have too much sense to be the dupes of such sophistry," proclaimed a newspaper correspondent. The Burrites could do nothing "so long as the people are influenced by reason."[31] And they were. They had to be. If the people were not sensible and perceptive enough to do what was right in the case of Aaron Burr, then the foundation of Ohio's democratic government was exploded. If people put individual interests above the security of the entire community, then democracy had produced only selfishness and anarchy. Or, as Regulus put it, "if the good sense and moral principles of the people cannot sufficiently check the impetuosity of the passions or the ambitions of aspiring men . . . a turbulent minority might keep up a constant state of discord and confusion, and might usurp the whole power of government."[32]

When Ohio's Regular Republicans realized that the Burr Conspiracy had disintegrated, they congratulated themselves and swore fealty to the government of the United States. The Ohio General Assembly's prompt action against "this lawless enterprise" convinced William Creighton, Jr., that Ohio had fully demonstrated "her patriotism and attachment to the General Government." He was also pleased by the great unanimity in the legislature. Indeed, Thomas Worthington agreed, "the Legislature of Ohio have done themselves immortal honour." More important, the people of the state had proved themselves worthy of self-government by resisting the blandishments of Burr. Wyllis Silliman admitted to having been much alarmed at first that Kentuckians or people like them might follow Burr. But he had been reassured. The people of Ohio were too patriotic, their eyes were too open; they saw clearly that their true interests lay with the American Union and not with "the infernal machinations of this American Cataline."[33]

As their immediate euphoria faded, Republicans discovered that sympathy for Burr was wider than they had suspected. When the Chillicothean Samuel Finley took wagons on a presidential commission to Pittsburgh in early December 1806, he was stunned by the "Multitudes" of Burr's "Agents and advocates." "I had no conception," he wrote to Worthington, "of the extent of Mr. Burr's preparations and design." So many "young men . . . in high Spirits" boldly proclaiming their connection with Aaron Burr was disconcerting to Finley. They could not possibly be aware of Burr's desperate plans, could they? John Bigger, Jr., of Lebanon, Ohio, thought it "crazy" that anyone might follow Burr. "What could tempt any men to such desperate measures against our Government the Lord only knows; A Government, where each of us may sit down, if not under our own Fig tree, yet beside well stored Barns and Corncribs and enjoy all the advantages from the protection of life and property, which can be expected from civil institutions on this side of the grave?"[34]

The aftermath of the Burr Conspiracy proved to be more of a trauma for Ohio's leaders than the event itself. In early 1807, Governor Tiffin and the state legislature were severely criticized for their arbitrary handling of the affair. "Notwithstanding the seeming union and patriotism of our people when this business first broke out," wrote Tiffin bitterly, "we have many, very many amongst us who are using every means to thwart the views of the government." Such men were attacking and ridiculing "those who are entitled to the highest encomiums for their vigilance and patriotism." So strong was the governor's sense of crisis that he told Thomas Worthington that "the salvation of Ohio almost depend[s] on you and a few others."[35]

By February, it was clear that some Ohioans sympathized with Burr and many disapproved of the state government's quick actions against him. Like other Regular Republicans, John McLean of Chillicothe expressed amazement that "Men living and enjoying the blessing of so good a Government should join Mr. Burr in his wicked designs." How was it to be explained? How was the popular support for Michael Baldwin and Elias Langham to be explained? What accounted for the presumptuous ambitions of men like Baldwin and Pritchard and Burr? To Chillicothe resident James Finley, Burr's success "in attaching so many of our Citizens to his interest," while mysterious, proved "forcibly, the doctrine of Human depravity." How could it be otherwise? The American governments were the freest in the world; all power was in the hands of the people. Anyone who would forsake "the glorious fabrick of Liberty and Happiness" for the doctrines and the "deadly poison" of a Burr had to be "naturally depraved."[36]

But the problem was not depravity. The problem was that Ohio consisted of a multitude of regional, economic, and political interests. Far from being a collection of isolated, relatively homogeneous communities that could govern themselves harmoniously, Ohio was a fluctuating mass of diverse peoples and divergent interests. Michael Baldwin was not depraved, even though Worthington sincerely believed that he was; he was simply different from Worthington. Their styles and values were antithetical. What the Jeffersonian Republicans faced in the first years of statehood was their own version of strife-ridden early Marietta. If Worthington had become like Rufus Putnam, Baldwin had become a more powerful version of the upstart Matthew Backus. And there were other men ready to assume the roles of James Varnum, Samuel Holden Parsons, and Manasseh Cutler.

The difficulty for Republican leaders like Tiffin and Worthington was that, unlike the Federalists, they were not prepared for society in the Ohio Valley to be so contentious and pluralistic. The founding fathers of Ohio had created a government that was to interfere in the affairs of individuals and local areas as little as possible. The rhetoric of statehood had set white males free to pursue their individual political and economic ambitions; it had sanctioned a frontier society—a scramble of autonomous men for positions and profits without any clear sense of the rules or contours of power. The results were, predictably, petty quarrels and vitriolic accusations of aristocracy and injustice. The democratic government of Ohio was designed to be a miniature version of the society of the state. It was not designed to govern a world in which there were legitimate and often irreconcilable differences of opinion, incompatible regional and individual interests, and an inadequate number of opportunities to satisfy the ambitions of Ohio's white males. Worthington, Massie, and Tiffin had been so immersed in their struggles to liberate themselves from the territorial government that they had not thought it necessary to create institutions to resolve and arbitrate disputes among themselves and their allies.

The Federalists had tried to deal with a world of contentious self-interested men by attempting to abbreviate the frontier stage of development. They recognized the increasing complexity of the American economy and American society, and, while they could not fully understand it, they accepted the need for some means of distinguishing among men and interests in a pluralistic society of independent men. The Federalists' solution was to make the national government the ultimate authority in the Northwest Territory; it would adjudicate disputes and guide Western society to the pinnacle of civilization. The system worked well in Marietta in the 1790s but had been rejected with the overthrow of the territorial government.

Now the Jeffersonian Republicans had to contend with a similar situation. The reaction to the Burr Conspiracy climaxed the growing sense of many prominent Ohioans that something was wrong in the new state. But they divided over precisely what was wrong and how to correct it.

Governor Tiffin and Senator Worthington continued to look for the causes of discord in the characters of men. Contentiousness, they asserted time and again, was the work of the depraved demagoguery of a Baldwin, a Langham, a Pritchard, or a Burr. Tiffin and Worthington's answer was to expose the evildoers through increased organization and publicity. Still trusting the people to make the right choices ultimately, they nonetheless argued that the mass of men needed some help, some guidance on occasion, to protect them from the designs of malicious Catalines.

Other Republicans and former Federalists, however, recognized that the problem lay in the nature of society and not in the characters of individual men. In a society that constantly urged men to have the greatest of expectations for themselves, that encouraged them to be as ambitious as Pritchard or as egalitarian as Baldwin, in a world that was as diverse and as complex as the Ohio Valley was rapidly becoming, there was a need for some reasonably objective authority to arbitrate the claims of self-interested men. The Federalists had intended that the national government would play that Olympian role. But, while the power of federal patronage remained an important key to the political strength of Worthington, the national government under the Virginia Dynasty of Jefferson, Madison, and Monroe was too emasculated to fulfill its prescribed function. Men seeking an alternative source to the will (that is, will in theory; wills, in practice) of the sovereign people would have to look elsewhere. They did. And what they found was the mysterious authority of the law.

7

Matters of Opinion
1807   1812

Between 1807 and 1812 the Jeffersonian Republican consensus in Ohio disintegrated over the degree to which men believed that popular sovereignty ought to be the source of authority in their society. Almost all of the state's political leaders agreed that democratic government had proved to be more chaotic than they had anticipated. But they could not agree on what, if anything, they should do about it. The Republican supporters of Governor Tiffin and Senator Worthington, who called themselves both Regular and Democratic Republicans, continued to uphold the supremacy of the Ohio legislature as the most direct and reliable voice of the people; their faith in popular government had been shaken but not destroyed. If there was excessive conflict in Ohio, it was simply because the people were not sufficiently informed about the men they were choosing to represent them. The solution to Worthington and Tiffin was obvious. They would develop and regularize political organization in Ohio to insure the election of Regular Republicans and to expose the demagogues and closet Federalists who were the causes of the perceived disorder in the state.

Other, more moderate, Republicans were coming to a conclusion that many Federalists had reached years earlier: some kind of authority was needed in a democratic society to adjudicate the differences that inevitably arose among independent men. Led by state Judges Samuel Huntington,

George Tod, and Calvin Pease, they began to call for a stronger role for the Ohio court system at the expense of the often unruly legislature. While the Regular Republicans got support from farmers and debtors, particularly in the middle regions of the state, the moderate Republicans were strong among professionals and merchants in urban areas and also among people in outlying regions who resented the Scioto Valley gentry's stranglehold on Ohio politics.

The split in the Republican ranks opened the way for a revival of Federalist fortunes. The Federalists had virtually retired from active politics in the years since statehood was achieved, but they remained a significant minority with strength in Marietta, the urban centers of the Miami Valley, the Quaker-dominated settlements of eastern Ohio, and among New Englanders in the Western Reserve. President Jefferson's experiment in commercial coercion, the Embargo of 1807, added numbers to the Federalist camp. Unable to command the support of a majority of Ohio's voters, the Federalists' appeal to approximately one-third of the state's electorate made them a powerful broker group in Ohio politics as long as the Republicans were divided.[1]

Not surprisingly, Ohio Federalists tended to support moderate Republican candidates in state elections. What the two groups shared was a distaste for the Regular Republicans' endorsement of a simple, popular government as the instrument of the will of the people; such a view seemed to them to be both naive and dangerous. A purely democratic government might work in a homogeneous society of virtuous people; but the increasingly heterogeneous society of Ohio required a more balanced form of government. Rufus Putnam of Marietta and Arthur St. Clair, Jr., of Cincinnati would endorse the moderate Republican Samuel Huntington for governor in 1808 because he represented a more democratic incarnation of the Federalist principles of the 1780s and 1790s. Ohio, like the rest of the United States, was a society of clashing interests and ambitions that needed institutions, whether they be the national government or the courts, to check and filter the decisions of popularly elected representatives in order to insure social order and justice. A world of autonomous men engaged in an open competition with nothing to distinguish among them but other men was anarchy.

The political battles that engulfed Ohio between 1807 and 1812 were bitter affairs. The motives that led men to choose sides in these struggles were complex and interrelated. Personality conflicts and political ambitions obviously influenced the choices they made. But the debates over the proper roles of courts and political organizations in the governing of Ohio also forced men to come to terms with the kind of society Ohio was becoming. To a large extent, their political decisions were the products of their understandings of the evolving nature of their increasingly pluralistic and interdependent world, and the ability of its residents to resolve their differences by themselves.

Judges have always occupied an anomalous position in a democratic society. In standing above society as the ultimate arbiter of conflicts, a strong court system is, almost by definition, a testament to the lack of consensus in a democracy and the failure of popular elections or legislative actions to resolve all disputes. By assuming a position of eminence, judges are cloaked with a prescience and integrity that ordinary men are assumed to lack. In Jeffersonian America, however, judges were still in the process of defining their responsibilities and powers.[2]

In the Northwest Territory, the three territorial judges had played both a legislative and a judicial role; with the governor during the first stage of territorial government they had made law as well as interpreted it. By endowing leading immigrants like Rufus Putnam with judicial authority, moreover, Congress had helped to legitimize its authority and that of its agents in the Ohio Country. The selection of Ohio Company associates and John Cleves Symmes as territorial judges had served to surround their purchases with an aura of fairness and regularity that squatters could never match. Of course, the Federalists had established a strong court system because they did not trust a government dependent upon popular sovereignty. But they also believed that tradition, precedents, and institutions contributed to the maintenance of social order and justice.

The future Jeffersonian Republicans, on the other hand, had settled in the Ohio Country with little interest in courts except as sources of local authority and status. Angered by the patronage system that governed access to power in the Northwest Territory, they eventually had become staunch defenders of the prerogatives of local justices of the peace. Believing that conflict was the work of evil men like Arthur St. Clair and not the inevitable product of a heterogeneous society, Republicans had seen courts as almost superfluous. Thus, the Ohio Constitution had created an extremely weak state court; its members were dependent for election and reelection on the general assembly and had to "ride like Post Boys," as one of them put it, to fulfill their duties.[3]

Given this lack of power and the hostility to courts as the last bastion of the Federalists evinced by the Republicans (on the national as well as the state level), it is not surprising that the early Ohio legislatures thoroughly dominated the state court system. Judges clearly felt intimidated by the assembly and with good reason. In 1805, the legislature removed William Irwin as associate judge of Fairfield County for putting private concerns above the public business. In 1806, Calvin Pease of Warren expressed reluctance in accepting Governor Edward Tiffin's appointment to the Ohio Supreme Court; Pease was afraid that the legislature would "at the next session think it proper to substitute another in my place" and that he would suffer in money and reputation.[4]

The 1805–6 session of the general assembly further weakened the state judiciary by repealing the application of the common law in Ohio. The motive of the legislators, according to Samuel Huntington (the future state judge and governor), was to discard "the disgraceful badge of remaining Servitude by being bound by British Statutes and Common Law."[5] But abolishing the common law did more than free Ohioans from their British heritage. It also increased the power of the assembly by eliminating an alternative authority to which opponents of legislative actions might have appealed for redress. Without the common law, and with the state judiciary thoroughly dependent upon the representatives of the people, the legislature was the final authority in Ohio. To many Republicans, such as Governor Tiffin and Senator Worthington, such a situation was entirely appropriate. Since the general assembly was a perfect reflection of the people, any check upon its power was inappropriate.

Ohio's few and disorganized Federalists, on the other hand, were not so pleased with the repeal of the common law. Zenos Kimberly of Jefferson County, for example, denounced the abolition as another "disorganizing Jacobinical procedure." In June 1806, the *Scioto Gazette* published a letter by "Lex" arguing that without the common law there were no precedents or rules left in Ohio. Oppression was now unavoidable, given the power of the legislature. Judges had been reduced to "mere tools, subservient to the ruling party." Lex greatly lamented the loss of "the binding force of common law, common honesty, common right, the birthright of every individual, the cement of friendship, the ligaments of society, the genius of humanity." Without traditional maxims what would hold the ever-expanding society of Ohio together? Even staunch Republicans like Samuel Huntington worried that "persons and property" might be left without protection unless something was substituted for the common law, or "unless Courts have the liberty so far to apply the principles of it, as to give a remedy where the Statute Law applies none."[6]

Federalists and some Republicans also feared that the legislature was putting too much power in the hands of ill-qualified justices of the peace who were easily swayed by the force of local public opinion. In 1804, the general assembly had extended the jurisdiction of justices of the peace to all cases involving fifty dollars or less in value. Governor Tiffin pronounced this act, increasing the authority of local officials, "a favorite law of many."[7] But is was not popular with the justices of the state court. In 1806, Judge Calvin Pease declared the act unconstitutional because it violated the seventh amendment of the United States Constitution (which limited the jurisdiction of justices of the peace to twenty dollars). Not only had Pease defied the Ohio legislature, he had done so with the authority of national, not state, law.[8]

A year later, Pease's colleagues, Samuel Huntington and George Tod, upheld his decision in the case of *Rutherford v. McFadden*. Denying the charge that the judges were trying to assume the role of legislators by declaring a law unconstitutional, Huntington contended nonetheless that the state supreme court had an obligation to protect the citizens of Ohio from the general assembly. If legislation was contrary to the federal Constitution, it was "the duty of the court to declare it *no law*." Only judges, Huntington argued, could protect the sanctity of the Constitution, and thus the rights of the people, from a potentially despotic legislature. If the assembly could pass whatever acts it wished, "then indeed is our constitution a blank paper; there is no guarantee for a single right to our citizens."[9]

Huntington and his colleagues were elevating constitutionalism to the level of common law; they were trying to sanctify the federal and state constitutions as authorities superior to the legislature. But they couched their argument in populist terms. By extending the authority of local justices to fifty dollars, Huntington declared, the legislature was violating the right of citizens to trial by jury.[10]

The first reaction of the Ohio General Assembly to Pease's original nullification of the act in 1806 had been mixed. A committee upheld the right of judges to declare laws unconstitutional, but pointed out that Judge Pease had made "an error in Judgment" in this particular case.[11] A sizable minority of the representatives wanted to impeach Pease for his defiance of the legislature, but the majority was unwilling to confront the court directly.

Politics soon made the issue a heated one. Governor Tiffin and Senator Worthington decided in 1807 to exchange offices. In January the legislature obligingly elected Tiffin to the senate. But Worthington delayed announcing his intention to run for governor for so long that other men seized the initiative. Marietta resident Return Jonathan Meigs, Jr., who had returned to Ohio in 1806 after serving as a judge in the Louisiana Territory, determined to seek the job. Meanwhile, some disgruntled Republicans and Federalists met in an impromptu Chillicothe caucus, organized by the unlikely duo of Michael Baldwin and Jacob Burnet, and nominated Nathaniel Massie for Governor. Worthington declined to challenge his old mentor Massie, and ran for a seat in the Ohio assembly. In the gubernatorial election, Meigs defeated Massie, but by a margin of fewer than two hundred votes (out of almost nine thousand cast). Angered by Meigs's close victory, Massie challenged it in the general assembly on the grounds that Meigs was not a legal resident of Ohio because he had been out of the state for so long. The legislature agreed with Massie and declared Meigs ineligible. It then appointed Thomas Kirker, a Massie supporter and the speaker of the house, to the governorship.[12]

Elected to a seat in the general assembly, Thomas Worthington was eager to rejuvenate and broaden his political base. The charges of aristocracy pinned on him by men like Baldwin and Pritchard had weakened Worthington's previously secure hegemony in Ohio politics. The issue on which he chose to consolidate his fortunes and to draw overt ideological lines was judicial review. The former senator had found a cause that he hoped would enable him to regain the mantle of a populist. In December 1807, a Worthington-led committee of the house of representatives drafted a resolution stating "That the judges of this state are not authorized by the constitution to set aside any act of the legislature, by declaring the law unconstitutional or null and void." The house passed the resolution by a vote of eighteen to twelve, but the senate rejected it.[13] Still, Worthington had once again assumed command of the political agenda in Ohio; the question of judicial review would be the major issue in state elections for the next five years.

Worthington obviously seized the initiative with the judiciary for personal political reasons. But there were important ideological considerations involved as well. The clamors of the first years of statehood had convinced Worthington that deceptive and selfish men had too much influence in the new state; he was certain that they were preparing the way for a revival of Federalism in Ohio. The leader of the statehood movement could not accept the fact that divisions and disagreements were natural parts of society. The territorial government had been responsible for discord before 1803; now malevolent men were trying to disrupt the harmony of the new state for personal gain. In asserting the power of judicial review, the Ohio judges were trying to revive Federalist principles, especially a reliance on the judgment of men set apart (or above) the rest of society in an institution relatively removed from popular control. Worthington intended to defeat them, as he had defeated St. Clair, by exposing them to the people. Simply appealing to "the good sense of the honest part of the community," as Congressman Jeremiah Morrow put it, "will keep the good old republican principles pretty much in fashion."[14]

Specifically, Worthington and Tiffin meant to develop the embryonic system of county conventions and legislative caucuses in Ohio. Republican organization on the local level, while rudimentary, had played an important role in state politics since the statehood movement. County conventions nominated candidates for offices and encouraged the potential supporters of those candidates to vote. The conventions, according to historian Donald J. Ratcliffe, "were attended by delegates elected by the people in their various townships at the time announced well in advance by the party committee at the county seat."[15] Less powerful, but still significant, was a caucus of Regular Republicans in the state legislature which met to choose candidates for state offices. As the congressional contest of 1806 had demonstrated, however, the nominations of the caucus were often ignored by many men. And there was a widespread feeling in Ohio in 1807 that caucuses and conventions were not as democratic as they appeared to be. On the contrary, many Republicans (and Federalists, of course) saw them as the means by which Worthington and Tiffin maintained their political hegemony.

Supporters of the moderate Republican Samuel Huntington exploited this hostility in the gubernatorial election of 1808. They accused Worthington and his allies of being aristocrats masquerading as democrats. Caucuses were a threat to the "freedom and independence" of voters because they allowed "one or two in our state or county to be our dictators."[16]

The election itself proved that the Regular Republican organization was not as strong as its opponents claimed. Huntington faced two Regular Republican candidates in 1808, Thomas Worthington and the incumbent Governor Thomas Kirker. The latter found strong support among men tired of Worthington's influence being the key to political offices in Ohio. Far from being dictatorial, Regular Republican organization was in disarray in 1808. There were too many men like Michael Baldwin and James Pritchard who were unwilling to defer to the judgments of their peers on every occasion.

Still, advocates of Worthington and Kirker found common ground on the question of judicial review. Regular Republicans worked hard to make the state court's assertion of its power to declare laws unconstitutional the overriding issue in the campaign. They reminded voters that Samuel Huntington was one of the judges who had engaged in the "unwarranted assumption of power to declare the acts of the legislature unconstitutional."[17] Accusing the judge's supporters of being Federalists, the Regular Republicans urged Ohioans to condemn "This aristocratical conduct of the judiciary" which had brought the state into "confusion" and a "lamentable state of oppression."[18]

A majority of voters apparently agreed with the Regular Republicans. But they divided their ballots between Worthington and Kirker, and Huntington was elected governor with approximately 45 percent of the vote.

The victor's supporters included the state's Federalists; both Rufus Putnam and Arthur St. Clair, Jr., endorsed him.[19] But the significance of the election of 1808 was less the victory of Huntington than the drawing of the lines of conflict for the bitter battle over judicial power which would dominate the meeting of the new legislature.

Worthington and his allies interpreted his defeat as further evidence of the fact that the major cause of the discord in Ohio was the behavior of a few corrupt demagogues. "The apparent Change in the Politicks of this State," argued Worthington supporter John Sloane of Canton, was the result of "the exertions of a few men" who sought office so fervently that they would even join with Federalists to obtain it.[20]

The Regular Republicans clearly saw the struggle against the judiciary as a continuation of their battle against the territorial government. Despite the lack of a widespread acceptance of two-party conflict as a legitimate activity and the frequent shifts of individual men from one camp to another, there was a remarkable ideological consistency to early Ohio politics. The fundamental issue was always the location of sovereignty, or the source of power, in a rapidly developing frontier society. The Federalists had tried to place it in the national government; the Jeffersonian Republicans in 1802 had insisted that sovereignty belonged to the people. But five years of Regular Republican government had not put the issue to rest. In 1808, Republicans were dividing among themselves (and still struggling with Federalists) over the extent to which ultimate authority should rest with the people. The significance of the judiciary issue was to redefine the Federalist argument for institutional restraint on the will of the people in populist terms. The judges and their defenders advocated positions with which Rufus Putnam was familiar, but they did so in ways that made their distrust of popular sovereignty palatable to a wider range of people.

Thomas Worthington and his allies were not wrong, then, to see the spectre of Federalism in support for the judges. Nor is it surprising that Regular Republicans attacked the state judiciary with a vehemence they had failed to muster since the ouster of Arthur St. Clair. In December 1808, the Ohio House of Representatives impeached Judges Calvin Pease and George Tod for "wickedly, wilfully and corruptly" declaring the law extending the jurisdiction of justices of the peace to fifty dollars unconstitutional. The judges were, said Ephraim Quimby of Warren, a class of men which was trying "to subvert the people's right to their own particular and exclusive interest."[21]

The judges' defenders asserted that "the independence of our judiciary" was "one of the grand pillars of our constitution" and attacked the attempt to "erect the Legislature into a powerful aristocracy" or "an infallible body" like the Pope. They saw the outcry against the judges as a movement to "bring all things back to a state of nature." To destroy the independence of the judiciary was "to introduce confusion into the system," to "destroy its symetry, and bring on a political dissolution." A correspondent to the *Ohio Gazette*, using the pseudonym "A Plough Jogger," contended that opposition to the court was intended to benefit the "kind of gentry" who operated as justices of the peace. Unlike the anticourt party, the court's defenders had a fear of the frailty of legislators and a dim view of the natural abilities of people. "The people scarcely ever read the laws," argued one. And even if they did, "a majority of them are not competent to make those nice distinctions which might be necessary for a legal investigation of the kind."[22]

In defending themselves against the charges, both Pease and Tod argued for the supremacy of the constitution. That document stood above the legislature and any of its decisions. "The people in their sovereign capacity," asserted Tod, "have given the constitution as a *rule* to guide and govern us." The constitution limited the legislature because its framers knew that "like all other men" legislators were "liable to err." If the assembly could pass one unconstitutional act, it could eventually oppress the people at will. After all, Ohio was a representative government, not a perfect democracy. Pease countered the legislature's claim that it spoke for the people by demanding how it came by a monopoly on truth. Who was infallible? All men are liable to err. What was more, men differ in opinion on occasion, and, at bottom, it was only a "matter of opinion who is right and who is wrong." Pease agreed that "no legitimate authority can be exercised by any one man or set of men over a state, without the consent of the governed." But the people of Ohio had delegated power to different branches because of the imperfections of men and because a direct expression of popular will "would inevitably end in anarchy or despotism." Once power was delegated, it could only be changed by the people, not by their representatives. For a constitution is "a law in its nature paramount to all other human laws—a law unalterable and unrepealable, except by the mighty hand of the people."[23]

However reasonable the judges' position may have sounded, they were completely misinterpreting the Ohio Constitution. In fact, Pease and Tod were developing a conception of human society which had more in common with Federalism than Republicanism. The Ohio Constitution had been written by men who had had an abiding faith in the ability of ordinary people to understand their interests and recognize their natural leaders. They assumed that the legislature would be the supreme institution of government; annually elected, it was to be a kind of a meeting of the people on a reduced scale. But Pease and Tod were rejecting the fundamental basis of Ohio's republican government. They were arguing not that almost everyone was good, moral, and capable of telling right from wrong, but that all men—not just the Burrs, the Baldwins, and the Federalists—were potentially depraved and that, as a consequence, there was a need for a society's best educated and tested men to adjudicate the inevitable conflicts of men. Because the legislature consisted of mortal men—indeed, because it was so close a reflection of the society it represented—it could not be endowed with the supreme power in the state. Five years of contentiousness had convinced some Ohioans of the necessity for a sophisticated and powerful legal system to exist in the state.

If the judges' view of human nature was more sophisticated (at least from a modern perspective), the legislators' position was more consistent with the state constitution. The Ohio House of Representatives declared the assembly supreme. Only the legislature could declare what "*shall* or *shall not* be law."[24] Only it was effectively the voice of the people. Only it was checked by annual elections. After all, as the newspaper correspondent "A Republican" put it, representatives were "organs of our will: To speak and act as we, *the people,* would speak and act, were we collectively present." Since the people and the legislature were virtually the same thing, the house contended that "there could be no tribunal above their authority." If judicial review were legitimately practiced, then the judges would have a legislative function. And that would be a usurpation of power. Finally, the house reminded the judges that they were elected by the assembly. They could not defy the will of the same body that gave them power.[25]

Despite what the Marietta lawyer William Woodbridge called the "fervour and irritability" of the legislature over the impeachments and the petitions of "several thousand citizens" of Ohio, nine senators voted not guilty. Thus, the two-thirds requisite for conviction was not achieved and Pease and Tod were acquitted. In bitter revenge, the house quickly passed an act extending the power of justices of the peace to all cases involving less than one hundred dollars.[26]

If the anticourt Republicans lost the impeachment trials, the judiciary question had become an issue with which they could rally voters. In the fall of 1809, the people of Ohio were called upon to defeat the "judicial aristocracy . . . the enemies of the people . . . this extra-judicial hydra—rear the monster no longer." And they did. In Ross County, Duncan McArthur routed the procourt candidate Joseph Kerr in the race for state senator. John Hamm of Chillicothe informed Major John Fuller that the results of

the elections for the assembly had left "The advocates for Judiciary infalli-
bility . . . all in the suds." Throughout the state, the court's opponents
did well. It was clear that "The next Legislature will have the strongest
Democratic majority ever known in this state."[27]

The new assembly quickly asserted its authority by passing a resolution
declaring all judicial seats vacant in 1810 because the constitution allowed
only a seven year term. By twisting the constitutional supremacy argument
back on the court's supporters, the legislators dismissed from office every
state official who had been appointed between 1803 and 1809. They then
proceeded to elect new judges who were more acceptable to the anticourt
party. When the work was done, Daniel Symmes gave a celebratory party.
"Thanks to a good destiny," rejoiced Hamm, "The Democracy of Ohio is
yet triumphant—the insidiousness of Quiddism and the wickedness of the
federalism to the contrary notwithstanding."[28]

Again, the judiciary issue provided the main point of division in the fall
elections. In 1810, the opposing candidates for governor were the moderate
Republican Return Jonathan Meigs and Thomas Worthington. Both sides
accused the other of being anarchic. In May, a *Scioto Gazette* correspondent using the pseudonym "Civis" accused the judges of causing "civil discord. It amounts," he wrote, "to an invitation to the people of this state to
rise in opposition to the constituted authority, and to commence a rebellion" that would indeed "consign to the tomb of oblivion, the best hopes of
a rising state, as yet in the morning of its existence." In reply, George Tod
argued that the Sweeping Resolution (as the measure declaring all judicial
seats vacant had been dubbed) was the work of "restless spirits who have
beguiled the better judgment of the representatives of the people."[29]

Worthington was presented to the voters as the true friend of the people.
A newspaper writer named "Logan" reminded the citizens of Ohio that
they were "freemen . . . governed by laws made mediately by" themselves. "You are not, as has been said, foes to your own liberties—you are
not your own worst enemies." The anticourt party appealed to the antilegal
instincts of the populace. Lawyers, said another correspondent named "A
Watchman," were "governed by self-interest" and the pursuit of "*fees.*"
While it was the "interest of the people to prevent law-suits," it was "the
interest of the lawyers to promote law-suits." The fifty dollar act had provided "an easy and cheap way of settling demands" by bringing "justice to
the door of every man." Writing to the *Scioto Gazette,* "A Backwoods
Man" decried the plots of "lawyers greedy after *fees*" who were attempting
to plunge the state "into perpetual confusion and uproar."[30] A Fourth of
July toast succinctly summarized the Worthington platform: "Democ-

racy—A Free and equal right of suffrage frequently exercised: Talents and integrity the only qualifications for office, and submission to the will of the majority."[31]

But the majority of Ohio voters refused to vote for Thomas Worthington in 1810; Meigs won the election with 9,924 votes to 7,731. The victory demonstrated the continuing strength of the moderate Republican-Federalist coalition. Meigs did well in the more commercial urban areas of the state, particularly Marietta and Dayton, while Worthington carried the Scioto Valley. The only consolation for Regular Republicans was the reelection of the popular incumbent, Jeremiah Morrow, to Congress. Morrow defeated the impeached judge, Calvin Pease.[32]

One of the major reasons for Meigs's success was the ability of his supporters to launch a populist attack on Worthington and his allies. They pointed out that the former senator's commitment to government by the will of the people was limited; Worthington trusted voters only so long as they were properly informed and organized. In particular, moderate Republicans attacked the formation of a wigwam, or local unit, of the secret national Society of St. Tammany in Chillicothe in March 1810. Members included Worthington, Edward Tiffin, and Daniel Symmes of Cincinnati. Within a year, there were other wigwams at Zanesville, Cincinnati, Zenia, Lancaster, and Warren. A national brotherhood that included many Republicans in other states, the Tammany Society had been "founded upon the purest principles of Political Virtue, and Genuine Patriotism" and was dedicated to making "the Number of the *Free and Independent* Citizens of Columbia . . . the number of brothers Constituting the Tammany Society."[33]

Worthington and Tiffin were the prime movers behind the Ohio wigwams. Disgusted by their inability to elect their candidates, Republicans had been forming township and county caucuses for years. The object was to bring some system into politics and to expose the evil and depraved candidates who might manage to mislead the public. The Tammany Society climaxed that effort. It was designed to fight "a perpetual war with the Evil Spirit" and to cement the harmonious bonds of union among true Republicans. With organization and a clear identification of candidates, wrote Grand Sachem J. V. Horne of Zanesville, "we may bid defiance to the slanders of our enemies, and the persecutions of that old monster Federalism." They would achieve "perfect liberty" at last.[34] The Tammany members were pledged to unite "in a body in support of such men and measures, as may be agreeable to the will of the majority; consistent with success; honorable to ourselves; and useful to the republic."[35] The members of the wigwams were admitted only after careful scrutiny and the rites kept secret in order to prevent the ambitious or insincere from infiltrating the ranks of the followers of St. Tammany. Like a more democratic version of the Society of the Cincinnati, the Tammany Society would educate the people and expose their enemies.

But, ironically, the formation of the Tammany Society was a crucial mistake on Worthington's part. For, as his opponents never tired of pointing out, a secret and exclusive organization had no place in a democratic society. Throughout the 1810 gubernatorial campaign, Meigs's supporters mocked the goals of the society and accused Worthington of trying to control popular decisions through his "tools and minions" and other "mere creatures of [his] will."[36] Defeated for governor, Worthington managed to win a seat in the United States Senate when the legislature met in December. Again, he met strong opposition and only defeated Samuel Huntington by four votes on the sixth ballot.[37]

In 1811, the growing attacks on the Tammany Society reversed the momentum gained by the anticourt party over the issue of judicial review. They were decried as a mysterious nobility plotting "Aristocracy, Monarchy, or Tyranny." All over the state the wigwams were subjected to virulent hostility. In Cincinnati, the *Liberty Hall* led the campaign against the Tammany Society. One correspondent went so far as to argue "that the *Burr* conspiracy emanated from the Tammany society, that it was the first effort of the Tammanites." The strong criticism of the potentially antireligious aspects of a secret brotherhood brought a serious division to the Chillicothe Methodist church. Joseph Collins, the minister, was forced to resign from the Chillicothe wigwam.[38]

The Tammany members continued to believe that they were synonymous with "*the sovereign people,*" as one Federalist sarcastically commented.[39] Republicans charged that their enemies were Federalists and demagogues who were plotting to "give judges the unlimited right to set aside law." Their detractors were merely men who had been denied offices through the operation of the county convention system. Because their opponents were so deceptive, argued the Tammany wigwams, they had to maintain secrecy and exclusivity. Only those of "*firm, uniform, Democratic-Republican principles,* and *good moral Character*" could be admitted to membership.[40]

The Tammany Society had been organized, as its founders claimed, "to connect in the indissoluble bonds of patriotic friendship, citizens of known attachments" to the United States and to republican principles. At the same time, the society would "suppress that disorganizing spirit produced and fostered by Aaron Burr and his associates, of whom we fear there is [*sic*] many whose heads are as yet uncovered."[41] In May 1811, Edward Tiffin delivered an oration defending the society as a collection of true Republicans trying to concentrate their strength and purity. The amount of abuse suffered by members of the society only showed how far "ignorance and prejudice may go towards dethroning reason, and suffering all the angry and turbulent passions to usurp its seat." Despite the hostility of some people, the brothers remained convinced that "time and a proper development of our principles and practice" would end the confusion.[42]

These proud protestations aside, the Regular Republicans had lost the initiative they had seized when they impeached the judges. They were now successfully labelled as aristocrats. Politically, Worthington had no choice but to seek an accommodation with the moderate Republicans. In the legislature of 1811, the Sweeping Resolution came within one vote of being repealed. In Worthington's home county of Ross, moderate Republicans such as Henry Brush and William Creighton ("an intriguing Burr-like double-faced kind of a character," John Hamm called him) swept into power. In the fall of 1811, the "great Conjuror" Creighton held a mock funeral for St. Tammany in Chillicothe. "The Tammany hobby horse," lamented Edward Tiffin, had been ridden "almost to death." Soon, all but one of the wigwams had disbanded and the legislature repealed the Sweeping Resolution in 1812. The judges had won.[43]

Republicans in Ohio reunited in 1811 and 1812. The likelihood of war with Great Britain and fears of Federalist victories in the races for the six congressional seats Ohio had been awarded after the census of 1810 provided the major incentives for Republican unity. The movement of the state government from Chillicothe to a permanent home in the new city of Columbus in 1816 helped to bury long-standing regional rivalries. Return Jonathan Meigs defeated Worthington in the gubernatorial election of 1814, but Worthington was appointed to Meigs's seat when President James Madison named the Ohio governor postmaster general of the United States.[44]

Worthington continued to believe that Ohio's problems and his personal political difficulties were the work of disorganizers and deceivers like Arthur St. Clair, Michael Baldwin, and Aaron Burr. Visiting Baldwin, who was dying from the effects of dissipation, in March 1810, Worthington could not help reflecting "on the miseries this young man has brought on himself." He expressed sorrow and regret that Baldwin's many talents had not been applied to the benefit of his fellow mortals and "his own good." The lawyer's life, Worthington concluded, had been little more than "a melancholy instance of the depravity of human nature."[45] To the end of his life, Worthington would find the keys to social harmony and individual happiness in the characters of men.

The explicit relationship between private and public behavior that Worthington drew in the case of Baldwin would echo throughout the nineteenth-century Midwest. The region's thoroughly pietistic culture would encourage people to find the sources of their failures within themselves. Like Michael Baldwin's inability to achieve the success his talents merited, their inability to fulfill all of their expectations about life would be attributed to their failure to control and discipline themselves.

But if the emerging culture of Ohio would emphasize the responsibility of each individual for his actions, the governing assumptions of the society about economic and political structures would closely adhere to the Federalist vision of the future of the West. Both the Federalists in the 1780s and the judges in 1808 had contended that human behavior was to a great degree the product of the environment; people acted differently in a variety of social, economic, and political contexts. The natural condition of men, moreover, was to be depraved in the sense that they were all self-interested. Thus, governments could not be established on a foundation of trust in popular sovereignty, for no such thing existed. A government that did not take into account the pluralistic as well as the democratic nature of Ohio's society, a government predicated on the belief that a natural harmony of interests could exist among egalitarian men, was a government out of step with the world.

Many Republicans reached a similar conclusion in the 1810s. The "Sovereigns," as Senator Joseph Kerr put it, "are not as they ought to be—and although they may individually be sensible that they do not possess all the qualification requisite, they are unwilling to have the appearance of acknowledging their weakness by pursuing measures pointed out by others."[46] The solution to this dilemma was to elaborate the assumptions that underlay the judges' assertion of judicial review and revise the ideological foundations of Ohio. A weak government may have been appropriate for a frontier society of people united in a defense of local interests against an allegedly tyrannical territorial government. But, as events in the second decade of the nineteenth century made clear, the era of the frontier was coming to a close. Ohio was becoming a place not far different from that envisioned by the Federalists in the 1780s—a heterogeneous society increasingly intertwined in the economic and political worlds of eastern America and Europe.

8

The Climax of a Liberal Society

1812   1819

In reacting against what they considered to be the excessive power of the
territorial government, Ohio's Jeffersonian Republicans had sanctioned
the existence of a society that met all the requirements of nineteenth-
century liberalism. Ohio had a weak government and a relatively open and
unregulated economy. No legally established institutions—no aristocracy,
church, or army—exercised extraordinary power. Each adult white male
was free to pursue his interests as he thought best. To a remarkable degree,
Ohio in the early nineteenth century was a society of autonomous men, a
political entity that had been born in a wholesale rejection of all institutional restraints on white males.[1]

But by 1812, the state's political gentry had discovered that a free society
could be as discordant and inequitable as any other. Their disillusionment
intensified during the War of 1812. In the Old Northwest, the war was
largely a disastrous enterprise; early efforts to conquer Canada failed dis-
mally and enthusiasm waned quickly. Many leading Ohioans, like their
counterparts on the national level, blamed military failures on the weakness of government and the excessive egalitarianism of soldiers. Americans
were too concerned with their own interests to discipline themselves in the
ways necessary to win a war. Militiamen elected officers less on the basis of
competence than on whether they allowed "every one to do as he pleased."

Even the officers were inordinately ambitious and jealous. "Every man," noted Carlos Norton in 1812, "wants to be an officer. We could raise three regiments of Colonels and captains."[2]

Still, the United States survived the War of 1812 and, in its aftermath, experienced an economic boom. Farmers in the Ohio Valley continued to produce an agricultural surplus. Banks mushroomed and emitted thousands of paper dollars, which men used to buy land and invest in schemes to make more money. The government sold land on easy credit terms. Prosperity seemed to be within the reach of everyone. Indeed, rarely in the history of the world has there been as much opportunity for as many individual white males as there was in the Ohio Valley in the 1810s. Economically, Ohio in the last half of the second decade of the nineteenth century appeared to be a shining proof of the possibilities of a liberal society.

But the prosperity of the boom times was artificial and collapsed quickly and violently in late 1818 and 1819. Fortunes built on credit were lost overnight. The causes of the sudden hard times lay in international economic conditions, the overly optimistic loan policies of banks throughout the United States, and the fluctuations of the market for goods and services. But for the citizens of Ohio, the Panic of 1819 brought a profound social and ideological, as well as economic, crisis.

Ultimately, the economic expansion and contraction of the late 1810s and 1820s demonstrated that the citizens of Ohio now lived in a web of interdependence with New York, Philadelphia, and London; decisions made by merchants and bankers in the cities of Europe could have stunning impact in Cincinnati, Marietta, and Chillicothe. The Ohio Valley had become a part of an international economy. It had not happened in the way that George Washington or Manasseh Cutler had hoped it would. But it had happened. And Ohio's political leaders would have to deal with that fact.

The Panic of 1819 also confirmed the judges' argument of the previous decade that Ohio was made up of a variety of peoples and interests. Reaction to the collapse divided men on economic, regional, cultural, and eventually political lines. It splintered forever the assumption on which the government of Ohio had been constructed in 1802: a democratic society produced not a natural harmony but a natural cacophony of interests. And the acceptance of the full implications of that reality would lead in the 1820s to demands for organizations of men to achieve shared goals in a society that resembled a bustling marketplace, and to plans for the thorough reform of both government and men in order to insure the peace and prosperity of everyone.

Tens of thousands of people poured down the Ohio River and across

Kentucky and Pennsylvania into Ohio in the 1810s. Most of them stopped in the state only for a brief respite before plunging on to settle in the new states of Indiana, Illinois, or Missouri. But those who chose to stay in Ohio combined with the reproduction of earlier settlers to double the population of the state between 1810 and 1820. Only thirty-two years after the Ohio Company associates had landed at the confluence of the Muskingum and Ohio rivers to begin the first permanent American settlement in the Northwest Territory, Ohio had a population of 581,295 and was the fifth largest state in the American Union.

Most of the new immigrants settled in or near previously developed parts of the state. Northwestern Ohio remained under uncertain jurisdiction while treaties were negotiated with defeated Indian tribes, and attracted few people. The Western Reserve in the northeastern corner of the state also grew slowly, largely because it was difficult to reach except by overland trails (a situation that the Erie Canal would soon correct). As late as 1820, Cleveland was a hamlet of only 606 citizens.[3]

The majority of the state's residents remained within the confines of the southern river valleys. The Miami Valley had one-fifth of Ohio's population in 1820. There was also growth in the central part of the state. On the upper Scioto River, Columbus was booming, as were Dayton and Springfield on the upper Miami, Zanesville on the Muskingum, and Lancaster on the Hocking.[4]

The vast majority of Ohioans continued to live on farms or in villages of 100 or fewer people. Only 35,000 lived in the 48 towns that exceeded 100 citizens in size. Of those towns, only Cincinnati, with 9,462 residents in 1815, could be judged a city. The census of 1820 reported that the exceedingly young population of Ohio (only 130,460 of its 581,295 citizens were males over eighteen) was overwhelmingly involved in some kind of agricultural activity.[5]

Despite the rural quality of life in Ohio, the regional dominance of growing communities such as Cincinnati, Columbus, Zanesville, Steubenville, and Chillicothe was of critical importance to the economic, social, and political structures of the state. While the permanent citizens of these towns numbered only in the few thousands, people for miles around were increasingly dependent on them. Places like Zanesville and Dayton served crucial roles as regional markets and centers of information. Most of the large landholders of the Scioto Valley lived outside of Chillicothe, for example, but their economic and political interests brought them to town frequently. Steubenville contained only two thousand residents in 1818, but its paper, woolen, and cotton mills, twenty-seven shops, sixteen taverns, and two banks served the needs of transients and a large regional population. Even more dramatically, Cincinnati dominated life in northern Kentucky and throughout the Miami Valley.[6]

In 1815, Cincinnati's leading booster, Dr. Daniel Drake, the son of a New Jersey emigrant to Kentucky, published the highly flattering *Picture of Cincinnati* to attract new residents to the town. But the strategic commerical location of Cincinnati needed little advertising. From a population of four thousand in 1814, Cincinnati had swelled to six thousand by 1816—and the number of residents was considerably augmented in summers by transient immigrants and laborers.[7]

The foundation of Cincinnati's economy was commerce. John Cleves Symmes, who died of cancer in 1814, had chosen his western purchase well. Drawing on the fertile fields of the Miami Valley, Cincinnati entrepreneurs (Daniel Drake counted seventy mercantile importers in the city in 1815) bought and processed tons of flour, pork, and whiskey for resale down the Ohio and the Mississippi rivers in New Orleans. Gorham A. Worth, the cashier of the city's branch of the Bank of the United States which opened in 1817, found "the great and unaccountable number of hogs" in Cincinnati stunning; the whole town seemed to be involved in the production of pork products.[8]

One of the major causes of Cincinnati's economic prosperity in the 1810s was the appearance of steamboats on the Ohio River. The first one, appropriately named the *New Orleans,* made its maiden voyage from Pittsburgh in 1811. In 1819, there were thirty-five steamboats operating on western rivers and nineteen more under construction. By making the transportation of goods more efficient and inexpensive and above all by making a return trip upriver from New Orleans easier, steamboats stimulated dramatic increases in trade. The Ohio River, once the domain of canoes and flatboats, marvelled Worth in 1817, had become "a mere business concern."[9]

Cincinnati's leading entrepreneurs quickly put the profits from commerce into large-scale manufacturing ventures. The growth of the city, the shortages experienced in earlier years and during the War of 1812, and the distances from overland markets in the East encouraged industrial development. By 1815, Cincinnati's breweries were processing forty to fifty thousand bushels of barley into beer every year. The Cincinnati Manufacturing Company had built a steam mill to use in what Drake called "an extensive woolen manufactury." The nine-story steam mill was three years in the building and cost the enormous amount of $120,000. It was designed to function as a woolen factory and to grind seven hundred barrels of flour a week. The new mill was the symbol of Cincinnati's prosperity and its campaign for self-sufficiency.[10]

The huge investments that lay behind these improvements were testaments to the incredible economic optimism of Cincinnatians. After long years of economic stagnation in the Ohio Valley (the result of frontier conditions, the Embargo, and, above all, the lack of specie or currency of any kind), the post–War of 1812 period was an era of heady economic confidence. People were buying land and borrowing money with few anxieties about the future.

Despite the plethora of economic opportunities, the chief beneficiaries of the good times were usually local notables with several (often interlocking) business enterprises. A relatively small group of men dominated the booming urban economy of Cincinnati, for instance. The Bell, Brass, and Iron Foundry (established in 1816), was one example; it employed 120 men, and was owned by a partnership that included William Henry Harrison, Jacob Burnet, James Findlay, and John H. Piatt. The trustees of the Cincinnati Manufacturing Company, which owned the huge steam mill, consisted of Samuel Davies and the owners of the Merino Sheep Company (Jacob Burnet, William Henry Harrison, James Findlay, William Barr, and Andrew Mack). The federal Land Office in Cincinnati was run by James Findlay and his assistant Peyton Symmes. And the three local banks were operated by the same men and their friends. Economic power easily translated into local political power. Jacob Burnet and his brother Isaac (Cincinnati's mayor from 1819 to 1831), James Findlay and his son-in-law, Common Pleas Court Judge George P. Torrence, and William Henry Harrison were the most powerful men in the city and the state. In the 1820s, the Ohio legislature would send both Jacob Burnet and Harrison to the United States Senate. These men and their friends and colleagues (including Martin Baum, O. M. Spencer, and Daniel Drake) were among the first settlers of Cincinnati and they had grown accustomed to having things their way.[11]

This local concentration of economic power had counterparts throughout the state: there were the Putnam and Woodbridge families in Marietta, Worthington and McArthur in Chillicothe, Belazeel Wells in Steubenville, and John Sloane in Canton. By dominating the regional economies, such men obtained strong influence in politics and society. But few people objected too strenuously to the power of these local elites in the late 1810s. There seemed to be enough prosperity for everyone.

Ohio's economic boom was part of a national phenomenon. The heady atmosphere created by the nation's fortuitous victory in the War of 1812 contributed to the sense of optimism, but the basis of American prosperity lay in European economic conditions. There the aftermath of the devastating Napoleonic wars and the effects of several bad harvests created an artificially high demand for American grain and cotton products. The possibilities of European profits brought a dramatic overexpansion in the American economy: increased demand abroad led to greater investments in land that could produce grain and cotton in the United States.

With confidence pervading the market, land speculation, long the province of gentlemen, became a national mania. Under the easy credit terms established by the Land Act of 1800, people began to buy huge amounts of land in the American West. They gave the government one-quarter of the purchase price and promised to pay the remainder in annual installments. The result was that many Americans went into debt. In 1815, only $3,000,000 was owed to the United States for payments on public land purchases; by 1819, the amount had risen to $16,794,795.[12]

The mushrooming of banks facilitated this land speculation (as well as investments in other entrepreneurial ventures). Throughout the nation, lending institutions calling themselves banks appeared wherever someone could afford a printing press. With little or no reserves of specie, these banks turned out thousands of dollars in paper currency, most of which were worthless. State governments chartered only a fraction of these institutions; nonetheless, the dramatic rise in the number of state chartered banks from 204 in 1815 to 400 in 1819 suggests the dimensions of the banking phenomenon. The Second Bank of the United States (BUS) encouraged the huge overextension of credit made possible by the operations of local institutions. Created by Congress in 1816 to bring order to the chaotic national economy and to the disorganized financial affairs of the national government, the Bank increased the speculative frenzy. Under its first president, William Jones, the Bank offered easy credit policies and gave little direction to the national economy.[13]

In many ways, the easy credit terms and the proliferation of banks had the effect of democratizing the American economy. They put sudden wealth within everyone's grasp; one needed little cash and few connections to obtain a bank loan that might become the basis of a great fortune. By making capital available to almost anyone, banks encouraged Americans to believe that equality of opportunity was a reality. Because paper money, unlike land or political offices, appeared to be an unlimited resource, it promised to remove the bases of jealousies and contentions and allow the harmonious coexistence of individual interest and social stability. If wealth could simply be created by banks, then there ought to be enough to satisfy the ambitions and desires of all. Paper money would put everyone's dreams within reach, eliminate almost all causes of social discord, and make America an open society in fact as well as in the imagination.

The prospects of easy wealth and easy lands were an unbeatable combination in attracting settlers to the West. Guidebooks and traveler's accounts beckoned people westward with zeal. The Ohio Country was indeed the promised land. There, labor was prized, slavery excluded, and morality championed. Land prices were low and the soil fertile. Above all, men could "acquire with their hands, independent fortunes for themselves and their children."[14] From all over the East, people flocked to the Ohio Valley. In New England, where "an excess of population, and the state of the times" had produced many unemployed men, the exodus was particularly strong. The number of people "from all parts of the world crowding on board the boats, arks, and rafts with their families" astounded James Kimball, an artisan from Salem, Massachusetts. He had "never imagined the emigration so great as it really is." The Englishman Morris Birkbeck described the situation succinctly in a famous comment in 1817. "Old America," he remarked, "seems to be breaking up and moving westward."[15]

These new immigrants came West with high expectations. In the post–War of 1812 prosperity, prior wealth or influential connections seemed unnecessary. Those who stayed in Ohio found a society that was a microcosm of the good times that were sweeping America. It was a world that offered a great deal to most people. It also worried its leading citizens.

Under the terms of the Land Act of 1800 (which was the legislative brainchild of Northwest Territory Representative William Henry Harrison), the price of federal land was established at two dollars per acre. Purchasers were allowed up to ten years to pay. With banks making cash available on a wide scale, it was easy to buy tracts that were beyond one's means. Such overextension worried Ohio's Republican leaders. But attempts by Senator Thomas Worthington in 1812 and at other times to abolish the credit provisions of the 1800 act and to sell federal land in small tracts for prices as low as one dollar failed. To have so many citizens of the country in debt to the government, warned Congressman Jeremiah Morrow as early as 1810, "will engender disaffection of the most dangerous kind—disaffection nerved by the powerful motives of interest."[16] Worthington and Morrow did not share their fellow citizens' faith that good times were going to be a permanent feature of American society.

But efforts to control the credit system failed. Eastern congressmen who feared depopulation if western land was too cheap and Ohio speculators opposed a price reduction by the federal government. Expensive government land meant that private sales would also be high. Congressional prices, argued Jacob Burnet, were "the standard by which the value of lands in this Country is estimated."[17] To allow them to fall would be to reduce the value of private property in Ohio. Thus, partly in order to protect their personal interests, leading Ohioans allowed a dangerous credit system to remain in operation.

By 1815, land prices in Ohio had risen to incredible heights. The inflation was particularly severe in towns. The establishment of Columbus as the state capital produced prices for town lots ranging from four hundred to one thousand dollars. And everyone bought such lots with the confident expectation that they would go much higher. Exuberance about the future was contagious. In March 1814, an enterprising citizen of Connecticut proclaimed to the inveterate entrepreneur and politician James Kilbourne that he was soon going to "commence the Building of the *City of Sandusky.* . . . All that is necessary to make it a great and important place," he confided to Kilbourne, was "some Governmental patronage, and Individual enterprise, perseverance and Industry." Even in Cincinnati John Cleves Symmes's grandson, John Cleves Short, found the people "grown mad about town property. Selling and speculating and valuing it at a price which nothing can justify." "An American may be proud of his liberty," wrote the perceptive English observer Adlard Welby in sum, "but the pride of a gentleman never stands in the way of a profitable speculation."[18]

In eastern Ohio and in the Scioto Valley, most of the best lands were already sold and consequently sales at the Steubenville, Marietta, and Zanesville federal land offices declined after 1815. But the total sales northwest of the Ohio River rose from 823,264 acres in 1814 to 1,414,952 in 1817, and again to 2,064,177 in 1819. More ominously, purchasers acquired much of this land on credit. By 1819, the total of unpaid balances owed to the government had reached $9,868,295 from an 1814 level of $2,134,989. The speculation was so tremendous that the *Liberty Hall and Cincinnati Gazette* complained that Americans had run out of new names for their new towns.[19]

Inflation produced good times between 1814 and 1818 for those who already owned farms as well as those who simply sought land. Prices skyrocketed under the pressure of the $100 million in bank notes in circulation in the United States in 1816. By 1818, enterprising farmers could sell a bushel of corn for fifty cents, and wheat for one dollar to a dollar and one-half per bushel. Flour brought anywhere from six and one-half to twelve dollars a barrel. And pork, the cheaply raised and easily preserved mainstay of the Ohio economy, went for four to seven dollars per hundred. No wonder Cincinnati's mercantile elite had such grandiose schemes for manufacturing establishments with the profits from such prices to fuel their imaginations.[20]

The foundation of the economic boom in Ohio, as in the rest of the United States, was the dramatic growth in the number of banks. By 1819, there were twenty-five state-chartered banks in Ohio and countless others operating without legal sanction. These institutions helped men such as

Alexander Bourne who wanted to make "*money* a little faster" than had been possible earlier in the state's history. The main obstacle to investments had been the lack of hard specie in the West. For years, even well-off men like Benjamin Ives Gilman and Paul Fearing of Marietta had had to sell land for livestock (in one instance, Fearing traded 1,688 acres for one ram) "because Cash, in this new Country, is almost out of the question." "There was no safety in promising money," recalled Moses Deming of life in the Western Reserve, so most payments were made "in cattle or grain."[21]

Local business elites created the earliest Ohio financial operations as means of consolidating their resources, raising money, and eliminating trade in scarce, bulky specie and in kind. In 1815, there were eight state-chartered banks in Ohio. They included the Bank of Chillicothe (1808), the Bank of Marietta (1808), the Miami Exporting Company (1807) in Cincinnati, the Western Reserve Bank (1812), the Bank of Steubenville, the Bank of Muskingum in Zanesville, the Dayton Manufacturing Company, and the Farmers and Mechanics Bank of Cincinnati. With the exception of the Miami Exporting Company, all of these institutions were chartered by the state of Ohio to run until 1818. During the War of 1812 and with the increased demand for a medium of exchange, these banks began to expand their operations by increasing the amount of bank stock and establishing branches.[22]

The proprietors of Ohio's banks generally supported the chartering of the Second Bank of the United States in 1816. As established institutions, Ohio's oldest banks wanted the stability and facility that the Bank promised to bring to national financial affairs. They hoped it would accommodate long distance transactions and bring some uniformity to financial dealings. Swallowing their traditional antipathy to the Bank, some Ohio Republicans and erstwhile Federalists saw the national institution as a necessary bulwark against the chaos experienced during the war and threatened by the nation's dramatic economic expansion. "Every day gives fresh evidence," argued a reluctant Congressman Jeremiah Morrow, "that public credit and finance cannot be supported without such an institution."[23]

But the major reason Ohio's chartered bankers supported the creation of the Second Bank of the United States was their growing fear of the economic and social implications of wildcat institutions like the infamous Owl Creek Bank of Mount Vernon and the Alexandrian Society of Granville. Most of these unchartered operations lacked the specie reserves requisite to make their loans secure. Acting with their eyes on the greatest possible profit, and with the faith that paper money was an unlimited commodity, they offered easy cash to almost anyone. For men who had not the advantages of a Thomas Worthington or a John Cleves Symmes, these banks were a godsend. "The rage for Bank Speculation" exceeded the bounds of reason, complained the Cincinnati Farmers and Merchants Bank president William Irwin. By printing and loaning money indiscriminately, wildcat banks were the means by which Ohioans intended to achieve universal prosperity. "Everybody," recalled the Methodist circuit rider James B. Finley, "went to banking . . . Tavern-keepers, merchants, butchers, bakers" —all became "bankers."[24]

Senator Joseph Kerr, who was as entrepreneurially minded as any citizen of Ohio, wanted to bypass banks altogether. Rather than create a new Bank of the United States, he recommended that the federal government simply issue treasury notes as legal tender. A bank, he argued, would benefit only a few people, while unlimited supplies of paper money would provide opportunities for everyone. Kerr was extraordinarily confident that the system would work. "What is to depress the Credit of Such paper," he demanded of a disapproving Thomas Worthington, "unless it is a dissolution of the Union?"[25]

Such ideas and the activities of wildcat banks threatened the personal interests of local business elites. They promised to fuel the anarchic ambitions that had already brought the state near chaos by convincing people they could have anything they wanted. Men like Worthington, Jacob Burnet, O. M. Spencer, David Chambers of Zanesville, and others supported the establishment of branches of the Bank of the United States in Ohio to put an end to "the promiscuous circulation of unauthorized bank paper." The national bank would give "our money system . . . a more stable and solid appearance." Consequently, all "The more stable and well founded banks" would support it.[26] Without the imposition of some restraint on wildcat banking, the economic and eventually the political control of leading Ohioans would be broken.

Chillicothe and Cincinnati's prominent men engaged in an intense competition for a BUS branch. The stockholders of the Bank of Chillicothe appointed Thomas Worthington (who had been corresponding for several years with John Jacob Astor of New York about the need for a national bank), Duncan McArthur, Thomas James, William Creighton, Jr., and Jesse Spencer as a committee to lobby for the establishment of a branch in their town. Cincinnatians also organized to protect their interests.[27] By the end of 1816, Governor Worthington had resolved the burgeoning competition by convincing BUS officials of the need for branches at both Chillicothe and Cincinnati. The directors of the Chillicothe branch included Edward Tiffin, Duncan McArthur, Samuel Finley, J. P. R. Bureau, William Creighton, Jr., Edward King, and Abram G. Claypool. In Cincinnati, Jacob Burnet, Martin Baum, James Findlay, John H. Piatt, William

Henry Harrison, and Daniel Drake were appointed directors of the branch bank.[28]

The efforts of Ohio's local gentries to restrain the expansions of unauthorized banks and unlimited paper currency were by no means solely directed at the establishment of the national bank in the state. By 1816, staunchly Republican newspapers such as the *Muskingum Messenger* (edited by the BUS partisan David Chambers) were pressing for reform of the state financial system. Unless the legislature acted soon, warned the *Messenger,* "the present progress of the *Banking mania,"* which was spreading "with an astounding rapidity . . . [and an] inundation of paper money . . . will totally unhinge the social system, and innumerable evils will follow in the train." Most people did not understand the danger; paper money was "the source of endless corruption, confusion, and distrust." In the same year, Governor Worthington also attacked the speculative fever in his messages to the legislature.[29]

The opponents of unlimited banking feared that an unrestrained development of the Ohio economy was potentially revolutionary. The social system that it threatened to "totally unhinge" was the one dominated by local gentries. Uncontrolled banks would put economic power in the hands of ordinary citizens and allow them to demand an end to the gentry's monopolization of land holdings, financial institutions, and political offices. They would, in fact, create an economic as well as a political democracy in the state. Or so Ohio's leaders feared. In any case, it would mean the end of the world as they had known it.

In February 1816, the Ohio General Assembly moved to relieve such fears by strengthening legal controls on all banks and their paper emissions. First, it reaffirmed a law passed by the previous assembly forbidding the circulation of unauthorized paper money. Second, in the Bonus Act of February 23, the assembly extended the charters of the state's original eight banks and created six new ones to run until 1843, if they all accepted several conditions. These provisions were designed to bring benefits to the state and to regulate their operations. Capitalized at no more than $500 thousand, the banks were forbidden to contract debts whose total exceeded three times their paid up stock; one-twenty-fifth of all stock was to be owned by the state of Ohio and its dividends were to be reinvested until Ohio owned one-sixth of the total stock of the bank; and finally, the banks, which were exempted from state taxation, were to open their books to the regular inspection of the state's agents. These actions worked both to provide the state government with a source of revenue without having to resort to taxation and to institute some form of control over the chartered banks.

All the banks accepted the legislature's terms for a charter extension, including new ones at Columbus, Lancaster, St. Clairsville, Mt. Pleasant, and West Union. So great was the demand for banks that the legislature chartered eleven more in the next two years. Again, the objective of chartering more banks was to answer the popular demand for more lending institutions while insuring at the same time that the state government would be able to regulate their operations.[30]

But the assembly's attempt to stem the popular current was futile. By the fall of 1816, the *Cincinnati Western Spy* reported that the law "seems generally to have been forgotten." The attractions of easy money were too great to be resisted. The cashier of the new BUS branch at Cincinnati, Gorham Worth, received a gala welcome in April 1817 from William Henry Harrison and James Findlay. Worth found Cincinnati to have "an air of life, a bustle and activity about it" and its hotels full of discussion about the public lands. Above all, he was impressed with the deafening cannon salute that greeted him—until he discovered that the Cincinnatians were not honoring him, but the money he carried with him.[31]

The celebration of money that seemed to consume all levels of Ohio society continued to worry prominent Ohioans. The chief object of Americans, lamented newspaper correspondent "Lancelot Wronghead," was "speculation—to obtain good bargains, their chief happiness."[32] But, according to several writers, the problem was deeper than the mere pursuit of money. The selfish behavior of Americans, like its institutional manifestation in wildcat banks, threatened the stability of the republic. The general defiance of legislative attempts to restrain the indiscriminate printing of paper money merely accentuated their fears, for they believed that when men refused to obey a law they were implicitly undermining the foundations of society. Whether the law was correct or not, argued "An Observer" in the *Liberty Hall,* it was the responsibility of citizens to respect the law or it would "no longer be our protection." Without respect for one law, the whole code would "be trampled upon, and it would be useless for us to elect men to enact laws for us to break and laugh at."[33]

The economic developments of the 1810s helped to blur the ideological distinctions among Ohio's political leaders. The reunification of Regular and moderate Republicans that had begun in 1811 continued after the War of 1812. Part of the motivation was personal interest. But a significant consideration was the fact that Ohio's leaders increasingly shared a fear about the ambitious and confident citizens of the state. It was as if proponents of banks and paper money had become like the squatters of the 1780s, defiant of anyone who attempted to control their interests. In the late

1810s, former enemies such as Thomas Worthington and the Federalist Jacob Burnet could find common cause in their opposition to unrestrained speculation.

Ohio's Republican leaders had not changed their minds overnight. But they had come to realize that the assumptions that had governed the Constitution of 1802 were no longer viable. Socially and economically, Ohio was becoming so complex that true individual independence and popular sovereignty were impossible. The personal positions of Ohio's local gentries, moreover, were intertwined with the protection of social and economic stability in the state.

It was in this spirit that Republicans like Worthington turned in the late 1810s to greater involvement of the state government in regulating the state's economy. It was also for this reason that they began to devise more formal methods of political organization. Republican and Federalist leaders no longer saw themselves as the leaders of a homogeneous society but as men with special interests to protect from the rest of society. To consolidate their positions and to bring stability to society as a whole, Ohio's leaders developed institutions like political county conventions and banks. Self-interest had even led them to welcome the rebirth of the BUS. These creations designed to compensate for the failure of Republican ideology, however, were becoming targets of democratic attack in the post–War of 1812 period.

The people who attacked the BUS and the state-chartered banks in the late 1810s were not motivated by an inherent dislike of the institutions themselves, but rather by a deep resentment at being excluded from the benefits of their operations. Joseph Kerr, a Scioto Valley surveyor and entrepreneur—and briefly a United States Senator (1814–16)—was a prominent leader of the antibank movement in Ohio. An assistant to Nathaniel Massie for a time, and a large landowner himself, Kerr became heavily involved in exporting the produce of the Scioto Valley. In 1811, he shipped $83,900 worth of pork, flour, and other products out of Chillicothe. Kerr's financial situation was always chaotic—he lived more in debt than out—but it was complicated by his contracts as a supplier of the army during the War of 1812. Kerr delivered supplies from Scioto Valley farms to the troops at Upper Sandusky and other locations. But the federal government was dilatory in paying Kerr and the contractor had to mortgage his lands and to borrow money in order to pay the farmers who had supplied him. By 1815, he owed thousands of dollars to the Banks of Marietta and Steubenville, including ten thousand dollars borrowed to buy army supplies.

The banks brought suit to recover their money and in the fall of 1816 Kerr was imprisoned for failure to pay a judgment against him. Again in

1818 the BUS had him put in jail for delinquency. Meanwhile, Kerr lost his land to his creditors and to several litigants who claimed he had obtained land through fraudulent entries. In 1821, Kerr sold what remained of his farm and bought a hotel in Chillicothe. After his candidate for president in 1824, Andrew Jackson, lost and with the hotel proving unprofitable, Kerr moved to Louisiana. There he proved more successful, developing a showplace plantation. Kerr died in 1837, one year after his similarly adventurous sons had died at the Alamo.[34]

Kerr never liked banks. As a senator elected to fill out Thomas Worthington's term in 1815 and 1816, he strongly opposed the chartering of the Second Bank of the United States. Banks, he believed, took advantage of anyone in order to satisfy their directors' voracious greed. Such institutions, he complained to an unsympathetic Worthington as early as 1814, "are calculated to dicieve; they promise all help until those dependent on them are, at full depth, involved." Ultimately, "those who are compeled to have money are compleatly in the power of the institution." "Incorporated bodies," Kerr concluded, led inevitably to "the Ultimate distruction of our free government." Such notions led him to challenge the Ohio legislature's right to charter banks and to insist that the BUS branches be subject to state control.[35]

Joseph Kerr had no animus against making money; indeed, he was constantly trying to expand his capital resources. If he opposed banks as monied institutions, he strongly supported the issuing of paper money by the federal government as a means of providing currency to all people on an equal and independent basis. Kerr's ideas on money were as inflationary as possible. What he resented about banks were the obstacles he thought they put before his speculations and the fact that they were run by men who were already economically and politically established.

Like so many other Ohioans, Joseph Kerr demanded a truly egalitarian society, one in which any man could get as much money as he needed for whatever he wanted. He did not understand that society and the economy were becoming too complex for the government to issue money indiscriminately. What would happen if everyone demanded specie for his paper at the same time? It was not the banks that were enslaving Joseph Kerr by making him financially dependent on them, but the interaction of his own financial ambitions with those of hundreds of other people.

Nonetheless, men who felt constrained by banks, or who felt themselves failing in some way, found it easy to attack the established banks and their directors as monsters and aristocrats. In the election of 1816, Governor Worthington was denounced for attending a BUS meeting in Philadelphia while in office. The only real issue of the campaign was Worthington's support of the national bank. Despite grumblings about the governor's close ties with the BUS, Worthington won a resounding victory over token opponents. But the new assembly's adamant refusal to charter sixteen new banks in the winter of 1817 raised a huge outcry.[36]

If the opponents of the Bank of the United States and local commercial elites were utopian in their goal of democratic prosperity through unrestrained economic expansion, their demands that the financial institutions of the state and nation be more responsive to popular needs were not without merit. They had a perfect right to expect Ohio's economic system to function in the open manner promised by its Republican rhetoric. Every town in the state, every group of men, felt itself inherently entitled to a legitimate bank. Failure to obtain a legislative charter for a bank in Canton, protested Thomas Rotch, one of the town's citizens, would bring ruin to many "enterprising" people. Too many banks was a danger, to be sure, but there was a clear need for more "progressive measures."[37] Rotch's opinions were not unique. As people felt the pinch of legislative restraint, which was attributed to the influence of chartered banks, they began to phrase their demands for an open banking system in democratic rhetoric.

In the *Muskingum Messenger* in January 1817, a writer using the pseudonym "Cato" advocated a totally laissez faire approach to banking. The legislature, he argued, had no business chartering banks in the first place. "Banks ought to be left with the people," subject to the natural movement of the economy. If a bank could not support its paper with specie, that inability alone would eventually put it out of business. By issuing charters, concurred another writer under the name "Equal Rights," the legislature was subsidizing the control of money by *"a privileged order."* "The first principles of power are in the people," a third writer, "Hampden," reminded the assembly.[38] In other words, the economic system of Ohio should be as democratic as its political system ostensibly was.

By the end of 1817, bank opponents were demanding that the people of Ohio exert their natural authority over the BUS branches in Chillicothe and Cincinnati by levying a tax on them. Over the protests of Worthington, Jacob Burnet, Duncan McArthur, and other traditional leaders, the Ohio House of Representatives resolved in January 1818 that a tax on the BUS branches was both expedient and constitutional. A year later, in the midst of a growing economic depression, the assembly levied a tax of fifty thousand dollars on the two branches and gave them six months to pay.[39]

Not only did people attack established banks as aristocratic bastions antithetical to popular interests, they criticized the system of county conventions and legislative caucuses that had evolved as a means of bringing order to Ohio politics. Such meetings, their opponents claimed with some truth, were merely devices to guarantee the election of gentry and their favorites. But the defenders of the caucus system argued that the reduction of a multiplicity of candidates to only two insured majority rule because one candidate would get more than half the vote. Previous competition and screening would also correct "the evils which ensue from the distraction of public sentiment at election" and end the horrifying practice of a candidate offering for office merely because he thinks himself qualified.[40]

But opponents of caucuses retorted that no group should decide which men ought to be presented to the people as a candidate for office. Just as legislative charters brought order to the economy by legally sanctioning only reliable institutions, caucuses gave an imprimatur to acceptable candidates. A great number of Ohioans found these attempts to bring system to the state's economy and politics undemocratic. They attacked the BUS and chartered banks as aristocratic and inequitable, and they labelled caucus decision as a usurpation of popular authority. A caucus was potentially "a powerful engine, by which the liberties of a nation may be jeopardized." In a free country, proclaimed the *Zanesville Express and Republican Standard*, "Every elector should vote for the candidate of his own choice."[41]

Populist attacks on monster banks and aristocratic domination were intense but infrequent before 1819. A growing number of people believed that society in Ohio was not as democratic as they had expected it to be, that land, trade, and politics were dominated by a relatively small group of men. But between 1814 and 1818 the widespread involvement in the booming prosperity of the Ohio Valley and the seemingly limitless opportunities offered by speculation and paper money made such things seem unimportant. They would soon be corrected by the natural economic growth of the state.

The contention of many that local oligarchies dominated Ohio, although exaggerated, was true. And, even more strongly than their critics, Ohio's local elites were worried about those people whose interests violently diverged from theirs. They were not opposed to making money, but they were greatly opposed to uncontrolled speculation involving anyone who wished to participate. Not only did it threaten to change their positions, the incredible speculative spirit of the 1810s was doomed to collapse. On some level, leading Ohioans sensed that the frenzied economic growth of the period could not be sustained, that not all people could obtain everything they wanted. The resources of the nation were not unlimited; even money was a finite commodity. If all bank depositors sought their holdings in specie at the same time, if all people sought to fulfill their most cherished dreams at the same time, there would be nothing for anyone but confusion and chaos. It was such a situation that finally occurred in the fall of 1818 when the entire superstructure of speculation collapsed. The causes of the crash, like the basis of the economic overexpansion, lay in events thousands of miles from Ohio. European demand for American foodstuffs and cotton, which had been artifically high between 1815 and 1818, suddenly fell with a good harvest and the stabilization of the postwar economy. In 1818, a British financial crisis led London banks to call for the repayment of all loans in specie. During the boom period, Americans had fallen heavily in debt to English merchants for manufactured goods and other products. The action of the British banks led to a serious drain on the limited specie holdings of American entrepreneurs and banks. In the United States, the demand of the Bank of the United States for payment of its loans in specie in order to meet its debts and those of the federal government intensified the crisis.

Called upon by the BUS for specie, the branches and state banks, many of which were dramatically overextended, made similar demands on their debtors. In Cincinnati, the local banks owed a total of $720 thousand to the BUS. Like banks throughout the nation, Ohio's local banks demanded that their debtors pay off their obligations. But the prosperity of the late 1810s had existed almost entirely on paper. The banks' debtors simply did not have the money, let alone the specie, to erase their loans. What specie there was in Ohio was quickly shipped to the East. Before anyone could catch his breath in the late summer and fall of 1818, the entire economic structure of Ohio collapsed. The years of instant prosperity were over.

Although the financial crisis that was labelled the Panic of 1819 struck people throughout the Ohio Valley, it was particularly severe in Cincinnati. The city that had been the greatest beneficiary of the boom was, inevitably, the greatest victim of its bust. From the middle of 1818, economic paralysis swept the city. Banks stopped specie payments; bankruptcies multiplied and the cashier of the BUS branch began prosecutions of debtors which resulted in the repossession of huge amounts of property. The city that had imported $1,619,030 worth of goods in 1817 purchased only $500,000 in 1819. "Persevering enterprize and hazard have been the leading features in the character of the people of Cincinnati," Rhode Island emigrant and lawyer William Greene told his fiancée, but "these have been carried to an extreme." The result was "a state of irretrievable bankruptcy."[42] The traveler James Flint reported in the summer of 1820 that Cincinnati had lost "the stir that animated it" two years earlier. Prices had fallen and empty houses vacated by people trying to escape creditors or seeking a fresh start elsewhere filled the city. Even the ever sanguine Daniel Drake admitted that Cincinnati did "not bloom . . . like the rose as heretofore. . . . How long it will be before we shall become retrogressive, in a decided degree," he warned his friend Edward Mansfield, "remains to be ascertained."[43]

The panic affected everyone in the city; there were literally no exceptions. The Cincinnati mercantile elite, even the directors of the BUS, suffered tremendous losses. Jacob Burnet—Arthur St. Clair's stalwart defender, a stockholder in the Miami Exporting Company, a director of the BUS branch, and a participant in numerous commercial ventures—lost eighty thousand dollars. Martin Baum, Cincinnati's leading entrepreneur, had to sell his home in order to meet his almost incomprehensible, by contemporary standards, debt of two hundred thousand dollars. Daniel Drake, who had invested on a smaller scale, also found himself deeply in debt. In the summer of 1819 Drake lived in a sixteen-square-foot cabin that he dubbed "Mount Poverty." Other leading citizens, like William Henry Harrison and James Findlay, were nearly ruined. Even the Presbyterian minister, Joshua L. Wilson, complained that he was "greatly involved in debt." "Most of the houses in the city are elegant," said the traveler Charles Sealsfield, "but they belong to the bank of the United States, which possesses at least two hundred of the finest houses in Cincinnati." The citizens of the city, he remarked, had forgotten "their actual means" in a "building mania."[44]

Although the losses of the Cincinnati gentry were spectacular, most of them managed to survive the panic and eventually to rebuild their fortunes. Other residents of the city were not so lucky. The failures of the town's leading entrepreneurs put hundreds of people out of work. The Cincinnati Iron Foundry closed its doors in early 1820, leaving more than a hundred men unemployed. Other commercial and industrial operations either closed or sharply reduced their operations. By early 1820, much of the city's population was out of work. Even artisans and shopkeepers, who were dependent on the demand of other citizens for income, found it difficult to keep their businesses going. In January 1820, a newspaper correspondent calling himself "A Friend of the Poor" urged the city to establish soup kitchens in each of Cincinnati's four wards to relieve the "many, very many" who were "actually suffering for the common comforts of life, particularly the articles of food and fuel." Within a month, such kitchens were open for the benefit of the poor. The depressed conditions persisted for years. In 1823, for example, Cincinnati was spending so much on poor relief that the town did not have enough money to repair roads.[45]

Outside of Cincinnati, the effects of the panic were less severe, but distress still pervaded all parts of the state that were in any way tied into the market economy. Banks failed or suspended specie operations throughout Ohio; many of the wildcat operations just disappeared. The precipitous decline in prices made farming unprofitable. Wheat that had been selling for one dollar to a dollar and one-half per barrel in 1815 brought only

127

twenty to seventy-five cents a barrel in 1819. Flour fell from six and one-half to twelve dollars a bushel, to a price of two and one-half to three dollars. By 1819, corn brought only twelve cents a bushel and pork only one and one-quarter to one and three-quarter dollars per hundred. As S. S. Tomlinson of Mt. Pleasant later recalled, "Very few products of the soil would command money."[46] Large farmers and rural entrepreneurs experienced hard times. Men like Duncan McArthur spent much of their time in the years after 1818 trying to salvage their farms and mills. Although able to borrow a needed twelve hundred dollars from the BUS in the spring in 1819, Thomas Worthington was unable to hire enough laborers to farm his land. That spring, the retired governor plowed for the first time in his life.[47]

The panic and subsequent depression reduced the flow of immigrants and the sales of public lands. Only 804,063 acres were sold by the United States government in 1820. But those who had already purchased land on credit were in a tough position. Generally, they had bought land with the expectation that money would continue to be easily available indefinitely. By 1819, obviously, that was no longer the case. Almost all of the specie in the Ohio Valley had been shipped to pay debts in the East and bank paper was almost worthless. In his study of public land policies, Benjamin Hibbard estimated that half of the men living in the Old Northwest in 1820 were in debt to the government for land. Very few of them had any means of paying what they owed. Eventually, the federal government had to pass relief acts to give men adequate time to pay or to allow them to return land for which they could not pay. The government also scrapped the credit system that was one of the major causes of the speculation.[48]

Thus, the Panic of 1819 and the five years of depression that followed it were a catastrophe for many residents of Ohio. The entire economy of the state not only came to a halt, much of the expansion experienced between 1814 and 1818 was reversed.

As men scrambled to recoup their fortunes or to feed their families, they gave a good deal of thought to what had happened to them. Modern Americans have become so inured to economic complexity and vagaries that it is difficult to comprehend the magnitude of the psychological and ideological crises produced by this first major national depression in American history. The events of the late 1810s stunned Ohioans. Economic events and movements that were international in scope and largely beyond their control had completely disrupted their world. Ironically, the pursuit of personal profit had created a society of interdependent rather than independent men.

9

Conflict and Consensus

1819   1824

While the Panic of 1819 provoked a variety of political and social reactions, its most immediate consequence was to shatter traditional patterns of political behavior by politicizing thousands of men who had previously taken little interest in elections. In the early 1820s, politics in Ohio lost its cohesion; there were no consistent divisions of voters along economic or party lines. The Federalists had long since ceased to be a powerful force in state elections and the Republicans were in disarray. Like the rest of the United States in the 1820s, Ohio was in an era of transition from what historians have called the first American party system to the second.

Still, if political loyalties were scrambled in the half-decade after 1819, there was a significant and consistent ideological cleavage between two points of view about the causes and ramifications of the Panic of 1819. The first is best described as populist; blaming the hard times on the corruption of local and national leaders and the excessive power of institutions like the Bank of the United States, its adherents tended to be middling people in the Cincinnati area who were hard hit by the Bank's contraction and farmers in subsistence areas that were relatively distant from the means (and prospective means) of access to national markets. In their version of the old Whiggish insistence on the inherent hostility between government and the people, these men saw the Bank of the United States, the United States

Supreme Court, and the system of political caucuses which had evolved in Ohio as institutions created by corrupt men to advance their own interests at the expense of the public good. Indeed, the Bank was what the *Cleaveland Register* called "a monster of iniquity . . . brought into existence under the administration of a short sighted chief magistrate, by a corrupt congress, who trampled on the constitution they had sworn to support in order to gratify their ambition for wealth." Since the people were vigilant guardians of their liberty, the corrupt Congress had chartered a Bank "with sufficient powers to bribe or terrify them into submission."[1] The panic, from this perspective, was a man-made disaster, a part of a larger scheme to rob Americans of their liberty by robbing them of the property that was the key to their independence. The only good thing about the economic collapse was that it had awakened Americans to a defense of their freedom from the agents of power; it had transformed long-standing ambivalence about the power of local gentries and national institutions into anger. That anger found expression in Ohio in a series of denunciations of corruption and power which reached a climax in support for the presidential candidacy of Andrew Jackson in 1824.

From the other point of view, the panic presented an opportunity to press for reforms of Ohio's society. Men of economic power and political influence in urban areas, people living in regions that stood to benefit from improvements in transportation, and a new group of young entrepreneur-politicians found the cause of the panic in the weakness, rather than the strength, of institutions and governments. Their response to depression was to initiate a program of systematic reform which would integrate the state into national economic, political, and social systems. The plans of these men resembled nothing so much as a state version of Henry Clay's American System—an effort to bring economic and social order to Ohio and to lead it into a prosperous, stable, and glorious future.

Recent historians have tended to describe this ideological division as a conflict between two Jeffersonian traditions—an Old Republican emphasis on the dangers of power and the belief of moderate Republicans that power could be used to improve society. The most prominent Old Republicans on the national level in the 1820s were Andrew Jackson and Martin Van Buren; moderate Republicans included Henry Clay and John Quincy Adams. The debates of the era did occur among Republicans and they did exacerbate a rift that had first appeared, both in Ohio and elsewhere, in the conflict over judicial review.[2] But what is striking is the degree to which the ideological split of the early 1820s continued the controversy between popular sovereignty and local autonomy, and government power and cosmopolitan development, which had characterized the struggles between Federalists and Jeffersonians. The Federalists may have faded as a political force, but the power of their ideas remained potent, largely because the growing complexity of Ohio's economy and society had convinced a significant group of men that an unregulated, liberal society would produce only chaos and degeneracy.

The panic, then, served to revive and clarify old issues. The major difference between the 1790s and the 1820s was that the debate now took place within an evolving consensus about the nature of society in the Ohio Valley. Indeed, by emphasizing the permanence of both individual independence and national interdependence it helped to solidify that consensus and to bring the era of the frontier, in which the assumptions that underlay and the rules that governed human behavior were in dispute, to an end.

As the effects of the panic intensified in late 1818 and early 1819, a large number of angry Ohioans engaged in a spirited defense of their liberty, which they defined as popular and local sovereignty. Their perceived opponents were corrupt political institutions, the Supreme Court, and particularly, the Bank of the United States. In fact, hostility toward the Bank was at a fever pitch in the winter of 1818–19. "If a monied aristocracy in Philadelphia" (the home of the Bank) could, "Through a simple order, . . . blight the prospects" of Ohioans, announced a group of enraged Cincinnatians in November 1818, then American "liberties are beset." The citizens of Ohio, warned future Jacksonian John McLean, had to protect themselves against this "Mammoth" institution.[3]

It was in this climate that the Ohio General Assembly voted in March 1819 to levy a tax of fifty thousand dollars per year on the two branches of the Bank of the United States in Ohio. Advocates of such a tax had been contending for years that the national bank should be subject to state taxation like all other banks. But the economic collapse made the issue a popular one. The two branches at Chillicothe and Cincinnati were given six months to comply with the decision of the assembly. Here was a classic confrontation between state and national authority, between local sovereignty and the developing national economy, which the Bank symbolized.[4]

What the legislators did not understand was that the Bank was as much a victim of the growth of international capitalistic networks as they were; it had had little more control over what had happened than the average American. Clearly, the Bank had been mismanaged and it had been extremely zealous in pressing for the payment of debts (especially in Cincinnati and its environs). But as William Jones, the president of the BUS explained, the Bank had been "compelled . . . to contract its operations and collect its resources from all quarters" because of the demands of its largely European creditors for payments on loans. The Bank, in short, stood in relation to Europe much as Ohio did to it.[5] What Ohioans were in fact protesting in their angry campaign against the Bank was their full involvement in a worldwide economy over which they had little control.

In the spring and summer of 1819, the attempt to tax the BUS involved the state in defiance of another national institution, the Supreme Court. In March 1819 the court denied the right of states to tax branches of the national bank in the case of *McCulloch v. Maryland*. James Wilson, one of Ohio's most strident critics of the Bank, summarized the decision in bold headlines in his newspaper, the *Western Herald:* THE UNITED STATES BANK, EVERYTHING! THE SOVEREIGNTY OF THE STATES, NOTHING!! Wilson went on to argue that the decision virtually returned the states to the status of territories.[6]

But the state of Ohio persisted in its efforts to exercise its authority over the BUS. In September, state auditor Ralph Osborn dispatched men to collect the tax that the branch directors had steadfastly refused to pay. On September 17, John L. Harper and two other men, acting in the name of the state, forcibly removed one hundred thousand dollars from the vault of the Chillicothe branch.[7]

This precipitous action sparked five years of legal controversy. The Bank obtained an injunction preventing Ohio from spending any of the money it had taken and sued the state for the return of its funds. In September 1820, ninety-eight thousand dollars were returned to the Bank while a suit to collect the other two thousand dollars continued. Finally, in 1824, the Supreme Court declared Ohio's tax unconstitutional because the officers of the national bank were acting as agents essential to the financial operations of the United States government.[8]

During the legal controversy, the Ohio General Assembly vehemently pressed its case against both the BUS and the Supreme Court. In December 1820, the legislators adopted almost unanimously a series of resolutions defending the right of a state to tax the Bank. They questioned the power of the Supreme Court to deal with the issue and criticized the *McCulloch* decision. In a strong assertion of Old Republican sentiment about the dangers of a powerful national government, they affirmed the Virginia and Kentucky Resolutions of 1798 and 1799 and their upholding of state sovereignty. But the legislators received little support outside of Ohio. Left alone in their fight, they passed a law withholding the state's protection from the branches of the Bank within its borders, a law that was apparently not enforced and was repealed in 1826.[9]

The struggle against the BUS, understandable as it was given the economic collapse, was quixotic at best. Many Ohioans saw the Bank in the same way Thomas Worthington had viewed the territorial government in

1802—a distant, corrupt obstacle to the fulfillment of the democratic aspirations of individual Americans. But taxing the branches and defying the Supreme Court were only briefly successful protests against the integration of the state and its citizens into an expanding international economic web. The Bank and the Supreme Court were not the causes of Ohio's dependence on people and developments beyond its borders; they were merely institutional manifestations of it. The collective ambitions of thousands of people to get land and make money had, ironically, made them more interdependent than independent. To attack the Bank or the Supreme Court was to proclaim, but not to preserve, the autonomy of local entities and individuals.

The Bank of the United States was not the only institution that many Ohioans perceived as corrupt and dictatorial in the early 1820s. One of the major effects of the panic was to focus attention on the system of caucus nominations which had developed in both Ohio and the United States as a whole. Begun as attempts to maintain solidarity in the face of Federalist challenges, county conventions and legislative caucuses had become effective means of bringing order and discipline to Republican ranks.[10] But in the second half of the 1810s, when the Federalists faded as a viable political force and the split among Republicans over the judiciary had healed, the rationale for the caucuses became less clear. Since there was no real opposition, the need for structured unanimity seemed artificial. In the boom times, moreover, many people found politics far less interesting than land speculation. Not surprisingly, then, the caucus system had degenerated into meetings of leading men who nominated each other for offices. In 1816, Thomas Worthington had been elected governor of Ohio against little more than token opposition; the same was true of Ethan Allen Brown in 1818 and 1820. A system that had begun as a way to advance the cause of democratic government had, partly through its own success, become undemocratic. There was a broad (and largely accurate) feeling in Ohio, as in the nation as a whole in the early 1820s, that caucuses worked not to the advantage of the popular will but to that of the small coterie of men who participated in them.[11]

The aftermath of the Panic of 1819 brought unprecedented numbers of men to the polls. For the first time since the struggle over the judiciary and the Tammany Society, political campaigns revolved around issues that provoked deeply emotional responses. Record numbers of voters turned out to vote in the state elections of 1822 and 1824; and over 130,000 men (or 90 percent of those eligible) cast ballots in the presidential election of 1828.[12]

A large part of the motivation of these new voters was their feeling that a corrupt aristocracy was using the power of government to destroy the liberties of the people. They perceived (again not inaccurately) a correspondence between economic and political gentries in Ohio; in Chillicothe and Cincinnati, for example, men who were prominent in local caucuses were also directors of the Bank of the United States. Hard times, as Donald J. Ratcliffe has argued, "had created in Cincinnati [and elsewhere] a widespread resentment against all politicians who were in a position to exploit public office for their own advantages."[13]

The combination of anger at both monster national institutions like the Bank and the perceived corruption of local elites produced political upheaval in several places. But the most dramatic example occurred in the area that was hit hardest by the panic—Cincinnati. There almost all local officials associated with banks were swept out of office in 1820. For years, the economy and government of Cincinnati had been dominated by men like Jacob and Isaac Burnet, James Findlay, Daniel Symmes, William Henry Harrison, Martin Baum, and others. Such a situation was acceptable to many men as long as there was prosperity. But when the economic system of the city collapsed, traditional leaders had to shoulder the responsiblity. Many people, reported the *Western Spy*, were determined "to submit no longer to the *abuses* of the banking system" and to the wishes of the local notables who dominated it.[14] There was in the minds of many Cincinnatians a clear divergence between the interests of the city's governors and the governed.

The most well-known case of political resentment against the traditional elite was the series of political contests between the Cincinnati lawyer James Gazlay and William Henry Harrison. Gazlay had been born in New York. He came to Cincinnati in 1813 and had earned a reputation as a friend to the downtrodden by publicly aiding debtors and by championing the cause of an Irish draymen against some local merchants. Harrison, on the other hand, was clearly a powerful local figure. The son-in-law of John Cleves Symmes, he was a director of the local branch of the Bank of the United States and a stockholder of the Miami Exporting Company. Harrison had also served as a territorial delegate to Congress and as Governor of the Indiana Territory. His gentry status was tempered somewhat by his reputation as an Indian fighter and the victor of the battle of Tippecanoe.

Gazlay and Harrison had three head-to-head political confrontations— an 1819 race for the state senate and the 1820 and 1822 campaigns for the congressional seat in the Cincinnati area. Gazlay constantly put Harrison on the defensive by attacking the Cincinnati gentry as unresponsive to popular wishes; his strident attacks attracted the support of middling and lower elements in the city's population. Harrison narrowly won the first two contests, largely on the basis of his support outside the city limits. But in 1822, Gazlay managed to defeat Harrison by successfully pinning the label of aristocrat on him. It was a lesson the future president of the United States would not forget.[15]

The discontent among many people in Cincinnati with the leadership of local gentry also affected national elections. In the presidential contest of 1824, the leading candidates for Ohio's sixteen electoral votes were De Witt Clinton of New York, Secretary of State John Quincy Adams of Massachusetts, and Henry Clay of Kentucky. Clinton's candidacy was stillborn because of his lack of support in his home state, while Adams was unable to inspire much enthusiasm except among natives of New England. By late 1823, in fact, most of the state's political leaders were solidly in the camp of Henry Clay. The Kentuckian was the choice of a majority of Ohio's congressmen and an unofficial state caucus.[16]

Clay was an imposing candidate in Ohio. As a resident of the neighboring state of Kentucky, he was a western favorite. He was also the advocate of internal improvements and a general American System that would make the United States more self-sufficient and powerful by breaking down obstacles to national economic development. Finally, the near unanimous support of Ohio's political leaders meant that Clay's campaign for voters would be well organized.

But Henry Clay also had a number of major liabilities in Ohio in 1824, the most important of which was his relationship with the Bank of the United States. Clay served as the Bank's lawyer in Ohio and Kentucky and had represented it in its suit to recover the tax Ohio had forcibly imposed on it. Just as ominous, Clay was a caucus candidate, a man chosen by a system in which leading men decided who they would propose to the people. On two important counts, then, Henry Clay qualified as the candidate of a corrupt aristocracy.

In contrast, Andrew Jackson of Tennessee had the appeal of a popular military hero and the appearance of being above political and economic machinations. Without the support of any major Ohio politician, except James Gazlay, the Hero of New Orleans did exceptionally well in Cincinnati and surrounding counties in 1824. Indeed, his late-appearing candidacy swept through the area like a tidal wave. "Strange! Wild! Infatuated!," wrote a stunned Cincinnati resident. "Two-thirds here are said to be for Jackson. But surely, in February last, his name was not mentioned in the Miami country."[17]

The sudden popular surge for Jackson frightened many leading citizens of Ohio. The "powerful excitement" for Jackson at a Cincinnati meeting, wrote William Greene, a Rhode Island-born protégé of Governor Ethan

Allen Brown, produced nothing but "disorder and confusion." There was enough "noise . . . to inflame the passions of an ignorant multitude." "My whole mind and soul revolt, now, against the very suggestion of Jackson's name." What was wrong with Andrew Jackson, according to another Cincinnatian, was that he was too often "too violent to be restrained by law."[18] Indeed, the general personified the wild and undisciplined American; his support resembled nothing so much as the speculation that had preceded the panic. Here was the spirit of defiant squatters, of impetuous Michael Baldwin.

Jackson did remarkably well, given his late start and weak organization, among the 40 percent of Ohio's eligible voters who participated in the election of 1824. He received 18,489 votes (or 37 percent of the total) and did especially well in counties severely affected by the panic. His best area was Cincinnati and Hamilton County, where the animus against the Bank was strongest. Clay, however, won the state with 19,255 votes (or 40 percent of the total).[19] In the House of Representatives, which had to decide the election since no candidate received a majority of the electoral votes, ten of Ohio's fourteen congressmen followed Clay's lead and supported John Quincy Adams, the eventual victor. They did so in the belief that what Allen Trimble, the speaker of the Ohio Senate, called the "reflecting part of the people"—those which another politician, John Johnston, described as the people "who are the best judges of qualification and who have the greatest Stake in the issue of the contest"—would support Adams, even if much of the populace preferred Jackson.[20]

Adams's election amid charges of a corrupt bargain with Clay, who became secretary of state, only confirmed the charges of Jackson's supporters that political leaders ignored the wishes of the people. And the new president's program of positive government action to improve the American economy and society further alienated men worried about the aggrandizement of national power. In 1828, Andrew Jackson won a resounding victory over Adams and carried Ohio's electoral votes.

While there was not an explicit connection among critics of the Bank of the United States, supporters of James Gazlay, and adherents of Andrew Jackson, all three movements made significant contributions to the establishment of the importance of political democracy in the evolving consensus about society and government in Ohio. Indeed, the Jacksonians took the notion of popular sovereignty and made it reality. Distrusting institutions and governments, they established the voting public as the primary source of authority. To that extent, they extended and institutionalized the democratic rhetoric of the Jeffersonian Republicans. Few men could publicly doubt in the 1820s, as Arthur St. Clair and Winthrop Sargent had in the 1790s, that all white men were entitled to equal participation in the political and economic affairs of the state. The democratic nature of Ohio's society was firmly entrenched; in fact, much of the political debate of the next century and a half would be about extending the right of voting to blacks and women.

But at the same time, the attack on the BUS and criticism of political corruption also represented largely negative and fleeting protests against the growing importance of national economic and political interdependence in the lives of ordinary people. The Jacksonians would be able to destroy the Bank and they helped to develop a more representative system of political conventions and party organizations to replace elitist caucus procedures. But they were more successful at democratizing the market and politics than they were at eliminating them.

In protesting the power of the Bank and in turning to a national military hero to seek redress in the federal government, Ohioans explicitly recognized the increasingly interdependent nature of their world and the power of people and institutions outside the state over individuals and governments within it. The Jacksonian movement, which began in a defense of local rights and popular sovereignty, ironically itself became a monument to the national character of American society. It was the Jacksonians, after all, who created the first thoroughly modern national political party in American history; the result of their campaign against the Bank was to open American society to entrepreneurial development that would tie Americans even more closely together. If the Jacksonians extended the democratic ideas of the Jeffersonians, making it clear that popular sovereignty was the sine qua non of American ideology and politics, they also transformed the Jeffersonian emphasis on local autonomy into an emphasis on the importance of national organization.[21]

The populist response to the Panic of 1819 was a critical contribution to the evolution of a consensus about the nature of government and society in Ohio. But just as significant was the response of a smaller group of local notables and professional politician-developers who saw the economic and political crises provoked by the panic as an opportunity to remake the world in which they lived.

To local gentries, the attacks on the Bank and the caucus system and the popular frenzy for Jackson were the logical extensions of the unruly behavior many Ohioans had been demonstrating for years. Like the political chaos of the first decade of statehood, the confusion of the War of 1812, and the wild speculation of the late 1810s, they were the characteristics of an unstructured and unstable society.

The panic focused an unease among local leaders about a thoroughly liberal society that had been growing for years. And no wonder, for they were subjected to constant challenges in a world in which there were no institutional restraints on the ambitions of individual men. In the mid-1810s, many local leaders had responded to their fears of social disintegration by organizing to reform human character. They had founded chapters of national organizations like the Washington Benevolent Society and the American Bible Society and established voluntary associations for the "Promotion of Good Morals." There was a strong religious impulse to these activities. But there was also the belief that thorough organization was necessary to counteract the centrifugal forces of American society; people had to learn to behave less as independent individuals and more like parts of an organic whole.

The reform efforts of local notables in Ohio's urban areas were manifestations of a national organizational impulse which had its roots in the Second Great Awakening. Voluntary associations of like-minded people were natural responses to the individualistic nature of a liberal society. But the effect of these organizations was, in the words of Donald G. Mathews, "to create a more integrated American society as opposed to a confederation of provincial societies." In tandem with men and women throughout the United States, Ohio's local leaders (many of them Congregationalists and Presbyterians) formed local units of national movements for moral reform, certain that only self-discipline could insure order in a society of theoretically autonomous individuals.[22]

The republican form of government, George Turner reminded the Marietta chapter of the Washington Benevolent Society in 1817, was "the most *precarious* form of government" because it allowed too much individualism. Such sentiments, of course, were to be expected from unreconstructed Marietta Federalists. But they were shared by prominent Republicans as well. As early as 1807, the Cincinnati physician and booster Daniel Drake had expressed a fear that man's "excessive attachment to animal gratification" would prevent progressive improvements in the condition of mankind; a free people were too naturally indolent and capricious.[23]

These men feared that the individualism of Ohioans would lead the state backward into barbarism instead of forward into civilization. Echoing Benjamin Rush's analysis of the stages of frontier settlement in the 1780s, they wondered whether Americans were reverting to primitive behavior. Were they concerned only with their own personal interests? Did they have no public spirit? Were they content to live like Indians in a state of disorganization and isolation? "The character" of Ohio and its "public sentiments," warned one orator, hung in the balance as never before. Without public-spirited actions to elevate the tone of society, the Ohio Valley would "relapse into its original rudeness."[24]

The local gentries of Ohio in the late 1810s sounded like the Ohio Company associates in the 1780s. They felt confronted by challenges not just to their economic and political status, but to the very nature of society. The new owners of the *Cincinnati Liberty Hall* proclaimed in 1816 their intention to secure "the stability" of society even if they had "to resist the popular current" on occasion. In calling for local road improvements, the *Cincinnati Western Spy* argued that "if certain individuals, as protectors and guardians" of the community's interests, could improve society without producing oppression, they had a duty to act. "To realize the security we have the right to claim" from government, said Bellamy Storer of Cincinnati succinctly in 1819, "there must be energy in those who are vested with power, and an assurance given them that they are not indebted to popular favor for the tenure of their offices."[25] Such sentiments ran directly contrary to the ideological assumptions that had produced the Ohio Constitution of 1802.

But times had changed. Ohio's local gentries were no longer as concerned with governing a society of autonomous individuals as they were with bringing order to a society of conflicting interests and passions. The ostensible purpose of the moral societies and reform efforts that appeared in Ohio in the decade after 1815 was to reverse the "*natural* and *judicial* tendency" of vice "not only to cut the sinews of society; but . . . to weaken the physical strength of a people."[26] On a deeper level, their goal was to remind the citizens of Ohio that they were parts of a larger, complex community; they had to be taught how to behave in an interdependent society. The speculative frenzy of the late 1810s and the panic had clearly demonstrated that the inability of any individual to control his ambitions and greed could affect "every branch of the community." Real happiness, Ohioans had to learn, would not come from pursuing "ambition, avarice, or sensuality, or in the indulgence of licentious passions."[27]

The men espousing such sentiments included both former Federalists and moderate Republicans. In Marietta, Rufus Putnam, William Rufus Putnam, Dudley Woodbridge, Samuel P. Hildreth, and Manasseh Cutler's son Ephraim all were active in reform efforts. In Chillicothe, William Creighton, Jr. (president of the local branch of the Bank of the United States), Duncan McArthur, the Presbyterian minister Robert G. Wilson, and Thomas Worthington formed an organization to encourage morality. Worthington's alliance with these men may seem strange given his long defense of popular sovereignty against both territorial Federalists and moderate Republican advocates of judicial review. But in the late 1810s, Worthington was an entrenched economic and political leader; he, like Creighton and the Putnams, had a great deal to lose to upstarts. The chaos of the War of 1812 and the proliferation of banks had convinced him of the dangers of a liberal or open society. Worthington in the late 1810s and the 1820s came to share the moderate Republicans' belief that the complex nature of Ohio's economy and society required greater government action and organizational efforts to temper the desires and reform the characters of the state's citizens. He did not want to see Ohio become a world of Michael Baldwins—passionate, undisciplined men who thought of nothing but personal interest.[28]

In Cincinnati, the same names that dominated the local economy and government appeared on the membership lists of nearly every organization for improvement; they included Jacob Burnet, Isaac Burnet, James Findlay, Martin Baum, Daniel Symmes, William Irwin, William Henry Harrison, and Daniel Drake. The influence of the Presbyterian church was especially strong in Cincinnati. Under the leadership of the Reverend Joshua L. Wilson, the congregation established what Daniel Aaron has called a "Presbyterian hegemony" in the city; prominent Presbyterians included Jacob Burnet, Martin Baum, James Findlay, and William Irwin.[29]

Despite the catastrophe of the panic and the political challenges to their positions in the early 1820s, what Walter Glazer describes as "a power elite" dominated Cincinnati. "A distinctively stable, select, and successful minority" of residents, argues Glazer after a thorough study of reform societies, monopolized positions on "the bank boards, city council, and the benevolent organizations."[30]

The early 1820s also saw the emergence of a new generation of politician-entrepreneurs. Advocating what amounted to a proto-Whig program of internal improvements under the auspices of the state government, they embraced an ideology that blended elements of both the Federalist and Republican visions of the West.

This new generation included Governor Ethan Allen Brown, Micajah T. Williams, Alfred Kelley, and Ephraim Cutler. The Connecticut-born Brown, the oldest of the group, had studied in the offices of Alexander Hamilton. An ardent admirer of De Witt Clinton of New York, his ambition was to build a canal system in Ohio which would rival the Erie Canal and link the Ohio River with New York City. Micajah T. Williams of Cincinnati had come to that city from North Carolina in 1812 at the age of twenty. An avid entrepreneur, politician, and part-owner of the *Western Spy,* Williams played "a key role in western transportation and banking from 1820 to 1843."[31] Alfred Kelley was a native of Connecticut who settled in Cleveland in 1810 when he was twenty-one years old. He, too, devoted his life to a series of economic ventures and promotions. Ephraim Cutler had migrated to the Ohio Company purchase in the 1790s, had been an active Federalist in Washington County, and was an influential member of the Ohio General Assembly in the 1820s.[32]

These men and several others in and out of politics constituted what Harry N. Scheiber has called a "cohesive elite group." They shared "a distinctive vision that transcended local concerns and embraced a view of statewide and regional possibilities." While they "did not fail to seize the main chance for themselves . . . they also devoted their efforts to seizing the opportunities for the community by mobilizing its government."[33] Brown, Williams, Kelley, and Cutler accepted the notion that government could use power to do good in the world. It is little wonder that so many of these men endorsed the presidential candidacies of Clinton, Adams, and Clay in 1824 or that they tended to prefer National Republican and Whig candidates to the Jacksonians in the 1830s. For they all shared the beliefs of John Quincy Adams that "The spirit of improvement is abroad upon the earth" and that the people entrusted men with power "upon condition that it shall be exercised to ends of beneficence, to improve the condition of himself and his fellow-men."[34]

The Panic of 1819 made the defects of the state government glaring to men worried about the effects of rapid demographic growth and economic speculation. In 1819, the Ohio House of Representatives urged that a constitutional convention be called to deal with the dramatic changes in the state. With the tremendous "increase of population and wealth," argued the legislators, "subjects of controversy have necessarily increased, contracts and crimes are alike multiplied. . . . We have banks, towns, merchants, speculators [who] have introduced luxury and idleness, and their concomitant vices." Since the representatives believed that Ohioans were not fully equipped to deal with the "new character" of "our employments and our amusements," it had "become necessary . . . to create additional restraints upon our actions."[35]

The principal goal of the convention advocates was to strengthen the state judiciary. They wanted to raise salaries and to give the state supreme court more power. In some ways, the proposed changes involved institutionalizing the de facto victory of the judiciary a decade earlier. But in the populist atmosphere of 1819, the idea of constitutional reform was too generally perceived, as James Wilson of Steubenville said, as "a maneuvre in the part of the lawyers to make a *splendid judiciary*." Other people feared that the convention would be used as a means of introducing slavery into Ohio. And in the fall of 1819 voters rejected the idea of a convention.[36]

Despite this setback the place of the judiciary in Ohio government was secure. Judges remained elected officials, responsible to the people on a regular basis. But they also had the power, if they wished to exercise it, to act as a check upon the legislature.

The panic also resulted in a state commitment to care for the indigent. Governor Worthington had warned of the growing number of poor people in Ohio as early as 1815. And in urban areas like Cincinnati there had long been calls for the establishment of poorhouses that would serve to relieve and isolate the poor. But these ideas met with little enthusiasm until the panic dramatically increased the number of unemployed and destitute people. In January 1821, the Ohio General Assembly created a system of poorhouses in each county to be supervised by seven directors.[37]

While the efforts to reform the judiciary and to care for the poor were significant, movements led by Brown, Williams, Cutler, and Kelley to build state supported and regulated systems of public education and internal improvements were far more successful. They saw these projects as investments in the economic future of Ohio. But they also saw them as ways of bringing order to both the deranged economy and society of the Ohio Valley.

Schools had been of primary concern to the Federalists. The Ordinance of 1787 had called for their promotion and granted land for their support. One of the first institutions established in Marietta by the Ohio Company associates was an academy. Manasseh Cutler devoted much of his time in the 1790s to the creation of a western university; that project, guided by Rufus Putnam, reached fruition in 1804 with the chartering of Ohio University in Athens.

Despite these efforts, education languished in early Ohio. The school lands reserved by the Northwest Ordinance were leased by the legislature in 1803 for fifteen years. Eventually, the state sold all the lands except those located in the Western Reserve. But even before that 1829 sale they produced little revenue because they were rented and sold for far too little money to support public schools. Above all, there was a widespread indifference to education. Ohio University did not even graduate a class until 1815, Miami University (founded in 1809) amounted to little, and local education for children and adolescents was limited to what the resources and inclinations of local citizens produced. As Rufus Putnam lamented in 1800, it was clear that with regard to education there was "no public spirit to be found . . . except only in the proprietors of the Ohio Company."[38]

Putnam exaggerated, of course. The moderate Republican defenders of the judiciary, for example, were also strong advocates of public education. "In a free government, where the rights of people are in their own keeping," argued Governor Samuel Huntington in 1810, "it is peculiarly necessary [that] they should have a correct knowledge of those rights." Both Huntington and his successor, Return Jonathan Meigs, annually urged the Ohio General Assembly to create a public school system. "Public opinion to be correct," said Meigs succinctly, "must be enlightened." Otherwise, "Tyrants would govern the ignorant."[39]

While the state legislature refused to act in the 1810s, there were strong efforts to establish school systems in urban areas. In Cincinnati, the lack of training for the young began to worry leading citizens. In 1814, after a competition for the honor between Presbyterians and Methodists, prominent citizens formed the Cincinnati Lancaster Seminary. Under the leadership of the Presbyterian minister Joshua L. Wilson, the school was organized as a joint stock company and capitalized at nine thousand dollars with subscriptions in twenty-five dollar shares. With loans from local banks, the seminary's seven directors erected a building on land donated by the Presbyterian church. The directors chose Jacob Burnet as their president and Daniel Symmes as their secretary. The academy opened on April 17, 1813, with four hundred and twenty students; a separate school was established for blacks.[40]

The purpose of the Cincinnati Lancaster Seminary was clear. "Without education," read the preamble to its constitution, "the mind cannot with facility comprehend those religious, moral, political and scientific principles, the operation of which is necessary to the dignity and happiness of man." Under the Lancastrian system (developed by the Englishmen Andrew Bell and Joseph Lancaster), teachers taught a packaged lesson to older, brighter students, or monitors, who then communicated it to other pupils. In this way, the Lancaster Seminary was to exemplify both economy and efficiency.[41]

As Ohioans became obsessed with the speculative mania of the late 1810s, worried citizens became more insistent in calling for the development of enlightening and disciplining institutions like the seminary. Americans were forfeiting their natural rights through dangerous self-indulgence. All true patriots, argued a *Western Spy* writer named "Bacon" in calling upon the legislature to create public academies in 1817, must regret "a people making money their god, intent alone upon its acquisition— forgetful of their own proper good, and by a sordid insensibility to the real honors and pleasures of intelligent beings." Schools were "virtuous and useful institutions" that fixed popular habits and principles so strongly that nothing could disturb them. Indeed, Bacon believed education was of such critical importance to the future of the republic that it could not be left to parents or local control. Experience had shown that if left to their own devices, "the mass of the people have remained in the darkest ignorance." So "sordid" was "the nature of the human heart" and so preferable was money to knowledge that few people would support education unless "the compulsory power of law" extracted financial support and demanded physical cooperation.[42]

Public schools, men like Bacon hoped, would discipline the young, teach them correct principles, and rescue them from greed and vice. In Ohio in the late 1810s, enlightened men found drinking and fighting too widespread; parents too often taught their children to pursue gratification and revenge rather than to obey laws and to respect other human beings. If those people who had grown up "in a state of ignorance and moral darkness" were to shape their children's character, warned a correspondent of the *Western Spy,* Ohio would be forever in "a state of degradation."[43] To avoid such a fate, leading Cincinnatians formed the Charity School Association in 1817 to teach poor children "an abhorrence of vice and a lasting love of virtue"; they also lobbied the assembly for a public school system.[44]

They did so not to provide a means for individuals to benefit and improve themselves, but as a response to their growing perception of society as disintegrating into wild self-indulgence. Without public education, another newspaper writer named "Q" bluntly stated in 1817, "our lives and property are insecure, government precarious, and social and political happiness at an end. And it is relatively thus, in proportion as the means of education is not within the control of the poorer class of society."[45] Education was the antidote to the poison of rampant individualism. If people were not properly trained at an early age, argued another correspondent of the *Western Spy* in 1818, "they will employ themselves in that which is low and criminal." So many people were "so intent upon money making" that children were growing up "like noxious and useless weeds, without culture, without knowledge, and without principles."[46]

These pre-1820 calls for public education met with little success. Even if children attended some school, lamented "E" in the *Western Spy,* parents often encouraged them to believe "that government in school is tyranny— respect for teachers, degrading." By the summer of 1817, the Cincinnati Lancaster Seminary had been all but abolished. The school had been in decline ever since its beginning because of the lack of consistent financial and popular support. The ubiquitous Dr. Daniel Drake attempted to turn the seminary into a college; in 1818, he raised twenty-nine thousand dollars from seven gentlemen. The college survived, but only barely, and its cause was not aided by the constant bickering of its faculty.[47]

In the state legislature, Governor Thomas Worthington's repeated calls for public schools were generally ignored. Without some sort of public education, "the poorer class" would be raised in "comparative ignorance," warned the father of Ohio's 1802 constitution, and thus would be "unable to manage with propriety, their private concerns, much less to take any part in the management of public affairs; and what is still more to be lamented, unacquainted with those religious and moral precepts and principles, without which they cannot be good citizens." The older Worthington became the more he echoed Manasseh Cutler.[48]

It was the Panic of 1819 that gave the movement for public education momentum. Just as for many Ohioans the depression brought home the necessity of asserting popular sovereignty, it made the dangers of "licentious disorder" readily apparent to Ohio's economic and political gentries. If public opinion was the supreme authority in a republic, wrote a Cincinnatian as the panic spread in the late fall of 1818, it had become dramatically disordered in recent years; it had been "bribed" by the "influence of riches" and formed in ignorance. As a result, there was "no ligament to secure political integrity, or civil security. In this order of things, government totters over the abyss of anarchy." If Ohio were to survive as a coherent entity, argued the Cincinnati Sunday School Association in the summer of 1818, its citizens had to learn to restrain their desires and to control their passions.[49] They needed, commented a writer in the *Western Spy* in the summer of 1819, to be disciplined. A properly developed sense of the law as well as common sense would force a man "to connect his own good with that of society, and to enjoy his own rights in a manner that will not injure his neighbors. . . . Hence," he concluded, "the aid of education should be called in to enforce self-government."[50]

Public schools, argued "Robert Raikes" in the same newspaper in 1822, would diffuse "pure morality and social order" throughout the community and thus increase the public safety and peace. By offering people the means of improving and advancing themselves, they would control the passions of men, "which even human laws are insufficient to restrain," and prevent "crimes which chiefly in the gloom of ignorance are engendered and cherished."[51]

By 1822, such arguments were common among Ohio's leading political figures. At a testimonial dinner for Henry Clay (presided over by William Henry Harrison), prominent Cincinnatians strongly urged the Ohio General Assembly to create a system of public schools. In the legislature, Ephraim Cutler assumed leadership of the public school movement. During the 1822 session, the House Committee on School Lands lauded public education as necessary for the survival of the republic; only with proper knowledge could people truly understand each other and live in harmony. The house approved the committee's recommendation that "a SYSTEM of education for common schools" be prepared by seven commissioners, including Cutler.[52]

The legislature rejected the first report of the commissioners, however. Many citizens continued to be reluctant to increase their taxes and to grant increased power to the state government. Partly, their caution stemmed from the economic hard times. But the public school movement, with its emphasis on uniformity and discipline, also ran counter to the principles on which the state of Ohio had been founded. It was potentially a serious infringement of local autonomy and an assault on the notion that the people, unaided, were, as Michael Baldwin had put it in 1802, "the only proper judges of their own interests." Many people were no more interested in sacrificing local and individual independence to become parts of an interdependent, cosmopolitan world in the 1820s than they had been in the 1790s.[53]

Ephraim Cutler attacked the taxation question in the 1824–25 legislature. He and his associates helped pass a major revision of the Ohio revenue system that, in Cutler's words, would help "to equalize the public burthens" among the various classes and sections of the state. With Cutler skillfully managing both bills, the passage of the new revenue act enabled the passage in February 1825 of an act creating a public school system. The bill laid an annual tax of one-twentieth of 1 percent for the support of schools and ordered township trustees to lay off school districts. The householders of each district were to elect three directors to build and maintain schools. Finally, no one was to be allowed to teach without a certificate from examiners to be appointed by the local Courts of Common Pleas.[54]

This act had little immediate impact; too much power was put in the hands of local authorities for the new system to work effectively. In 1835, the Ohio General Assembly had to revise the act drastically. But the 1825 bill was the critical step in getting Ohio publicly committed to one of the most important goals of the Northwest Ordinance of 1787. The state's leaders, anxious about the growing complexity of society and the unruliness of its citizens, had embarked on a statewide system of public education for the purpose of training Ohioans to be responsible citizens in a national, commercial republic.

The 1824–25 session of the Ohio legislature also passed an act authorizing the digging of a canal to connect the waters of Lake Erie with those of the Ohio River. The primary reason for undertaking this enterprise was to improve the state's economy. By connecting the Ohio River with the Great Lakes, a canal would allow the relatively inexpensive and fast shipment of agricultural products to New York City and the East via the recently opened Erie Canal. Ohioans would no longer be dependent on the New

Orleans market for imports and exports. Canals would also spur the economic development of the central and northern parts of the state. They would bring a degree of order to an economy seriously disrupted by the Panic of 1819.

But canals, as men like George Washington and Manasseh Cutler had argued in the 1780s, were more than economic enterprises. Improved communication and transportation would not only enable man to conquer nature, but to conquer himself as well. Internal improvements were a means of counteracting the disintegrating tendencies produced by the geographic expansion of America. They would, through frequent intercourse, overcome the parochialism of isolated, self-interested individuals and localities. To build a direct link between Cincinnati and New York was to recognize and encourage their mutual economic and cultural dependence; it would announce to the world that Ohioans valued being part of larger economic and political networks. A state-developed canal system was in this sense a reversal of the insistence of the founders of the state of Ohio on the supremacy of local authority and individual independence.

Republicans had never opposed internal improvements. As part of Ohio's admission to the Union, the federal government had established a 3 percent fund to provide for internal improvements. But little was done for a decade and a half after 1803, largely because of fears of huge expenses and state control.[55]

The War of 1812 gave a spur to movements to improve the "interior *communication,*" which "will forever bind the Union."[56] Cincinnatians began to discuss improving the navigation of the Ohio River and Governor Worthington urged the legislature to undertake the repair and improvement of Ohio's roads. In 1816, an Ohio legislative committee praised New York's venture in the construction of the Erie Canal; leading Ohioans generally expressed enthusiasm for the project. Such men begged the Ohio legislature to consider a similar canal and to improve roads. Ohioans, they believed, had to rise above selfish interests, local prejudices, and the fear of huge financial investments.[57]

All the ills of the world, argued a correspondent of the *Western Spy* in 1818, were traceable to the evil of selfishness. But internal improvements would reverse that tendency by bringing people closer together economically, and thus, intellectually and emotionally. Canals would make the economic interests of different parts of the state and the nation so inextricably interwoven that one could not act without considering the impact on another. Roads, wrote another correspondent of the *Spy* that same year, "have a powerful agency, in the formation of moral, political, commercial, and agricultural character of a people." If villages, like families or individuals, were isolated, without frequent communication with others, their citizens became narrow and intolerant, "considering themselves the center of perfection, the arbiters' of right and wrong." Isolation made people "esteem the universe as made for their sole purpose . . . while the dreams of fancy and the vagaries of the imagination, hurry the mind into every wild extravagance." By encouraging exchanges of goods and ideas, internal improvements were effective in counteracting the evils of localism and selfishness. They "produce a uniformity of sentiments," a homogeneity of interests. [58]

If education would discipline people, canals would force them to recognize the interdependence of a complex society. Internal improvements would allow, even stimulate, men to make money by lowering shipping costs and increasing the number and accessibility of markets. Better roads and canals would also add to the glory of the state of Ohio. The Ohio Canal, claimed its leading advocate Governor Ethan Allen Brown in 1819, was "a project so grand and magnificent" that its effect was almost incalculable. "Roads and canals are veins and arteries to the body politic," Brown told the legislature, diffusing "supplies, health, vigor and animation to the whole system." But even more important, internal improvements would help to create a harmony of interests among Ohioans that did not naturally exist. They would reduce the regional and selfish causes of rivalries and bickerings. They would make Ohioans so aware of the complexity of the world, of their economic dependence on events and people in other parts of state and the nations, that they would find it in their best interest to tailor their appetites for fame and fortune to the parameters established by society. To prosper in a modern society, men would have to adjust their goals to the standards of the world about them. No longer could they plunge into the wilderness to begin anew or to escape the competitive and impersonal aspects of a market economy. Canals would bring men and their interests into a tightly interdependent system. [59]

As with the supporters of a public school system (which itself was an internal improvement), the advocates of canals were a decided minority before 1825. But the depression of 1819–24 began to change that situation by giving the boosters of canals the arguments that they would help reverse the balance of trade with the East, bring specie to the West, and end the depression. Internal improvements, argued Governor Brown, would reduce the cost and difficulty of taking goods to markets and thus remove "one principal obstruction to the removal of the commercial distress." [60] Brown's advocacy of canals in the early 1820s had the support of Jacob Burnet, Daniel Drake, William Greene, and other leading Ohioans. As William Steele of Cincinnati told Brown in December 1820, "this is the most favourable time for such an undertaking that we will probably see for twenty years to come."[61] Ohioans were in such deep distress that they would probably be willing to try any remedy.

But the depression made immediate action impossible simply because of the amounts of money required. There was also a sizable opposition to the project of a grand canal linking the Ohio River and Lake Erie. "The magnitude and novelty of the enterprise" combined with the fear of incurring a huge debt to make many legislators wary of such grandiose schemes. Above all, there was the problem of what Micajah T. Williams called sectional jealousies. If a canal was built, every part of the state wanted it to pass through their region. Nobody in the Miami Valley wanted to contribute to the construction of a canal that would go through the Scioto or Muskingum valleys. In its origins, at least, the project of a canal from river to lake was producing the very kind of bickerings it was designed in part to reduce.[62]

Nonetheless, the advocates of the project continued to exert pressure on the Ohio General Assembly. Men like Brown, Williams, and Alfred Kelley emphasized the benefits of canals to the entire community. Both farmers and merchants would profit and the entire community would be rescued from an unstable economy. Canals were a more effective method of relieving economic distress than any "schemes of paper credit." The efforts of the canal lobby met with success in 1822 when the legislature appointed seven commissioners (including Kelley, Worthington, Brown, and Williams), to investigate the feasibility of a Lake Erie-Ohio River canal.[63]

The commissioners hired engineers to inspect the Erie Canal and to survey a possible route for the Ohio Canal. They also discussed the securing of loans from eastern banks. In January 1824, the committee reported that, given the success of the Erie Canal, there was no reason for Ohio to delay. In advocating the construction of a canal, the committee devoted the bulk of its report to statistical enumeration of the financial benefits and the potential costs. But the commissioners also reflected on the moral and political advantages of the project.

One of the major intangible benefits of the Ohio Canal would be the promotion of pride in one's state and nation. This increase in patriotism would help to unite Ohioans. For patriotism was "the secret chain, which binds together in one great family, the numerous individuals of which a state or a nation is composed, the secret spring which makes them alive to the general interest of the community: to its honor and reputation, and ready to make personal sacrifices for the promotion of the public good." Without such a spirit, "a state is composed of a multitude of uncongenial spirits" and filled with the kinds of "clashing interests [and] jealous animosities" that had too much characterized the state of Ohio. By embarking on the building of a canal, Ohioans could concentrate their energies and "even flatter their laudable ambition," by working for the promotion of "a common interest." Thus, internal improvements would improve society as well as the economy. Canals and roads would link people together and make them more aware of each other; utlimately, they would be more willing to channel their ambitions and desires into the service of the community as a whole.[64]

Throughout 1824, "the canal spirit," as commissioner Alfred Kelley called it, grew in Ohio. It was encouraged by a strong campaign in the state press orchestrated by Micajah T. Williams and by the state's gradual economic recovery. Above all, the visible success of the Erie Canal erased doubts about the feasibility of the project, and the passage of the ad valorem taxation system relieved some of the financial worries. In January 1825, after years of effort, the legislature passed a bill authorizing the construction of a canal from Lake Erie to the Ohio River via the Scioto Valley.[65]

The nearly simultaneous adoption of a public school system and a system of internal improvements by the same legislature was not coincidental. Both were responses to perceptions of a related economic and social disintegration; both were efforts to integrate Ohio into a larger world. There was, recalled participant Caleb Atwater, "a perfect coincidence of views" among the advocates of both measures. For all were dedicated to correcting "the wretched state of things" in Ohio with a "great revolution in our civil policy."[66]

The Panic of 1819 produced significant political conflicts in Ohio which would eventually coalesce into the Jacksonian-Whig party system of the 1830s and 1840s. But the debates of the early 1820s also revealed a growing consensus about government and society which drew from both Jeffersonian and Federalist legacies. The populist protests against the Bank and the caucus system helped to entrench democratic elections and equal access to power as political shibboleths. The success of the public school and canal movements committed the power of the state government to guiding Ohio and its citizens into responsible roles as parts of a national system. After the 1820s, few could deny for long that the residents of Ohio were independent only to the extent that their interdependence with the rest of the American and European worlds allowed them to be.

Conclusion:
"Ohio Has Behaved Nobly at Last"

E ight thousand people gathered just outside Newark, Ohio, at eleven in
the morning on July 4, 1825. They were there to witness the breaking of
ground to initiate construction of the Ohio Canal linking Lake Erie and the
Ohio River. It was a festive occasion, replete with cannon salutes, an elaborate dinner, and plenty of toasts. Dignitaries in attendance included Governor Jeremiah Morrow and former governors Ethan Allen Brown and
Thomas Worthington. Thomas Ewing, a future United States senator,
gave the major address of the day. But the man who attracted the most
attention was a visitor from the state of New York, Governor De Witt
Clinton.[1]

The father of the Erie Canal was on a triumphal tour of Ohio. Warmly
received by local leaders in towns throughout the state, Clinton recipro-
cated with praise for the enterprise Ohio had demonstrated in undertaking
the building of a canal. He welcomed the prospect of "an easy and prosperous intercourse" between the Ohio Valley and the great cities of the Atlantic world. "Your Dorados or mountains of gold," Clinton told the citizens
of Cincinnati, "are to be seen, not in the follies or fictions of ignorance and
fatuity, but in the cultivation of a vast inland trade, now at your command,
and opening still more extensively for your benefit."[2]

At the Newark ceremony, Ohio Governor Morrow and New York Governor Clinton stood facing each other and simultaneously shoved spades into the earth. It was a significant moment. Even though the canal system would take years to complete, involve Ohio in a web of debts, and be made obsolete almost immediately by railroads, the groundbreaking symbolized Ohio's commitment to state-supported development in the name of commercial progress and national unity. The joint appearance of Morrow and Clinton represented the commonality of interests between the East and the Ohio Valley.

During his trip, Clinton marvelled at the extent of Ohio's urban and economic development. He was not alone. By the 1820s, it was rare for men and women not to remark on the rapid pace at which Ohio had grown. In 1825, it was the fourth most populous state in the American Union with a population of over 700,000. Cincinnati was a major metropolis of the republic. In his speech at the Newark ceremony, Thomas Ewing noted that projects like canals were usually "the achievements of national maturity, after ages of progressive improvement had passed away." But Ohio had "not grown up like other nations, by the slow and gradual increase of a stationary people." Its citizens exhibited "at once, all the vigor and freshness of youth, the strength and firmness of manhood, and the wisdom of age."[3] In other words, Ohio had passed through the stages from barbarism to civilization described by Benjamin Rush in the 1780s in an incredibly short period of time. What had been the wilderness home of Indians and squatters in the 1780s was now the scene of farms and cities, commerce and manufactures; what had been a troublesome, even potentially treasonous, region in the 1780s and 1790s had become an integral part of the United States.

Between 1780 and 1825, against the background of almost unparalleled demographic and economic growth, Ohio had experienced severe ideological and political conflicts. The primary cause of the turmoil was the lack of consensus in a pluralistic, frontier society. The ideological foundations of government, in particular, had vacillated between complete distrust and complete faith in popular sovereignty.

In the territorial government established by the Northwest Ordinance of 1787, the Federalists had attempted to control the development of the Ohio Valley. They wanted settlement to be deliberate; they valued social order and national authority above individual liberty and local prerogatives. The Federalists' efforts inspired a coalition of local interests to push for statehood on a platform of popular sovereignty and local autonomy. Not surprisingly, the state government created by the Constitution of 1802 was in many ways the ideological antithesis of the territorial government. In reaction to the latter's power, the former was practically impotent. But what was a powerful opposition ideology proved to be a less than effective way of governing a dynamic and pluralistic state, as many Republicans realized during the Burr Conspiracy and the struggle over the role of the state judiciary.

Neither the Federalist nor the Republican vision of the future of the Ohio Valley was foolish or naive. The problem with both was that they were inappropriate for the kind of society emerging in Ohio. The Federalists' insistence on national authority and vertical patronage was out of touch with the deep-seated attachment of frontiersmen to local rights. But the Jeffersonian Republicans erred in the opposite direction; they failed to understand the need for regulation and arbitration in a pluralistic society of autonomous individuals in pursuit of fame and fortune. Neither absolute power nor absolute liberty could effectively govern Ohio.

The citizens of Ohio reached a basic consensus about government and society only when they abandoned the extremes of individual and local independence, and national control and institutional authority. That finally happened in the decade after 1815, particularly after the Panic of 1819 when many people confronted the full extent of their dependence on people and events beyond the Ohio Valley. While demanding popular sovereignty as an American birthright, the citizens of Ohio had little choice but to entrust power to institutions like state governments, courts, and schools to channel individualism into social order.

Ultimately, the Federalist emphasis on designing the world and governments to shape people was as important in nineteenth-century Ohio as the Jeffersonian Republican insistence on democratic elections. It would be simplistic to argue that the reformers of the 1820s were Federalist clones. Unlike the plans of the 1780s, the schemes of the 1820s did not force improvement on people, but offered participation in them as a means of self-enhancement. The proponents of public schools and canals not only accepted the innate and irreversible individualism of Americans, they tried to harness it as the key to reorganizing society.

Despite these important differences, the goals underlying the reforms of the 1820s were remarkably similar to those that had motivated the founders of Marietta and the authors of the Northwest Ordinance. They included a commitment to elevating the quality of society in an effort to prevent a regression into the chaos and degeneracy of a world where men acted in complete isolation from each other. And they held a similar vision of the future of the Ohio Valley—a highly structured society of responsible human beings fully integrated into the economic and cultural worlds of the East and Europe.

Rufus Putnam and Manasseh Cutler would have been far from comfortable had they been able to attend the groundbreaking ceremony in July 1825. But they deserved to be there. The decision to build a canal was, as the editor of the *National Intelligencer* wrote, "striking evidence of the hardy enterprise of the Sons of the West, who, after taming the Savages by their valor, and subduing the forests by their labor, conquer time and space by their intelligence." Ohio, said Governor Clinton succinctly, "had behaved nobly at last."[4]

Notes

Preface

[1] See John R. Howe, "Republican Thought and the Political Violence of the 1790s," in *Essays on the Early Republic, 1789–1815,* ed. Leonard Levy (Hinsdale, Ill.: Dryden Press, 1974), 144–60.

[2] For studies of American attitudes about the West, see Henry Nash Smith, *Virgin Land: The American West as Symbol and Myth* (Cambridge: Harvard University Press, 1950); Durand Echeverria, *Mirage in the West: A History of the French Image of American Society to 1815* (Princeton: Princeton University Press, 1957); Richard Slotkin, *Regeneration Through Violence: The Mythology of the American Frontier, 1600–1860* (Middletown, Conn.: Wesleyan University Press, 1973); Arthur K. Moore, *The Frontier Mind: A Cultural Analysis of the Kentucky Frontiersman* (Lexington: University of Kentucky Press, 1957); Annette Kolodny, *The Land Before Her: Fantasy and Experience of the American Frontiers, 1630–1860* (Chapel Hill: University of North Carolina Press, 1984); and Lester H. Cohen, "Eden's Constitution: The Paradisiacal Dream and Enlightenment Values in Late Eighteenth-Century Literature of the American Frontier," *Prospects* 3 (1977): 83–107.

[3] See Howard Lamar and Leonard Thompson, eds., *The Frontier in History: North America and Southern Africa Compared* (New Haven: Yale University Press, 1981), Introduction; Don Harrison Doyle, *The Social Order of a Frontier Community: Jacksonville, Illinois, 1825–1870* (Urbana: University of Illinois Press, 1978), Introduction; Richard Hofstadter, *The Progressive Historians: Turner, Beard, Parrington* (New York: Alfred A. Knopf, 1969), part 2; Lee Benson, *Turner and Beard: American Historical Writing Reconsidered* (Glencoe, Ill.: Free Press, 1960); and Frederick Jackson Turner, *The Frontier in American History* (New York: H. Holt, 1920).

[4] See R. R. Palmer, *The Age of the Democratic Revolution*, 2 vols. (Princeton: Princeton University Press, 1958); Joyce Appleby, *Capitalism and a New Social Order: The Republican Vision of the 1790s* (New York: New York University Press, 1984); Nathan O. Hatch, "The Christian Movement and the Demand for a Theology of the People," *Journal of American History* 67 (1980): 545–67; Alfred F. Young, *The Democratic-Republicans of New York, 1763–1797* (Chapel Hill: University of North Carolina Press for the Institute of Early American History and Culture, 1967); Eric Foner, *Tom Paine and Revolutionary America* (New York: Oxford University Press, 1976); Sean Wilentz, *Chants Democratic: New York City and the Rise of the American Working Class, 1788–1850* (New York: Oxford University Press, 1984); Rhys Isaac, *The Transformation of Virginia, 1740–1790* (Chapel Hill: University of North Carolina Press for the Institute of Early American History and Culture, 1982); Edward Countryman, *A People in Revolution: The American Revolution and Political Society in New York, 1760–1790* (Baltimore: Johns Hopkins University Press, 1981); Gary B. Nash, *The Urban Crucible: Social Change, Political Consciousness, and the Origins of the American Revolution* (Cambridge: Harvard University Press, 1979); and Alfred F. Young, ed., *The American Revolution: Explorations in the History of American Radicalism* (DeKalb, Ill.: Northern Illinois University Press, 1976).

[5] See Richard Buel, Jr., "Democracy and the American Revolution: A Frame of Reference," *William and Mary Quarterly*, 3d ser., 21 (1964): 165–90; Bernard Bailyn, *The Ideological Origins of the American Revolution* (Cambridge: Belknap Press, 1967); Gordon S. Wood, *The Creation of the American Republic, 1776–1787* (Chapel Hill: University of North Carolina Press for the Institute of Early American History and Culture, 1969); J. G. A. Pocock, *The Machiavellian Movement: Florentine Political Thought and the Atlantic Republican Tradition* (Princeton: Princeton University Press, 1975); John R. Murrin, "The Great Inversion, or Court versus Country: A Comparison of the Revolution Settlements in England (1688–1721) and America (1776–1816)" in *Three British Revolutions: 1641, 1688, 1776*, ed. J. G. A. Pocock (Princeton: Princeton University Press, 1980), 368–453; Linda Kerber, *Federalists in Dissent: Imagery and Ideology in Jeffersonian America* (Ithaca, N.Y.: Cornell University Press, 1970); Gerald Stourzh, *Alexander Hamilton and the Idea of Republican Government* (Stanford: Stanford University Press, 1970); Charles Royster, *A Revolutionary People at War: The Continental Army and American Character, 1775–1783* (Chapel Hill: University of North Carolina Press for the Institute of Early American History and Culture, 1979); and Drew R. McCoy, *The Elusive Republic: Political Economy in Jeffersonian America* (Chapel Hill: University of North Carolina Press for the Institute of Early American History and Culture, 1980).

[6] See Jeffrey P. Brown, "Frontier Politics: The Evolution of a Political Society in Ohio, 1788–1814" (Ph.D. diss., University of Illinois at Urbana, 1979); and Donald J. Ratcliffe, "The Experience of Revolution and the Beginnings of Party Politics in Ohio, 1776–1816," *Ohio History* 85 (1976): 186–230. For a full discussion of the historiography of early Ohio politics see the Essay on Sources.

1 Congress v. Squatters, 1780–1786

[1] David Howell to William Greene, December 24, 1783, Edmund C. Burnett, ed., *Letters of Members of the Continental Congress* (Washington, D.C.: Carnegie Institution of Washington, 1934), 7:397.

[2] On congressional land policy and the future Northwest Territory in the 1780s, see Robert Berkhofer, "Jefferson, the Ordinance of 1784, and the Origins of the American Territorial

System," *William and Mary Quarterly,* 3d ser., 29 (1972): 231–62; Peter S. Onuf, "Liberty, Development, and Union: Visions of the West in the 1780s," *William and Mary Quarterly,* 3d ser., 43 (1986): 179–213; Jack Ericson Eblen, *The First and Second United States Empires: Governors and Territorial Government, 1784–1912* (Pittsburgh: University of Pittsburgh Press, 1968), chap. 1; Peter S. Onuf, *The Origins of the Federal Republic: Jurisdictional Controversies in the United States, 1775–1787* (Philadelphia: University of Pennsylvania Press, 1983), esp. 149–209; Jack N. Rakove, *The Beginnings of National Politics: An Interpretative History of the Continental Congress* (Baltimore: Johns Hopkins University Press, 1979), 353–54; and Thomas P. Abernethy, *Western Lands and the American Revolution* (New York: D. Appleton-Century, 1937).

³ James Tilton to the President of Delaware, February 20, 1784, in Burnett, *Letters* 7:446. See also Merrill Jensen, *The New Nation: A History of the New Nation During the Confederation* (New York: Alfred A. Knopf, 1950), 28–84; E. James Ferguson, "The Nationalists of 1781–1783 and the Economic Interpretation of the Constitution," *Journal of American History* 56 (1969): 241–61; Robert Berkhofer, "The Ordinance of 1784," in *The Old Northwest in the American Revolution: An Anthology,* ed. David Curtis Skaggs (Madison: State Historical Society of Wisconsin, 1977), 392–419; and "Ordinance of April 23, 1784," in Henry Steele Commager, ed., *Documents of American History* (New York: Appleton-Century-Crofts, 1963), 122–23.

⁴ Daniel Brodhead to William Moore, December 3, 1781, in C. W. Butterfield, ed., *Washington-Irvine Correspondence* (Madison, 1882), 194n; William Irvine to Moore, December 3, 1781, ibid., 231; Irvine to George Washington, April 20, 1782, ibid., 109. See also Jack M. Sosin, *The Revolutionary Frontier, 1763–1783* (New York: Holt, Rinehart, and Winston, 1967), 1–19.

⁵ Petition of Kentucky Settlers, in Archer B. Hulbert, ed., *Ohio in the Time of the Confederation* (Marietta, Ohio: Marietta Historical Commission, 1918), 138–39. Helpful discussions of frontier life and attitudes can be found in Patricia Watlington, *The Partisan Spirit: Kentucky Politics, 1779–1792* (New York: Atheneum for the Institute of Early American History and Culture, 1972), esp. 11–34; Malcolm J. Rohrbough, *The Trans-Appalachian Frontier: People, Societies, and Institutions, 1775–1850* (New York: Oxford University Press, 1978); and Beverley W. Bond, Jr., *The Foundations of Ohio* (Columbus: Ohio State Archaeological and Historical Society, 1941). While the following works do not deal directly with the Ohio Valley, they are valuable discussions of life in the Southern backcountry. See Richard R. Beeman, *The Evolution of the Southern Backcountry: A Case Study of Lunenburg County, Virginia, 1746–1832* (Philadelphia: University of Pennsylvania Press, 1984); Robert D. Mitchell, *Commercialism and Frontier: Perspectives on the Early Shenandoah Valley* (Charlottesville: University Press of Virginia, 1977); Carl Bridenbaugh, *Myths and Realities:Societies of the Colonial South* (Baton Rouge: Louisiana State University Press, 1952), 119–96; Forrest McDonald and Grady McWhiney, "The Antebellum Southern Herdsman: A Reinterpretation," *Journal of Southern History* 41 (1975): 147–66; and John Solomon Otto, "The Migration of the Southern Plain Folk: An Interdisciplinary Synthesis," *Journal of Southern History* 51 (1985): 183–201, esp. 192–93.

⁶ Petition to Settle Ohio Lands, in Hulbert, *Ohio in the Confederation,* 95, 96.

⁷ James Henretta, "Families and Farms: *Mentalité* in Pre-Industrial America," *William and Mary Quarterly,* 3d ser., 35 (1978): 9; Petition to Congress, April 11, 1785, in Hulbert, *Ohio in the Confederation,* 104, 105.

⁸ W. H. Hunter, "The Pathfinders of Jefferson County," *Ohio Archaeological and Historical Society Publications* 6 (1898): 175.

⁹ "Biographical Sketch of Isaac Williams," in Samuel P. Hildreth, *Biographical and Histor-*

Notes to Chapter 1

ical Memoirs of the Early Pioneer Settlers of Ohio (Cincinnati, 1852), 131–44; John McDonald, *Biographical Sketches of General Nathaniel Massie, General Duncan McArthur, Captain William Wells, and General Simon Kenton* (Dayton, 1852); and Joseph Doddridge, "Notes on the Settlement and Indian Wars of the Western Parts of Virginia and Pennsylvania," in Samuel Kercheval, *A History of the Valley of Virginia* (Woodstock, Va., 1850), 164–263; see also Stanley Elkins and Eric McKitrick, "A Meaning for Turner's Frontier: Democracy in the Old Northwest," *Political Science Quarterly* 69 (1954): 321–53.

[10] Dorsey Pentecost to James Wilson, June 26, 1783, "A Plan for the Western Lands, 1783," *Pennsylvania Magazine of History and Biography* 60 (1936): 289, 291.

[11] George Washington to Henry Knox, December 5, 1784, in John C. Fitzpatrick, ed., *Writings of George Washington* (Washington, D.C.: Government Printing Office, 1938), 28:4; Washington to Jacob Reed, November 3, 1784, ibid., 27:486.

[12] Washington to James Duane, September 7, 1783, ibid., 27:133, 136.

[13] New York delegates to George Clinton, September 19, 1783, in Burnett, *Letters* 7:300–301; Report of Congressional Committee on Indian Affairs, September 22, 1783, in Berkhofer, "The Ordinance of 1784," 398.

[14] Virginia delegates to Benjamin Harrison, November 1, 1783, in Burnett, *Letters* 7:365.

[15] See Joseph W. Ernst, "With Compass and Chain: Federal Land Surveyors in the Old Northwest, 1785–1816," (Ph.D. diss., Columbia University, 1958), 4–78; and William D. Pattison, "The Survey of the Seven Ranges," *Old Northwest*, Skaggs, 375–90.

[16] See John Parker Huber, "General Josiah Harmar's Command: Military Policy in the Old Northwest," (Ph.D. diss., University of Michigan, 1968), esp. 59–68.

[17] Samuel Holden Parsons to William S. Johnson, December 3, 1785, in Charles S. Hall, *Life and Letters of Samuel Holden Parsons* (Binghamton, N.Y.: Otseningo Publishing Co., 1905), 479; Parsons to Johnson, November 26, 1785, William S. Johnson Papers, Manuscripts Division, Library of Congress.

[18] Josiah Harmar to the Secretary at War, August 10, 1786, in William H. Smith, *The St. Clair Papers: The Life and Public Services of Arthur St. Clair* (Cincinnati, 1882), 2:16. The title "Secretary at War" was used in official correspondence during the years of the Confederation.

[19] Winthrop Sargent, Diary, August 7, 1786, Winthrop Sargent Papers, Massachusetts Historical Society, Boston; John Mathews to [?], 1787, Marietta College Archives, Marietta, Ohio.

[20] Commissioners of Indian Affairs to Harmar, January 24, 1785, Smith, *St. Clair Papers* 2:3.

[21] John Amberson, "Advertisement," March 12, 1785, Smith, *St. Clair Papers* 2:5n; John Armstrong to Harmar, April 13, 1785, ibid., 4. See also Randolph C. Downes, "Ohio's Squatter Governor: William Hogland of Hoglandstown," *Ohio Archaeological and Historical Society Publications* 43:273–82.

[22] Armstrong to Harmar, April 12, 1785, in Hulbert, *Ohio in the Confederation*, 107; Armstrong to Harmar, in Harmar to the President of Congress, May 1, 1785, Smith, *St. Clair Papers* 2:4.

[23] Harmar to the Secretary at War, June 1, and October 22, 1785, Smith, *St. Clair Papers* 2:6, 12.

[24] Richard Butler, October 1, 1785, quoted in Hunter, "Pathfinders of Jefferson County," 138.

[25] Harmar to the Secretary at War, July 12, 1786, Smith, *St. Clair Papers* 2:14; Levi Munsell to Ephraim Cutler, August 17, 1842, in Julia P. Cutler, ed., *Life and Times of Ephraim Cutler* (Cincinnati, 1890), 133.

²⁶ Sargent, Diary, August 7, 1786, Sargent Papers.

²⁷ Petition of Wicom Hougland and others to Congress, April 11, 1785, in Hulbert, *Ohio in the Confederation*, 104, 105. See also Theodore Roosevelt, *The Winning of the West* (New York, 1889–96), 3:234.

2 Planning the Republic: The Federalists and the Ohio Country, 1786–1788

¹ McCoy, *Elusive Republic*, 133, 134. See also the studies of American attitudes toward the West and economic development in Julian P. Boyd, "Thomas Jefferson's Empire of Liberty," *Virginia Quarterly Review* 24 (1948): 538–44; Appleby, *Capitalism and a New Social Order*, chaps. 3 and 4; Foner, *Tom Paine and Revolutionary America*, 101–6; Kerber, *Federalists in Dissent*, esp. 152–53; Pocock, *The Machiavellian Moment*, 511–12, 534–35; Stourzh, *Alexander Hamilton*, chaps. 4 and 5; Robert Berkhofer, "Space, Time, Culture, and the New Frontier," *Agricultural History* 38 (1964): 21–30; Cohen, "Eden's Constitution," 83–107; and especially Onuf, "Liberty, Development, and Union."

² On Congress and the West in the 1780s, see Onuf, *Origins of the Federal Republic*, 149–209; and Eblen, *First and Second American Empires*, chap. 1.

³ Dwight Foster, Benjamin Heywood, and Daniel Class to Rufus Putnam, July 9, 1788, in Rufus Putnam Papers, Marietta College Archives; Samuel Holden Parsons to George Washington, April 21, 1788, quoted in Hall, *Samuel Holden Parsons*, 519. On the Federalist persuasion, see Wood, *Creation of the American Republic*, 519–64; Stourzh, *Alexander Hamilton*; Kerber, *Federalists in Dissent*; Richard H. Kohn, *Eagle and Sword: The Federalists and the Creation of the Military Establishment in Amercia, 1783–1802* (New York: Free Press, 1975); Royster, *A Revolutionary People at War*; and Charles Royster, *Light-Horse Harry Lee and the Legacy of the American Revolution* (New York: Alfred A. Knopf, 1981).

⁴ An earlier version of parts of this chapter appeared in Andrew R. L. Cayton, " 'A Quiet Independence': The Western Vision of the Ohio Company," *Ohio History* 90 (1981): 5–32. See also Samuel P. Hildreth, *Pioneer History* (Cincinnati, 1848); Rohrbough, *Trans-Appalachian Frontier*, 66–70; and Randolph Downes, *Frontier Ohio, 1788–1803* (Columbus: Ohio State Archaeological and Historical Society, 1935), chap. 2.

⁵ See Marc Egnal, "The Origins of the Revolution in Virginia: A Reinterpretation," *William and Mary Quarterly*, 3d ser., 37 (1980): 401–28; Onuf, *Origins of the Federal Republic*; Abernethy, *Western Lands and the American Revolution*; and Sosin, *Revolutionary Frontier*, 20–82, 151–60.

⁶ See McCoy, *Elusive Republic*, 18–22; and Gordon S. Wood, ed., *The Rising Glory of America, 1760–1820* (New York: G. Braziller, 1971), 14–19.

⁷ See David Freeman Hawke, *Benjamin Rush: Revolutionary Gadfly* (Indianapolis: Bobbs-Merrill, 1971), 304–6.

⁸ John W. Harpster, ed., *Pen Pictures of Early Western Pennsylvania* (Pittsburgh: University of Pittsburgh Press, 1938), 196–200.

⁹ See, for example, Beverley W. Bond, Jr., *The Civilization of the Old Northwest: A Study of Political, Social, and Economic Development, 1788–1812* (New York: Macmillan, 1934), 9–12; and Archer B. Hulbert, ed., *The Records of the Original Proceedings of the Ohio Company* (Marietta, Ohio: Marietta Historical Commission, 1917), 1:ciii.

¹⁰ See Wood, *Creation of the American Republic*, 471–518; and Royster, *A Revolutionary People at War*, 295–368.

¹¹ See Robert F. Jones, "William Duer and the Business of Government in the Era of the American Revolution," *William and Mary Quarterly*, 3d ser., 32 (1975): 393–416, esp. 404–7; and Jensen, *The New Nation*, 355–59.

Notes to Chapter 2

[12] See Sidney Kaplan, "Pay, Pension, and Power: Economic Grievances of the Massachusetts Officers of the Revolution," *Boston Public Library Quarterly* 3 (1954): 15–34, 127–42; and Sidney Kaplan, "Veteran Officers and Politics in Massachusetts, 1783–1787," *William and Mary Quarterly,* 3d ser., 9 (1952): 29–57.

[13] Manasseh Cutler to Winthrop Sargent, October 6, 1786, quoted in Kaplan, "Veteran Officers," 43.

[14] James Varnum, "An Oration Delivered at Marietta, July 4, 1788" (Newport, 1788), in Hildreth, *Pioneer History,* 507; Cutler to Nathan Dane, March 16, 1787, in William Parker Cutler and Julia Perkins Cutler, eds., *Life, Journals, and Correspondence of Rev. Manasseh Cutler* (Cincinnati, 1888), 1:507.

[15] James M. Varnum, "Ministerial Oppression, with The Battle of Bunker Hill: A Tragedy," 1775, Harris Collection, John Hay Library, Brown University, Providence, Rhode Island. See Royster, *A Revolutionary People at War,* for a discussion of the impact of the war for independence on the officer corps. See also Fred Anderson, *A People's Army: Massachusetts Soldiers and Society in the Seven Years' War* (Chapel Hill: University of North Carolina Press for the Institute of Early American History and Culture, 1984), for a superb analysis of the military heritage of men like Rufus Putnam.

[16] Parsons to Colonel Root, August 29, 1779, in Hall, *Samuel Holden Parsons,* 266.

[17] Hall, *Samuel Holden Parsons,* 581; Parsons to his wife, October 18, 1788, ibid., 533.

[18] Hildreth, *Early Pioneer Settlers of Ohio,* 235. See also Rufus Putnam to George Washington, April 5, 1784, Rowena Buell, ed., *Memoirs of Rufus Putnam* (Boston: Houghton, Mifflin, 1903), 224–25.

[19] "Petition of settlers of Belpre, the Northwest Territory to George Washington," March 14, 1793, Samuel Prescott Hildreth Papers, Marietta College; "Copy of an Address from Abraham Whipple to Congress," Whipple Papers, Rhode Island Historical Society, Providence.

[20] C. M. Storey, ed., *Massachusetts Society of the Cincinnati: Minutes of all Meetings of the Society up to and including the meeting of October 1, 1825* (Boston: Published for the Society, 1964), xxviii.

[21] George Blazier, ed., *Joseph Barker: Recollections of the First Settlement of Ohio* (Marietta, Ohio: Marietta College, 1958), 50. See also Mrs. L. A. Alderman, *The Identification of the Society of the Cincinnati with the First Authorized Settlement of the Northwest Territory at Marietta, Ohio, April 7, 1788* (Marietta, 1888), 24.

[22] Storey, *Massachusetts Society,* xxvi.

[23] Parsons to Alexander McDougall, August 20, 1783, quoted in E. James Ferguson, *The Power of the Purse: A History of American Public Finance, 1776–1790* (Chapel Hill: University of North Carolina Press for the Institute of Early American History and Culture, 1961), 156n. See also Wallace E. Davies, "The Society of the Cincinnati in New England, 1783–1800," *William and Mary Quarterly,* 3d ser., 5 (1948): 3–25.

[24] Cutler to Sargent, June 16 and November 6, 1786, Winthrop Sargent Papers. See also Wood, *Creation of the American Republic,* 391–467.

[25] Benjamin Tupper to Henry Knox, April 1787, quoted in Kaplan, "Veteran Officers," 55.

[26] Buell, *Rufus Putnam,* 103; Cutler to Sargent, October 6, 1786, quoted in Kaplan, "Veteran Officers," 49.

[27] Varnum, "Oration," 506; Sargent, Diary, July 19, 1786, Sargent Papers; [?] Freeman to Sargent, April 4, 1786, quoted in Benjamin Harrison Pershing, "Winthrop Sargent: A Builder in the Old Northwest," (Ph.D. diss., University of Chicago, 1927), 24.

[28] Putnam to Fisher Ames, 1790, in Buell, *Rufus Putnam,* 246; Manasseh Cutler, *An Explanation of the Map. . . .* (Salem, 1787), 21.

[29] See Hugh Cleland, *George Washington in the Ohio Valley* (Pittsburgh: University of Pittsburgh Press, 1955), for a collection of Washington's writings on the region. For an insightful discussion of the relationship between personal and public interests with regard to Western lands, see Royster, *Light-Horse Harry Lee*, 66–83.

[30] Putnam to George Washington, February 28, 1791, in Clarence E. Carter, ed., *The Territorial Papers of the United States* (Washington, D.C.: Government Printing Office, 1934), 2:338; Varnum, "Oration," 506; Parsons to William S. Johnson, November 24, 1788, in Hall, *Samuel Holden Parsons*, 534.

[31] James Monroe to Thomas Jefferson, May 11, 1786, in Stanislaus Hamilton, ed., *The Writings of James Monroe* (New York, 1898), 1:127; and ibid., July 16, 1786, 1:140–41.

[32] Washington to James Madison, March 31, 1787, in Fitzpatrick, *Writings of George Washington* 29:190–92. See also, Wood, *Creation of the American Republic*, 391–564.

[33] John Jay to Thomas Jefferson, April 24, 1787, in Julian P. Boyd, ed., *The Papers of Thomas Jefferson* (Princeton: Princeton University Press, 1950–), 11:313–14; Barthelemi Tardiveau to Josiah Harmar, August 6, 1787, Gayle Thornbrough, ed., *Outpost on the Wabash: Letters of Brigadier General Josiah Harmar and Major John Francis Hamtramck* (Indianapolis: Indiana Historical Society, 1957), 29; Jefferson to Madison, June 20, 1787, in Boyd, *Papers of Jefferson* 11:481.

[34] "Report of the Secretary at War Relative to Intruders on the Public Lands," April 19, 1787, in Carter, *Territorial Papers* 2:27; Henry Knox to the President of Congress, April 16, 1787, ibid., 26.

[35] Washington to Hugh Williamson, March 15, 1785, in Fitzpatrick, *Writings of Washington* 28:108.

[36] Parsons to Oliver Ellsworth, May 20, 1789, in Hall, *Samuel Holden Parsons*, 558; Cutler, *Explanation of the Map*, 14.

[37] Cutler, Journal, July 27, 1787, in W. P. Cutler and J. P. Cutler, *Manasseh Cutler* 1:304; Samuel Osgood, July 25, 1787, ibid., 300; Richard Henry Lee to Washington, July 15, 1787, in James C. Ballagh, ed., *The Letters of Richard Henry Lee* (New York: Macmillan, 1914), 2:425.

[38] Cutler, Journal, July 21, 1787, in W. P. Cutler and J. P. Cutler, *Manasseh Cutler* 1:296.

[39] On St. Clair's life, see Smith, *St. Clair Papers*, passim.

[40] Varnum, "Oration," 506; Marietta citizens to St. Clair, in Hildreth, *Pioneer History*, 512.

[41] The literature on the Northwest Ordinance is voluminous. The most important works include Onuf, *Origins of the Federal Republic;* Eblen, *First and Second United States Empires*, chap. 1; "Editorial Note on the Northwest Territory," Boyd, *Papers of Jefferson* 18:159–78; Robert Berkhofer, "The Northwest Ordinance and the Principles of Territorial Evolution," in John P. Bloom, ed., *The American Territorial System* (Athens, Ohio: Ohio University Press, 1973), 45–55.

[42] St. Clair quoted in Hildreth, *Pioneer History*, 510. See also Rohrbough, *Trans-Appalachian Frontier*, 68–76.

[43] Hildreth, *Pioneer History*, 273–74.

[44] Cutler, *Explanation of the Map*, 14; Varnum, "Oration," 507.

[45] Putnam to Fisher Ames, 1790, in Buell, *Rufus Putnam*, 246; Washington to the Marquis de Lafayette, February 7, 1788, in Fitzpatrick, *Writings of Washington* 29:412; Hulbert, *Records of the Ohio Company* 1:15, 20. See also John Reps, *Town Planning in Frontier America* (Princeton: Princeton University Press, 1969), 282–91.

[46] Solomon Drowne, "An Oration, Delivered at Marietta, April 7, 1789," (Worcester, 1789), in Hildreth, *Pioneer History*, 522; Hulbert, *Records of the Ohio Company* 2:209.

[47] Hulbert, *Records of the Ohio Company* 1:51. See also Reps, *Town Planning*, 285.

⁴⁸ Cutler to Ebenezer Hazard, September 18, 1787, in W. P. Cutler and J. P. Cutler, *Manasseh Cutler* 1:331; Hulbert, *Records of the Ohio Company* 2:80.

⁴⁹ Cutler, *Explanation of the Map*, 16.

⁵⁰ Varnum, "Oration," 505; Putnam to Ames, 1790, in Buell, *Rufus Putnam*, 247.

⁵¹ Cutler, *Explanation of the Map*, 16. On shipbuilding in Marietta, see Archer B. Hulbert, "Western Ship-Building," *American Historical Review* 21 (1916): 720–33.

⁵² Cutler, *Explanation of the Map*, 20.

⁵³ Ibid., 21; Thomas Wallcut to George Minot, October 31–November 3, 1789, "Journal of Thomas Wallcut," George Dexter, ed., *Proceedings* (Boston: Massachusetts Historical Society, 1879–80), 17:175; Drowne, "An Oration," 522, 521.

⁵⁴ Wallcut to Minot, October 31–November 3, 1789, "Journal," 175.

3 Establishing the Authority of the National Government, 1788–1798

¹ John D. Barnhart, *Valley of Democracy: The Frontier versus the Plantation in the Ohio Valley, 1775–1818* (Lincoln: University of Nebraska Press, 1953); Robert Wiebe, *Opening of American Society*, 132; Bernard Bailyn et al., *The Great Republic: A History of the American People* (Boston: D.C. Heath, 1977), 397; and Elkins and McKitrick, "A Meaning for Turner's Frontier," 349. Some parts of this chapter were previously published in Andrew R. L. Cayton, "The Contours of Power in a Frontier Town: Marietta (Ohio), 1788–1803," *Journal of the Early Republic* 6 (1986).

² Eblen, *First and Second United States Empires*, 317; Downes, *Frontier Ohio*, 149.

³ Arthur St. Clair to George Washington, August 1789, in Carter, *Territorial Papers* 2:212.

⁴ "Report of the Secretary at War to the President," June 12, 1789, in Carter, *Territorial Papers* 2:196; James Backus to Elijah Backus, May 11, 1788, Backus-Woodbridge Papers, Ohio Historical Society; John May, Journal, May 22, 1788, in Dwight Smith, ed., *The Western Journals of John May: Ohio Company Agent and Business Adventurer* (Cincinnati: Historical and Philosophical Society of Ohio, 1961), 98; "Narrative of John Heckewelder's Journey to the Wabash in 1792," *Pennsylvania Magazine of History and Biography* 12 (1888): 42.

⁵ Major John F. Hamtramck to Josiah Harmar, August 31, 1788, in Thornbrough, *Outpost on the Wabash*, 114, 115.

⁶ Parsons to William S. Johnson, October 27, 1785, in Hall, *Samuel Holden Parsons*, 475; "Report of the Secretary at War: Indian Affairs," May 2, 1788, in Carter, *Territorial Papers* 2:104; Jonathan Dayton to John Cleves Symmes, September 12, 1788, in Beverley W. Bond, Jr., ed., *The Correspondence of John Cleves Symmes, Founder of the Miami Purchase* (New York: Macmillan for the Historical and Philosophical Society of Ohio, 1926), 203.

⁷ Bond, *Foundations of Ohio*, 243–48; Treaty of Fort McIntosh, January 21, 1785, and "Instructions to the Governor of the Territory of the United States Northwest of the River Ohio," in Smith, *St. Clair Papers* 2:2, 37.

⁸ Rufus Putnam to George Washington, June 16, 1783, in Buell, *Memoirs of Rufus Putnam*, 218, 217.

⁹ Putnam to John Heckewelder, February 19, 1788, Putnam Papers; Josiah Harmar to the Secretary at War, March 9, 1788, in Smith, *St. Clair Papers* 2:42; St. Clair to the Secretary at War, January 27, 1788, ibid.; Report of the Secretary at War to Congress, July 10, 1787, in Carter, *Territorial Papers* 2:31–32.

¹⁰ Harmar to Hamtramck, February 15, 1789, in Thornbrough, *Outpost on the Wabash*, 150; Hamtramck to Harmar, August 31, 1788, ibid., 116.

11 Henry Knox to St. Clair, December 19, 1789, in Carter, *Territorial Papers* 2:225. See also Bond, *Foundations of Ohio,* 312–16.

12 Harmar to Joseph Howell, Jr., June 6, 1790, in William H. Denny, "Military Journal of Ebenezer Denny," *Memoirs of the Historical Society of Pennsylvania* 7:457.

13 These events have been examined so thoroughly elsewhere that there is no need to recount them in detail here. See, among many others, Francis Paul Prucha, *The Sword of the Republic: The United States Army on the Frontier, 1783–1846* (New York: Macmillan, 1969), 20–40; Kohn, *Eagle and Sword;* R. David Edmunds, *Tecumseh and the Quest for Indian Leadership* (Boston: Little, Brown, 1984); and Paul David Nelson, *Anthony Wayne: Soldier of the Early Republic* (Bloomington: Indiana University Press, 1985).

14 "Narrative of John Heckewelder's Journey," 471; *History of Washington County, Ohio* (Cleveland, 1881), 362–66; Thomas Wallcut to St. Clair, 1790, "Journal," 182n.

15 Report of Police Committee, March 19, 1789, Hildreth Papers.

16 Solomon Drowne to Levi Wharton, January 21, 1792, in William Drowne, "A Brief Sketch of the Life of Solomon Drowne, M.D.," Drowne Papers, Rhode Island Historical Society. See also, among many studies of the general developments described above, McCoy, *Elusive Republic;* Gordon S. Wood, ed., *The Rising Glory of America, 1760–1820* (New York: G. Braziller, 1971), Introduction; Countryman, *A People in Revolution;* Robert Gross, *The Minutemen and Their World* (New York: Hill and Wang, 1976); Foner, *Tom Paine and Revolutionary America;* Isaac, *Transformation of Virginia;* and Appleby, *Capitalism and a New Social Order.*

17 Cutler to John May, December 15, 1788, in E. J. Benton, ed., *Side Lights on the Ohio Company of Associates from the John May Papers* (Cleveland Western Reserve Historical Society, 1917), *Tracts* 97:137. See also T. T. Belote, *The Scioto Speculation and the French Settlement at Gallipolis* (Cincinnati, 1894); Archer B. Hulbert, "The Method and Operations of the Scioto Group of Speculators," *Mississippi Valley Historical Review* 1 (1915): 502–15, 2 (1916): 56–73; and Jones, "William Duer and the Business of Government," 404–7.

18 "Letter to the Other Associates," Newport, September 20, 1788, in Benton, *Side Lights,* 117.

19 Cutler, Journal, August 21, 1788, in W. P. Cutler and J. P. Cutler, *Manasseh Cutler* 1:412; Cutler to the Ohio Company Agents, November 19, 1788, in Benton, *Side Lights,* 129, 132.

20 Putnam to Cutler, May 16, 1788, in W. P. Cutler and J. P. Cutler, *Manasseh Cutler* 1:378.

21 Thomas Stovey to Putnam, April 12, 1788, Marietta College Archives; Parsons to his wife, June 1, 1788, in Hall, *Samuel Holden Parsons,* 521; Putnam to Mr. Foster, June 30–July 1, 1788, Marietta College Archives. See also John May, Journal, July 7, 1788, in Smith, *John May,* 51.

22 Putnam to Mr. Foster, June 30–July 1, 1788, Marietta College Archives; Putnam quoted in Buell, *Rufus Putnam,* 106.

23 Parsons to Cutler, January 23, 1789, in W. P. Cutler and J. P. Cutler, *Manasseh Cutler* 1:441; and ibid., December 11, 1788, 1:440; Cutler to Sargent, September 28, 1789, quoted in Josephine Phillips, "The Naming of Marietta," *Ohio Archaeological and Historical Quarterly* 55 (1946): 134; Sargent, Diary, November 25, 1789, Sargent Papers.

24 Wallcut quoted in Phillips, "Naming of Marietta," 135; May, Journal, July 14, 1789, in Smith, *John May,* 122; Putnam to Cutler, August 12, 1790, in W. P. Cutler and J. P. Cutler, *Manasseh Cutler* 1:464.

25 John Mathews to Putnam, August/September, 1789, Hildreth Papers.

[26] Parsons to William S. Johnson, November 24, 1788, in Hall, *Samuel Holden Parsons,* 535.

[27] William Jackson to George Turner, December 23, 1789, in Carter, *Territorial Papers* 2:227; Knox to Sargent, November 9, 1789, ibid., 223; and St. Clair to Washington, May 1, 1790, ibid., 248.

[28] Sargent to Washington, November 27, 1789, in Carter, *Territorial Papers* 2:225; and St. Clair to Alexander Hamilton, August 9, 1793, ibid., 459.

[29] "Memorandum of Absences of Governor Arthur St. Clair," 1798, in Carter, *Territorial Papers* 2:648 (Sargent estimated St. Clair had been absent for a total of five and a half years); Jefferson to George Turner, August 9, 1793, ibid., 459.

[30] Sargent to Washington, July 6, 1792, in Carter, *Territorial Papers* 2:406; Sargent to John Cleves Symmes, February 6, 1793, ibid., 406; Sargent to St. Clair, February 6, 1793, ibid., 431; Sargent, Diary, February 10, 1794, Sargent Papers.

[31] Washington to Jefferson, March 10, 1793, in Carter, *Territorial Papers* 2:444; Washington to Jefferson, April 5, 1793, ibid., 450; St. Clair to Jefferson, August 9, 1793, ibid., 457; and Sargent to the Secretary of State, August 5, 1797, ibid., 618.

[32] St. Clair to Sargent, December 1, 1796, in Carter, *Territorial Papers* 2:413–14.

[33] See Smith, *St. Clair Papers* 2:70–74.

[34] St. Clair to Jefferson, December 14, 1794, ibid., 332, 333.

[35] Edmund Randolph to Washington, January 4, 1794, in Carter, *Territorial Papers* 2:472.

[36] Buell, *Rufus Putnam,* 100, 99.

[37] Putnam to Ames, 1790, ibid., 243, 244; Putnam to Knox, August 21, 1792, ibid., 325; and Putnam to Washington, February 28, 1791, in Carter, *Territorial Papers* 2:339.

[38] Putnam to John Mathews, 1794, Hildreth Papers; Putnam to [?], August 30, 1794, Putnam Papers.

[39] See Carl E. Prince, *The Federalists and the Origins of the U.S. Civil Service* (New York: New York University Press, 1977), for a general discussion of the Federalist patronage policy and appointments. See also Leonard D. White, *The Federalists: A Study in Administrative History* (New York: Macmillan, 1947); Wood, *Creation of the American Republic;* and Stourzh, *Alexander Hamilton,* 195–220.

[40] See *History of Washington County, Ohio,* 111–14, 359, for lists of appointments.

[41] Putnam to Timothy Pickering, January 15, 1789, Putnam Papers.

[42] Ibid.

4   An Alliance Of Local Interests, 1790–1798

[1] Petition to Congress from Citizens of the Territory, 1799, in Carter, *Territorial Papers* 3:50. See also Watlington, *Partisan Spirit,* and Mary K. Bonsteel Tachau, *Federal Courts in the Early Republic: Kentucky, 1789–1816* (Princeton: Princeton University Press, 1978).

[2] "A Friend to the People," *Cincinnati Western Spy and Hamilton Gazette,* September 24, 1801.

[3] On the national Jeffersonian movement, see Appleby, *Capitalism and a New Social Order;* Lance Banning, *The Jeffersonian Persuasion: Evolution of a Party Ideology* (Ithaca, N.Y.: Cornell University Press, 1978); and McCoy, *Elusive Republic.*

[4] "Cincinnati," *Centinel of the North-Western Territory,* April 25, 1795.

[5] See William Hutchinson, "The Bounty Lands of the American Revolution in Ohio" (Ph.D. diss., University of Chicago, 1927). See also Downes, *Frontier Ohio;* Barnhart, *Valley of Democracy,* 121–60; Rohrbough, *Trans-Appalachian Frontier,* 64–88; and Bond, *Civilization of the Old Northwest.*

⁶ *Autobiography of Rev. James B. Finley, or, Pioneer Life in the West*, ed. W. P. Strickland (Cincinnati, 1854), 107.

⁷ Hutchinson, "Bounty Lands," 197; David M. Massie, *Nathaniel Massie: A Pioneer of Ohio* (Cincinnati, 1896), 171.

⁸ Massie, *Nathaniel Massie*, 102, 14–29.

⁹ Ibid., 18, 19.

¹⁰ Nathaniel Massie, Sr., to Massie, October 4, 1788, Nathaniel Massie Papers, Ohio Historical Society; Massie, *Nathaniel Massie*, 30–31, 29.

¹¹ Massie to [?], December 3, 1795; and Massie to John Graham, April 4, 1797, Massie Papers.

¹² Thomas Worthington to his wife, May 17, 1797, in Sarah Anne Worthington Peter, *Private Memoir of Thomas Worthington* (Cincinnati, 1882), 23.

¹³ Hutchinson, "Bounty Lands," 197.

¹⁴ Alfred Byron Sears, *Thomas Worthington: Father of Ohio Statehood* (Columbus: Ohio Historical Society, 1958), 3–22; Massie to Worthington, July 20, 1797, Thomas Worthington Papers, Ohio Historical Society. See also Peter, *Private Memoir*, 3–22.

¹⁵ See William Edward Gilmore, *Life of Edward Tiffin, First Governor of Ohio* (Chillicothe, 1897).

¹⁶ "Duncan McArthur," in John McDonald, *Biographical Sketches* (Dayton, 1852), 71–182, 92–93; Marie Dickore, *General Joseph Kerr of Chillicothe, Ohio* (Oxford, Ohio: Oxford Press, 1941), 1–8; and W. H. Burtner, Jr., "Charles Willing Byrd," *Ohio Archaeological and Historical Quarterly* 41 (1932): 237–40.

¹⁷ Massie, MS, 1796; and Joseph Watkins to Massie, April 28, 1796, Massie Papers; James Ross to Worthington, May 19, and April 1, 1801, Worthington Papers.

¹⁸ Watkins to Massie, August 27, 1796, Massie Papers; Worthington to the Electors of Ross County, August 26, 1802, *Chillicothe Scioto Gazette*, August 28, 1802.

¹⁹ R. K. Meade to Arthur St. Clair, May 4, 1789, in Smith, *St. Clair Papers* 2:114; Strickland, *James Finley*, 11; Peter, *Private Memoir*, 33, 31.

²⁰ Charles Willing Byrd to Massie, May 4, and June 13, 1801, Massie Papers.

²¹ Gilmore, *Edward Tiffin*, 1–5; Sears, *Worthington*, 43. See also Peter, *Private Memoir*, 23.

²² James B. Finley, *Sketches of Western Methodism*, ed. W. P. Strickland, (Cincinnati, 1854), 87, 106.

²³ Ibid., 198, 89, 88; Elmer T. Clark, ed., *The Journal and Letters of Francis Asbury* (Nashville: Abingdon Press, 1958), 2:575–76. See also Donald G. Mathews, *Religion in the Old South* (Chicago: University of Chicago Press, 1977); William W. Sweet, ed., *Religion on the American Frontier* (Chicago: University of Chicago Press, 1946), vol. 4, *The Methodists*, 154; and Hatch, "The Christian Movement."

²⁴ John Sale to Edward Dromgoole, February 20, 1807, in Sweet, *Religion on the Frontier*, 4:160; Frederick Bonner to Dromgoole, July 19, 1807, ibid., 170; and Peter Pelham to Dromgoole, June 20, 1807, ibid., 165.

²⁵ See Smith, *St. Clair Papers* 2:376, 386–87.

²⁶ See Massie to Worthington, July 13, 1798; and Manchester Inhabitants to the Acting Governor, in Massie to Worthington, July 20, 1797, Worthington Papers.

²⁷ St. Clair to Massie and other Justices of Adams County, June 29, 1798, Smith, *St. Clair Papers* 2:425n, 426n.

²⁸ Worthington to St. Clair [draft; 1798?], Worthington Papers.

²⁹ "Speech of Governor St. Clair to the Legislature," December 19, 1799, in Smith, *St. Clair*

Papers 2:478; see also Journal of Executive Proceedings, September 3, 1798, in Carter, *Territorial Papers* 3:513.

[30] See Bond, *Correspondence of John Cleves Symmes*, 17–21.

[31] Symmes to Mr. and Mrs. Peyton Short, April 28, 1797, in Beverley W. Bond, Jr., ed., *The Intimate Letters of John Cleves Symmes and His Family* (Cincinnati: Historical and Philosophical Society of Ohio, 1956), 51, 52.

[32] See Benjamin H. Hibbard, *A History of the Public Land Policies* (New York: Macmillan, 1924), 56–81; and Malcolm J. Rohrbough, *The Land Office Business: The Settlement and Administration of American Public Lands, 1789–1837* (New York: Oxford University Press, 1968), 3–25.

[33] See Bond, *Correspondence*, 149, 158, 159.

[34] Memorial to Congress by Citizens of the Territory, July, 1799, in Carter, *Territorial Papers* 3:36; St. Clair to Timothy Pickering, July, 1799, in Smith, *St. Clair Papers* 2:445.

[35] Petition to Congress by Citizens of the Territory, 1799, in Carter, *Territorial Papers* 3:43; St. Clair to Joseph Parks, December 13, 1798, in Smith, *St. Clair Papers* 2:436, 437.

[36] See Carter, *Territorial Papers* 3:29–30, 178–179; see also the comments of Elkins and McKitrick, "A Meaning for Turner's Frontier," 341, 350.

[37] "Candidres," *Cincinnati Western Spy,* September 24, 1799.

[38] See Downes, *Frontier Ohio*, 62–63, 129–30, 181; Bond, *Civilization of the Old Northwest,* 12; Richard C. Wade, *The Urban Frontier: Pioneer Life in Early Pittsburgh, Cincinnati, Lexington, Louisville, and St. Louis* (Cambridge: Harvard University Press, 1959), 22–27; Bond, *Foundations of Ohio,* 290–301.

[39] On the importance of the army to the economy of the Northwest Territory in the 1790s, see Randolph C. Downes, "Trade in Frontier Ohio," *The Mississippi Valley Historical Review* 16 (1929–30), 467–94, esp. 476–79.

[40] "Narrative of John Heckewelder's Journey," 42; Jacob Burnet, *Notes on the Early Settlement of the North-Western Territory* (Cincinnati, 1847), 36, 37.

[41] See Hildreth Papers, vol. 2, no. 43.

[42] "Manlius," *Centinel,* November 9, 1793.

[43] "Manlius," *Centinel,* November 30, 1793.

[44] "Anticipation," *Centinel,* August 23, 1794.

[45] Sargent to St. Clair, February 6, 1793, in Carter, *Territorial Papers* 2:433.

[46] Ibid., 434; St. Clair to Edmund Randolph, May 9, 1793, in Smith, *St. Clair Papers* 2:316; Proclamation of Governor Arthur St. Clair, August 6, 1793, in Carter, *Territorial Papers* 2:456.

[47] Sargent to Lt. Prior, October 25, 1792, in Carter, *Territorial Papers* 3:386.

[48] Sargent, Diary, September 8, 1794, Sargent Papers.

[49] Sargent, Diary, September 9, 10, 18, 23, 1794, Sargent Papers.

[50] Sargent to Timothy Pickering, September 30, 1796, quoted in Pershing, "Winthrop Sargent: A Builder of the Old Northwest," 46–47; Sargent, Diary, February 13, 1795, and July 16, 1794, Sargent Papers. See Downes, *Frontier Ohio*, 127–46.

[51] "Dorastus," *Centinel,* January 13, 1795.

[52] "Territory of the United States Northwest of the River Ohio, Circular, December 30, 1797," in J. P. Cutler, *Ephraim Cutler,* 320.

5   "The Only Proper Judges Of Their Own Interests," 1798–1803

[1] See Appleby, *Capitalism and a New Social Order;* Banning, *Jeffersonian Persuasion;* Richard E. Ellis, *The Jeffersonian Crisis: Courts and Politics in the Young Republic* (New

York: Oxford University Press, 1971); Ronald P. Formisano, *The Transformation of Political Culture: Massachusetts Parties, 1790s–1840s* (New York: Oxford University Press, 1983); Howe, "Republican Thought and Political Violence," 147–65; David Hackett Fischer, *The Revolution of American Conservatism: The Federalist Party in the Era of Jeffersonian Democracy* (New York: Harper and Row, 1965), 201–26; and McCoy, *Elusive Republic.* On the Ohio statehood movement, see Peter S. Onuf, "From Constitution to Higher Law: The Reinterpretation of the Northwest Ordinance," *Ohio History* 94 (1985): 5–33; Barnhart, *Valley of Democracy,* 138–60; Ratcliffe, "The Experience of Revolution"; Sears, *Thomas Worthington,* v–viii, 52–67; and Downes, *Frontier Ohio,* 147–252.

² Thomas Worthington to Nathaniel Massie, March 5, 1802, Massie Papers; John Smith to Worthington, January 17, 1803, Worthington Papers; Worthington to Thomas Jefferson, January 30, 1802, in Smith, *St. Clair Papers* 2:569. See also Banning, *Jeffersonian Persuasion,* 133–40.

³ Arthur St. Clair to James Ross, December, 1799, in Smith, *St. Clair Papers* 2:482; Winthrop Sargent to Timothy Pickering, August 14, 1797, in Carter, *Territorial Papers* 2:622.

⁴ Michael Baldwin to the Electors of Ross County, *Scioto Gazette,* August 28, 1802. On Baldwin, see Andrew R. L. Cayton, "The Failure of Michael Baldwin: A Case Study in the Origins of Middle Class Culture on the Ohio Frontier," *Ohio History,* 95 (1986): 34–48.

⁵ See Downes, *Frontier Ohio,* 147–252.

⁶ "Reply of the House of Representatives to the Governor," September 30, 1799, in Smith, *St. Clair Papers* 2:464.

⁷ Downes, *Frontier Ohio,* 177–252, sees the developing controversy between St. Clair and his opponents in regional terms—Cincinnati v. Chillicothe v. Marietta.

⁸ Worthington to Massie, December 27, 1799, Massie Papers.

⁹ Worthington, uncompleted MS, [1799?], Worthington Papers; William Henry Harrison to Massie, January 17, 1800, in Massie, *Nathaniel Massie,* 156.

¹⁰ See election returns in *Cincinnati Western Spy,* October 22, 1800.

¹¹ "Answer of the House of Representatives," November, 1800, in Smith, *St. Clair Papers* 2:513. See also Sears, *Thomas Worthington,* 56.

¹² John Cleves Symmes to Griffen Greene, January 21, 1802, Hildreth Papers.

¹³ "A Countryman," "Number II," *Scioto Gazette,* February 19, 1801.

¹⁴ John Brown to Worthington, February 20, 1801, Worthington Papers; Worthington to Return Jonathan Meigs, February 23, 1801, Hildreth Papers; "Important," *Scioto Gazette,* January 8, 1801.

¹⁵ "The Governor's Reply to the Answer of the House of Representatives," November 17, 1800, in Smith, *St. Clair Papers* 2:515.

¹⁶ "A Friend to Liberty and the Rights of Man," *Scioto Gazette,* November 27, 1800.

¹⁷ St. Clair to James Ross, December, 1799, in Smith, *St. Clair Papers* 2:483, 482; St. Clair to Paul Fearing, December 25, 1801, ibid., 550; "A Friend to Liberty and the Rights of Man," *Scioto Gazette,* November 27, 1800.

¹⁸ "Address of Governor St. Clair to the Territorial Legislature at the Opening of the Second Session, at Chillicothe, November 5, 1800," in Smith, *St. Clair Papers* 2:505.

¹⁹ "At a Meeting of the Inhabitants of Marietta," January 12, 1801, *Scioto Gazette,* January 29, 1801.

²⁰ See Downes, *Frontier Ohio,* 186–200.

²¹ William Rufus Putnam to Fearing, January 3, 1802, Paul Fearing Papers, Marietta College.

²² St. Clair to Fearing, January 15, 1802, Hildreth Papers. See also Sears, *Thomas Worthington,* 68–70; and Massie, *Nathaniel Massie,* 78.

²³ Robert Oliver to Griffen Greene, December 29, 1801, Hildreth Papers; St. Clair to James Ross, January 15, 1802, in Smith, *St. Clair Papers* 2:556; St. Clair to Fearing, January 15, 1802, Hildreth Papers. See also "Depositions," *Scioto Gazette*, January 2, 1802; and Sears, *Thomas Worthington*, 70–71.

²⁴ Samuel Finley to St. Clair, December 28, 1801, *Scioto Gazette*, January 2, 1802. See also Sears, *Thomas Worthington*, 70–71; Edward Tiffin to Worthington, January 18, 1802, Worthington Papers; Massie to Worthington, January 18, 1802, in Smith, *St. Clair Papers* 2:560; and Burnet, *Notes on the Early Settlement*, 333–34.

²⁵ Dudley Woodbridge to Ephraim Cutler, December 29, 1801, J. P. Cutler, *Ephraim Cutler*, 56n.

²⁶ Worthington to Abraham Baldwin, November 30, 1801, quoted in Sears, *Thomas Worthington*, 64; Worthington to Massie, January 25, 1802, Worthington Papers.

²⁷ J. Darlinton to Fearing, March 29, 1802, Fearing Papers. See also Baldwin to Worthington, March 25, 1802; James Pritchard to Worthington, March 23, 1802; James Caldwell to Worthington, March 8, 1802, all in Worthington Papers.

²⁸ Worthington to Massie, March 5, 1802, Massie Papers.

²⁹ Worthington to Jefferson, January 30, 1802, in Smith, *St. Clair Papers* 2:565–70; Worthington and Massie to Thomas Jefferson, February, 1802, Massie, *Nathaniel Massie*, 79.

³⁰ See Sears, *Thomas Worthington*, 73–85; R. C. Downes, "Thomas Jefferson and the Removal of Governor St. Clair in 1802," *Ohio Archaeological and Historical Society Publications* 36 (1927): 62–77; Noble E. Cunningham, Jr., *The Jeffersonian Republicans in Power* (Chapel Hill: University of North Carolina Press for the Institute of Early American History and Culture, 1963), 196–200; and Dumas Malone, *Jefferson the President: First Term, 1801–1805* (Boston: Little, Brown, 1970), 243–44.

³¹ Samuel Finley to Worthington, February 12, 1802, quoted in Sears, *Thomas Worthington*, 79.

³² Ross County election returns are in *Scioto Gazette*, October 16, 1802. Tiffin led the list with 905 votes; Grubb was fourth with 621. Hamilton County returns are in the *Western Spy*, October 20, 1802. Ninety-nine people received votes. The Republican ticket had been announced in the *Western Spy*, August 28, 1802.

³³ Sears, *Thomas Worthington*, 94–108; and Barnhart, *Valley of Democracy*, 153–60.

³⁴ Nathaniel Macon to Worthington, September 1, 1802, Worthington Papers; "An Address," *Western Spy*, July 17, 1802. See also "Journal of the Convention," *Ohio Archaeological and Historical Quarterly* 5 (1897): 80–132.

³⁵ F. R. Aumann, "The Development of the Judicial System of Ohio," *Ohio Archaeological and Historical Society Quarterly* 41 (1932): 201–5.

³⁶ Burnet, *Notes on the Early Settlement*, 350–69; Sears, *Thomas Worthington*, 104–5; and Caleb Atwater, *A History of the State of Ohio, Natural and Civil* (Cincinnati, 1838), 169, 171–75.

³⁷ "Governmental Election," *Scioto Gazette*, December 18, 1802; Sears, *Thomas Worthington*, 90–91; and Massie, *Nathaniel Massie*, 108.

³⁸ John Amberson, "Advertisement," March 12, 1785, in Smith, *St. Clair Papers* 2:5n; Michael Baldwin to the Electors of Ross County, August 28, 1802, *Scioto Gazette*, September, 1802.

³⁹ Downes, *Frontier Ohio*, 216–25.

⁴⁰ Ibid.

⁴¹ Buell, *Memoirs of Rufus Putnam*, 126.

6   Catalines And Contentiousness, *1803–1807*

¹ See Malone, *Jefferson the President*, 244; and Cunningham, *Jeffersonian Republicans in Power*, 196–200. On Ohio politics from 1803 and 1808, see Ratcliffe, "Experience of Revolution," 200–204; William T. Utter, *The Frontier State, 1803–1825* (Columbus: Ohio State Archaeological and Historical Society, 1942), 3–120; Sears, *Thomas Worthington*, 108–202; and Jeffrey P. Brown, "The Ohio Federalists, 1803–1815," *Journal of the Early Republic* 2 (1982): 261–63.

² Benjamin Tupper to Thomas Worthington, February 20, 1804; and George Granger to Worthington, March 25, 1805, Worthington Papers.

³ Abraham Shepherd to Worthington, February 13, 1799; and William Creighton to Worthington, December 27, 1802, Worthington Papers.

⁴ J. Brown to Worthington, March 19, 1799, Worthington Papers. Some parts of this chapter previously appeared in Cayton, "Failure of Michael Baldwin." See also "Michael Baldwin," *History of Ross and Highland Counties* (Cleveland, 1880), 73–74.

⁵ Sears, *Thomas Worthington*, 68, 78; Blennerhassett quoted in *History of Ross and Highland Counties*, 73.

⁶ "Baldwin," *History of Ross and Highland Counties*, 73, 74.

⁷ See Bertram Wyatt-Brown, *Southern Honor: Ethics and Behavior in the Old South* (New York: Oxford Univ. Press, 1982); E. P. Thompson, "Patrician Society, Plebeian Culture," *Journal of Social History* 7 (1974): 382–405; and Isaac, *Transformation of Virginia*.

⁸ Baldwin to Worthington, April 2, 1802, Worthington Papers.

⁹ Edward Tiffin to Worthington, December 24, 1802, and January 9, 1803, Worthington Papers.

¹⁰ Tiffin to Worthington, December 8, 1803; and George Hoffman to Worthington, December 30, 1803, Worthington Papers.

¹¹ Duncan McArthur to Worthington, January 2, 1804; and Tiffin to Worthington, January 13, 1804, Worthington Papers.

¹² Tiffin to the General Assembly, December 4, 1804, *Journal of the House of Representatives of the State of Ohio; Being the First Session of the Third General Assembly* (Lexington, 1805), 8. See election returns in *Scioto Gazette*, November 12, 1804.

¹³ Tiffin to Worthington, December 18, 1804, Worthington Papers.

¹⁴ Tiffin to Worthington, December 18, 1806; and John Smith to Worthington, March 26, 1802, Worthington Papers.

¹⁵ John J. Wells to Worthington, December 29, 1802; Tiffin to Worthington, December 8, 1803; and William Creighton to Worthington, December 31, 1802, Worthington Papers.

¹⁶ Baldwin to the Citizens of Ohio, *Scioto Gazette*, May 21, 1803.

¹⁷ Worthington, Diary, April 16, 1803, Thomas Worthington Papers, Manuscripts Division, Library of Congress, Washington, D.C. See also Jan Lewis, *The Pursuit of Happiness: Family and Values in Jeffersonian Virginia* (New York: Cambridge University Press, 1983).

¹⁸ "An Oration Delivered the Fourth of July last, before the Republicans of Cincinnati, by Mr. Matthew Nimmo," *Western Spy*, July 20, 1803.

¹⁹ "A Republican," *Scioto Gazette*, November 19, 1804. An excellent discussion of the evolution of political organization in early Ohio is Ratcliffe, "The Experience of Revolution."

²⁰ Thomas Gibson to James Findlay, October 16, and November 5, 1805, Torrence Papers, Cincinnati Historical Society.

²¹ James Pritchard to Worthington, January 24, 1806, Worthington Papers.

²² See Samuel Huntington to Worthington, February 15, 1806, Worthington Papers.

²³ Worthington to Nathaniel Massie, February 16, 1806, Worthington Papers; "An Old Citizen of Ross," *Scioto Gazette,* May 22, 1806.

²⁴ "A Friend to the People," *Western Spy,* September 23, 1806; and "Brutus," ibid., October 7, 1806.

²⁵ "Tom Tough," *Scioto Gazette,* September 4, 1806. See Ratcliffe, "The Experience of Revolution," 203.

²⁶ See Thomas Perkins Abernethy, *The Burr Conspiracy* (New York: Oxford University Press, 1954), esp. 101–18; Walter F. McCaleb, *The Aaron Burr Conspiracy* (New York: Argosy-Antiquarian, 1966), esp. 207–8; Leslie Henshaw, "The Aaron Burr Conspiracy in the Ohio Valley," *Ohio Archaeological and Historical Publications* 24 (1915): 121–37; and Milton Lomask, *Aaron Burr: The Conspiracy and Years of Exile* (New York: Farrar, Straus, and Giroux, 1982).

²⁷ Henry Dearborn to Tiffin, November 26, 1806; and Tiffin to Matthew Nimmo, December 10, 1806, Edward Tiffin Papers, Ohio Historical Society.

²⁸ Tiffin to Nimmo, December 17, 1806, Tiffin Papers.

²⁹ "The Fredonian," *Scioto Gazette,* October 9, 1806.

³⁰ "Sydney—No. II," *Western Spy,* October 21, 1806; and "Regulus," *Scioto Gazette,* November 6, 1806.

³¹ "The Fredonian, Number IV," *Scioto Gazette,* November 6, 1806.

³² "Regulus," *Scioto Gazette,* November 13, 1806.

³³ William Creighton, Jr., to Worthington, December 18, 1806; Worthington to Massie, January 29, 1807; and Wyllis Silliman to Worthington, January 20 and 6, 1807, Worthington Papers.

³⁴ Samuel Finley to Worthington, December 18, 1806, Worthington Papers; and John Bigger, Jr., to James Findlay, January 17, 1807, Torrence Papers.

³⁵ Tiffin to Worthington, January 25, 1807, Worthington Papers.

³⁶ John McLean to Worthington, February 6, 1807; and James Finley to Worthington, January 31, 1807, Worthington Papers.

7 Matters Of Opinion, 1807–1812

¹ See Brown, "The Ohio Federalists," 264–73; Ratcliffe, "Experience of Revolution," 204–11; and Ellis, *The Jeffersonian Crisis.* The interpretation presented in this chapter is especially indebted to Ellis. See also, on American politics in general in the early nineteenth century, Fischer, *Revolution of American Conservatism;* and Ronald P. Formisano, "Deferential-Participant Politics: The Early Republic's Political Culture, 1789–1840," *American Political Science Review* 68 (1974): 473–84.

² On judges and the law in the Early Republic, see James Williard Hurst, *Law and the Conditions of Freedom in the Nineteenth Century United States* (Madison: University of Wisconsin Press, 1956); Morton J. Horwitz, *The Transformation of American Law, 1780–1860* (Cambridge: Harvard University Press, 1977); William E. Nelson, *Americanization of the Common Law: The Impact of Legal Change on Massachusetts Society, 1760–1830* (Cambridge: Harvard University Press, 1975); Perry Miller, *The Life of the Mind in America: From the Revolution to the Civil War* (New York: Harcourt, Brace, and World, 1965), 99–265; and Tachau, *Federal Courts in the Early Republic.*

³ Daniel Symmes to Samuel Huntington, February 22, 1805, Samuel Huntington Papers, Ohio Historical Society.

⁴ Committee Report on William Irvine's Impeachment, February 18, 1805, *Journal of the*

House of Representatives of the State of Ohio 3:152; Calvin Pease to Edward Tiffin, March 7, 1806, Tiffin Papers.

5 Huntington to Thomas Worthington, December 10, 1805, Worthington Papers.

6 Zenos Kimberly, quoted in Sears, *Thomas Worthington*, 143; "Lex," *Scioto Gazette*, June 5, 1806; Huntington to Worthington, December 10, 1805, Worthington Papers.

7 Tiffin to Worthington, January 3, 1807, Worthington Papers.

8 See Sears, *Thomas Worthington*, 142–45; William T. Utter, "Judicial Review in Early Ohio," *Mississippi Valley Historical Review* 14 (1927): 3–24; and William T. Utter, "Ohio and the English Common Law," *Mississippi Valley Historical Review* 16 (1929–30): 321–33.

9 Huntington, Opinion in *Rutherford v. McFadden*, Supreme Court for Jefferson County, *Scioto Gazette*, October 15, 1807.

10 Ibid. See also Jeffrey P. Brown, "Samuel Huntington: A Connecticut Aristocrat on the Ohio Frontier," *Ohio History* 89 (1980): 420–38.

11 Tiffin to Worthington, January 9, 1807, Worthington Papers.

12 On the Burnet-Baldwin caucus, see Tiffin to Worthington, February 5, 1807, Worthington Papers; Sears, *Thomas Worthington*, 139–42; John Mathews, Levi Whipple, et al. to Nathaniel Massie, September 15, 1807, in Massie, *Nathaniel Massie*, 94; and "Communication," *Western Spy*, September 21, 1807. On the Meigs-Massie controversy, see Massie to the General Assembly of the State of Ohio, December 14, 1807, Massie Papers, Massie, *Nathaniel Massie*, 94–100; and Sears, *Thomas Worthington*, 139–42.

13 House Resolution quoted in Sears, *Thomas Worthington*, 144.

14 Jeremiah Morrow to Worthington, February 19, 1808, Worthington Papers.

15 Ratcliffe, "Experience of Revolution," 201.

16 "An Elector," *Marietta, Ohio Gazette and Virginia Herald*, September 22, 1808.

17 "Honestus," *Western Spy*, October 8, 1808.

18 "Horastus," *Scioto Gazette*, September 23, 1808.

19 Brown, "Ohio Federalists," 267–68.

20 John Sloane to Worthington, November 13, 1808, Worthington Papers.

21 *Journal of the Senate of the State of Ohio in Cases of Impeachments* (Chillicothe, 1809), 14, 15, 16; Ephraim Quimby to Worthington, December 24, 1808, Worthington Papers.

22 "Plough-Jogger," *Ohio Gazette*, November 10 and 17, 1808.

23 George Tod's Answer, January 9, 1809, *Journal of Impeachments*, 61, 62, 63, 64, 62; Calvin Pease's Answer, February 1, 1809, ibid., 28, 30, 35, 32.

24 Reply of the House to Tod, January 14, 1809, ibid., 81, 89.

25 "A Republican," *Scioto Gazette*, September 11, 1809; *Journal of Impeachments*, 90, 83, 87, 88.

26 William Woodbridge to Paul Fearing, February 12, 1809, Fearing Papers; *Journal of Impeachments*, 44–47, 97–100.

27 "A Farmer," *Scioto Gazette*, October 2, 1809; John Hamm to Major John Fuller, October 1, 1809, John Fuller Papers, Ohio Historical Society.

28 Hamm to Fuller, October 1, 1809, Fuller Papers. See also Resolution, January 6, 1810, *Journal of the House of Representatives of the State of Ohio, First Session of the Eighth General Assembly* (Chillicothe, 1810), 142; Sears, *Thomas Worthington*, 149–50; Atwater, *History of the State of Ohio*, 182–86; Salmon P. Chase, ed., *The Statutes of Ohio and the Northwestern Territory* (Cincinnati, 1833), 41.

29 "Civis," *Scioto Gazette*, May 9, 1810; George Tod, quoted in "Justice," *Scioto Gazette*, May 9, 1810.

30 "Logan," *Scioto Gazette*, May 9, 1810; "A Watchman," *Scioto Gazette*, July 4, 1810; and "A Backwoodsman," *Scioto Gazette*, July 11, 1810.

[31] Worthington quoted in "Fourth of July," *Zanesville Muskingum Messenger*, July 7, 1810.

[32] Sears, *Thomas Worthington*, 152; Brown, "Ohio Federalists," 273.

[33] Members listed in Tammany Society Papers, Chillicothe Wigwam, 1807–1905, Ohio Historical Society; Chillicothe Society to the Tammany Society of Pittsburgh, June 18, 1810, ibid.

[34] J. Van Horne to Thomas Scott, March 25, 1811, Tammany Society Papers.

[35] Chillicothe Society to Pittsburgh Society, June 18, 1810, Tammany Society Papers.

[36] "A Democrat," *Muskingum Messenger*, August 25, 1810.

[37] Carlos A. Norton to Worthington, December 15, 1810, Worthington Papers.

[38] James Armstrong to *Western Spy*, July 6, 1811; "A Republican," *Liberty Hall*, February 13, 1811; and Joseph L. Collins to the Grand Sachem, July 15, 1811, Tammany Society Papers.

[39] A. Bourne to Paul Fearing, July 11, 1811, Fearing Papers.

[40] "Communication," *Muskingum Messenger*, July 3, 1811; and Samuel Williams to Wilson Elliott, August 20, 1811, Tammany Society Papers.

[41] James Heaton, *Liberty Hall*, May 29, 1811.

[42] "Anniversary Oration delivered before the Tammany Society," by Edward Tiffin at the Chillicothe Court House, May 13, 1811, Tammany Society Papers. See also *Constitution of the Tammany Society or Columbian Order* (Chillicothe, 1810); and "Oration Delivered before the Tammany Society of Cincinnati on the 12th May, 1814, Being the Anniversary of the Order, by Thomas Henderson," *Liberty Hall*, June 4, 1814.

[43] Hamm to Worthington, July 5, 1811; and Tiffin to Worthington, October 31, 1811, Worthington Papers. See also *Journal of the House of Representatives of the State of Ohio, Ninth General Assembly* (Chillicothe, 1811), 160–61.

[44] Brown, "Ohio Federalists," 273–74.

[45] Worthington, Diary, March 8, 9, 1810, Thomas Worthington Papers, Manuscripts Division, Library of Congress.

[46] Joseph Kerr to Worthington, March 3, 1815, Worthington Papers.

8 The Climax of a Liberal Society, *1812–1819*

[1] See Alexis de Tocqueville, *Democracy in America*, ed. J. P. Mayer (1835, vol. 1, and 1840, vol. 2; reprint, New York: Anchor Books, 1969). For powerful discussions of the liberal tradition in America, see Richard Hofstadter, *The American Political Tradition and the Men Who Made It* (New York: Alfred A. Knopf, 1948), v–xi, 3–17; Louis Hartz, *The Liberal Tradition in America: An Interpretation of American Political Thought Since the Revolution* (New York: Harcourt, Brace, 1955); and John Patrick Diggins, *The Lost Soul of American Politics: Virtue, Self-Interest, and the Foundations of Liberalism* (New York: Basic Books, 1984); and Appleby, *Capitalism and a New Social Order*.

[2] W. A. Trimble to Thomas Worthington and Alexander Campbell, December 24, 1812; and Carlos Norton to Worthington, April 17, 1812, Worthington Papers. For an overview of the War of 1812 in the Old Northwest, see Reginald Horsman, *The Frontier in the Formative Years, 1783–1815* (New York: Holt, Rinehart, and Winston, 1970), 166–77.

[3] William T. Utter, *The Frontier State*, 391.

[4] Ibid.

[5] Ibid., 322, 393, 392. For discussions of Ohio's society in the early nineteenth century, see Lee Soltow, "Inequality Amidst Abundance: Land Ownership in Early Nineteenth Century America," *Ohio History* 88 (1979): 133–51; Robert E. Chaddock, *Ohio Before 1850: A Study*

of the Early Influence of Pennsylvania and Southern Populations in Ohio (New York: Columbia University Press, 1908); and James M. Miller, *The Genesis of Western Culture: The Upper Ohio Valley, 1800–1825* (Columbus: Ohio State Archaeological and Historical Society, 1938).

[6] See Wade, *The Urban Frontier;* Daniel Aaron, "Cincinnati, 1818–1838: A Study of Attitudes in the Urban West," (Ph.D. diss., Harvard University, 1942), esp. v–vii; and Steven J. Ross, *Workers on the Edge: Work, Leisure and Politics in Industrializing Cincinnati, 1788–1890* (New York: Columbia University Press, 1985), chap. 1.

[7] Daniel Drake, *Natural and Statistical View, or Picture of Cincinnati and the Miami Country* (Cincinnati, 1815).

[8] Ibid., 150; Gorham A. Worth, "Reprint of 'Recollections of Cincinnati,' " *Quarterly Publications of the Historical and Philosophical Society of Ohio* 11 (1916): 32.

[9] Worth, " 'Recollections,' " 21. See also R. Carlyle Buley, *The Old Northwest: Pioneer Period, 1815–1840* (Bloomington: Indiana University Press, 1950), 1:421–22.

[10] Drake, *Natural and Statistical View*, 145–46; Wade, *Urban Frontier*, 56–58.

[11] Harry Stevens, *The Early Jackson Party in Ohio* (Durham: Duke University Press, 1957), 9–14; Aaron, "Cincinnati"; Wade, *Urban Frontier*, 53–59.

[12] Thomas H. Greer, "Economic and Social Effects of the Depression of 1819 in the Old Northwest," *Indiana Magazine of History* 44 (1948): 229. See also Rohrbough, *Land Office Business*, 89–136.

[13] Bray Hammond, *Banks and Politics in America: From the Revolution to the Civil War* (Princeton: Princeton University Press, 1957), 227–85. See also Douglass C. North, *The Economic Growth of the United States, 1790–1860* (Englewood Cliffs, N.J.: Prentice-Hall, 1961).

[14] Atwater, *History of the State of Ohio*, 351.

[15] James Miller to James Kilbourne, February 3, 1815, James Kilbourne Papers, Ohio Historical Society; James Kimball, "A Journey to the West in 1817. Notes on Travel by a Salem Mechanic on his Way to the Ohio Fifty Years Ago," *Historical Collections of the Essex Institute* 8 (1868): 235; Morris Birkbeck, *Notes on a Journey in America* (London, 1818), 31. See also Buley, *Old Northwest* 1:1–58, 94–564; Frederick Jackson Turner, *Rise of the New West, 1818–1829* (New York: Harper and Brothers, 1906), 65–82; and George Dangerfield, *The Era of Good Feelings* (New York: Harcourt, Brace, 1952), 105–21.

[16] Jeremiah Morrow quoted in Buley, *Old Northwest* 1:107.

[17] Jacob Burnet to Worthington, March 17, 1812, Worthington Papers.

[18] John Kerr to Worthington, July 1, 1812, Worthington Papers; L. Wildman to Kilbourne, March 12, 1814, Kilbourne Papers; John Cleves Short to Ethan Allen Brown, Ethan Allen Brown Papers, Ohio Historical Society; Adlard Welby, *A Visit to North America*, in *Early Western Travels, 1748–1846*, ed. Reuben G. Thwaites (Cleveland: A. H. Clark Co., 1904), 12:227. See also Goodwin Berquist and Paul C. Bowers, *The New Eden: James Kilbourne and the Development of Ohio* (Lanham, Md.: University Press of America, 1983).

[19] Buley, *Old Northwest* 1:125.

[20] Ibid., 123, 124.

[21] A. Bourne to Paul Fearing, July 27, 1811, Fearing Papers; Gilman and Fearing to David Humphreys, April 24, 1810, Hildreth Papers; Deming, Autobiography, Moses Deming Papers, Ohio Historical Society.

[22] Utter, *Frontier State*, 270–71; and Mary Lou Conlin, *Simon Perkins of the Western Reserve* (Cleveland: Western Reserve Historical Society, 1968), 66–74.

[23] Morrow to Worthington, December 24, 1814, Worthington Papers.

[24] William Irwin to James Findlay, March 20, 1814, Torrence Papers; Strickland, *Rev. James B. Finley*, 273.

25 Joseph Kerr to Worthington, November 16, 1814, Worthington Papers.

26 "The United States Bank," May 30, 1816, *Muskingum Messenger.*

27 John Evans to Worthington, August 26, 1816, Worthington Papers; *Western Spy,* September 20, 1816.

28 Worthington to William Jones, November 20, 1816, Worthington Papers. On the branch directors, see Chandler Price to Worthington, October 13, 1817, ibid.; and *Western Spy,* February 20, 1819.

29 "The Ohio Legislature v. Unchartered Banks," *Muskingum Messenger,* January 8, 1816; Sears, *Thomas Worthington,* 199.

30 Utter, *Frontier State,* 270–73.

31 *Western Spy,* September 13 and 27, 1816; Worth, " 'Recollections,' " 26, 27, 30, 27.

32 "Lancelot Wronghead," *Western Spy,* March 7, 1817.

33 "An Observer," *Liberty Hall and Cincinnati Gazette,* March 3, 1817; "A Citizen," *Muskingum Messenger,* December 12, 1816.

34 Dickore, *General Joseph Kerr,* 41–74, 83–89, 97–103.

35 Kerr to Worthington, October 14, 1814, Worthington Papers. On banking and attitudes toward banking, see Hammond, *Banks and Politics;* and Buley, *Old Northwest* 1:565–88.

36 "Our Governor—Again," *Western Spy,* November 15, 1816; Sears, *Thomas Worthington,* 200–202.

37 Thomas Rotch to Worthington, January 15, 1817, Worthington Papers.

38 "Cato," *Muskingum Messenger,* January 16, 1817; "Equal Rights," ibid., February 6, 1817; and "Hampden," ibid., March 20, 1817.

39 See E. L. Bogart, "Taxation of the Second Bank of the United States by Ohio," *American Historical Review* 17 (1912): 312–31.

40 "Town Meeting," *Western Spy,* August 30, 1816; "The Delegation System," *Muskingum Messenger,* October 24, 1816.

41 *Western Spy,* November 1, 1816; "Farmers and Mechanics," *Zanesville Express and Republican Standard,* October 5, 1815.

42 Wade, *Urban Frontier,* 171; William Greene to Abby Lyman, October 23, 1820, Greene-Roelker Papers, Cincinnati Historical Society.

43 James Flint, *Letters from America,* in Thwaites, *Early Western Travels* 9:238; Drake to Edward Mansfield, April 21, [1819?], Jared Mansfield Papers, Ohio Historical Society. On the Panic of 1819, see Hammond, *Banks and Politics,* 257–85; Samuel Rezneck, "The Depression of 1819–1822, A Social History," *American Historical Review* 39 (1933–34), 28–47; Greer, "Economic and Social Effects of the Depression"; Murray N. Rothbard, *The Panic of 1819: Reactions and Policies* (New York: Columbia University Press, 1962); Buley, *Old Northwest* 1:565–88; and Dangerfield, *Era of Good Feelings,* 175–96.

44 Edward D. Mansfield, *Memoirs of the Life and Services of Daniel Drake, M.D.* (Cincinnati, 1855), 132–34, 102–5, 115–19, 135–37; J. L. Wilson to R. Boal, Jr., May 12, 1818, in W. W. Sweet, ed., *Religion on the American Frontier* (New York: Harper and Brothers, 1936), vol. 2, *The Presbyterians,* 731–32; Charles Sealsfield, *The Americans as They Are* (London, 1828), 5.

45 "A Friend to the Poor," quoted in Wade, *Urban Frontier,* 172.

46 Buley, *The Old Northwest* 1:129; S. S. Tomlinson, quoted in W. H. Hunter, "The Pathfinders of Jefferson County," *Ohio Archaeological and Historical Society Publications* 6 (1898): 255.

47 Volume 29, Duncan McArthur Papers, Manuscripts Division, Library of Congress, passim.

⁴⁸ Hibbard, *History of Public Land Policies*, 94. See also Rohrbough, *Land Office Business*, 137–56.

9   Conflict and Consensus, 1819–1824

¹ *Cleaveland Register*, December 29, 1818, quoted in Buley, *Old Northwest* 1:589–90.

² See Ellis, *The Jeffersonian Crisis*, 277–84; Robert V. Remini, *Andrew Jackson and the Course of American Freedom, 1822–1832* (New York: Harper and Row, 1981), 12–38; Robert Kelley, *The Cultural Pattern in American Politics: The First Century* (New York: Alfred A. Knopf, 1979), 160–66; McCoy, *Elusive Republic*, 248–59; and Robert Dawidoff, *The Education of John Randolph* (New York: W. W. Norton, 1979). The best discussion of Ohio politics in the early 1820s is Donald J. Ratcliffe, "The Role of Voters and Issues in Party Formation: Ohio, 1824," *Journal of American History* 59 (1979): 847–71.

³ *Liberty Hall*, November 17, 1818; John McLean to Ethan Allen Brown, January 9, 1819, Brown Papers.

⁴ See E. L. Bogart, "Taxation of the Second Bank," 312–31; Buley, *Old Northwest* 1:588–94; and Utter, *The Frontier State*, 302–12.

⁵ William Jones to Thomas Worthington, November 25, 1818, Worthington Papers. See also Hammond, *Banks and Politics in America*, 251–85.

⁶ Wilson in *Western Herald and Steubenville Gazette*, March 20, 1819, quoted in Utter, *Frontier State*, 302.

⁷ Utter, *Frontier State*, 306–7.

⁸ Ibid., 309. See also Buley, *Old Northwest* 1:590–91.

⁹ Utter, *Frontier State*, 311–12. See also Buley, *Old Northwest* 1:591–94.

¹⁰ See Ratcliffe, "Experience of Revolution," 186–230.

¹¹ See Ratcliffe, "Role of Voters and Issues in Party Formation," passim.

¹² Ibid., 850, 865.

¹³ Ibid., 860. See also Stephen C. Fox, "Politicians, Issues and Voter Preference in Jacksonian Ohio: A Critique of an Interpretation," *Ohio History* 86 (1977): 155–70; Donald J. Ratcliffe, "Politics in Jacksonian Ohio: Reflections on the Ethnocultural Interpretation," *Ohio History* 88 (1979): 5–36; and Stevens, *Early Jackson Party*.

¹⁴ "Radical Reform," *Western Spy*, August 17, 1820; and "Reform of the Banks," *Western Spy*, September 7, 1820.

¹⁵ See Utter, *Frontier State*, 310; Stevens, *Early Jackson Party*, 21–28, 43–47; and Aaron, "Cincinnati," 77.

¹⁶ Ratcliffe, "Role of Voters and Issues in Party Formation," passim; Stevens, *Early Jackson Party*, passim.

¹⁷ H. D. Ward to Ephraim Cutler, April 14, 1824, in J. P. Cutler, *Ephraim Cutler*, 189.

¹⁸ William Greene to Ethan Allen Brown, January 12, 1824, Brown Papers; John C. Wright to Cutler, January 12, 1824, in J. P. Cutler, *Ephraim Cutler*, 186.

¹⁹ Ratcliffe, "Role of Voters and Issues in Party Formation," 853; Stevens, *Early Jackson Party*, 137–42.

²⁰ Allen Trimble to Duncan McArthur, December 22, 1824, McArthur Papers; John Johnston to Brown, December 15, 1824, Brown Papers.

²¹ See Michael Wallace, "Changing Concepts of Party in the United States: New York, 1815–1828," *American Historical Review* 74 (1968): 453–91; Richard Hofstadter, *The Idea of a Party System* (Berkeley: University of California Press, 1970), esp. 212–71; Marvin Meyers,

The Jacksonian Persuasion (Stanford: Stanford University Press, 1957); Arthur M. Schlesinger, Jr., *The Age of Jackson* (Boston: Little, Brown, 1945); Lee Benson, *The Concept of Jacksonian Democracy* (Princeton: Princeton University Press, 1961); and Lynn Marshall, "The Strange Still-Birth of the Whig Party," *American Historical Review* 72 (1967): 445–68.

22 Donald G. Mathews, "The Second Great Awakening as an Organizing Process, 1780–1830: An Hypothesis," *American Quarterly* 21 (1969): 27. See also T. Scott Miyakawa, *Protestants and Pioneers: Individualism and Conformity on the American Frontier* (Chicago: University of Chicago Press, 1964); Paul Johnson, *A Shopkeeper's Millenium: Society and Revivals in Rochester, New York, 1815–1837* (New York: Hill and Wang, 1978); and Doyle, *Social Order of a Frontier Community.*

23 George Turner, *An Oration, Pronounced Before the Washington Benevolent Society of the County of Washington, State of Ohio, On the 22d, February, 1817* (Marietta, 1817), 5; Daniel Drake, "Address Before the Cincinnati Lyceum," 1807, Torrence Papers. See also Henry D. Shapiro and Zane L. Miller, eds., *Physician to the West: Selected Writings of Daniel Drake on Science and Society* (Lexington: University Press of Kentucky, 1970).

24 "Oration by Nathaniel Wright, esq., on the 4th instant," *Western Spy,* July 11, 1818; *Western Spy,* July 4, 1818.

25 *Liberty Hall,* December 30, 1816; "Local," *Western Spy,* August 2, 1816; and "Oration Delivered by Bellamy Storer, Esq. at the First Presbyterian Church in Cincinnati, on Monday the 5th instant," *Western Spy,* July 10, 1819.

26 Samuel Robbins, *An Address to "The Society in Marietta for the Promotion of Good Morals," Delivered at their Annual Meeting, June 5th, 1815* (Marietta, 1815), 10, 11, 10.

27 Ephraim Cutler, *An Oration, Delivered Before the Washington Benevolent Society, at Marietta, on the 22nd of February, 1814* (Zanesville, 1814), 4.

28 Utter, *Frontier State,* 384.

29 Aaron, "Cincinnati," 155, 273, 253–80, and Appendix. See also Harry Stevens, "Bank Enterprisers in a Western Town, 1815–1822," *Business History Review* 29 (1955): 139–156.

30 Walter Glazer, "Voluntary Associations in Cincinnati," *Historical Methods Newsletter* 5 (1972): 158, 155, 156.

31 John S. Still, "Ethan Allen Brown and Ohio's Canal System," *Ohio Historical Quarterly* 66 (1957): 22–56; and Harry N. Scheiber, "Entrepreneurship and Western Development: The Case of Micajah T. Williams," *Business History Review* 37 (1963): 345.

32 See Harry N. Scheiber, "Alfred Kelley and the Ohio Business Elite, 1822–1859," *Ohio History* 87 (1978): 365–92; J. L. Bates, *Alfred Kelley* (Columbus, 1888); and J. P. Cutler, *Ephraim Cutler,* passim.

33 Scheiber, "Alfred Kelley," 367, 366. See also Harry N. Scheiber, *Ohio Canal Era: A Case Study of Government and the Economy, 1820–1861* (Athens, Ohio: Ohio University Press, 1969).

34 John Quincy Adams quoted in Dangerfield, *Era of Good Feelings,* 348. Not all of the men who supported internal improvements in Ohio in the early 1820s became Whigs in the 1830s. Still, their ideological viewpoints had much in common with the ideology described in Daniel Walker Howe, *The Political Culture of the American Whigs* (Chicago: University of Chicago Press, 1979), esp. 11–42; and Thomas Brown, *Politics and Statesmanship: Essays on the American Whig Party* (New York: Columbia University Press, 1985), esp. 1–21, 215–9.

35 "Ohio Convention," Committee Report, House of Representatives, January, 1819, *Western Spy,* July 31, 1819.

36 James Wilson to Brown, March 4, 1819, Brown Papers. See also "The Election," *Scioto Gazette and Fredonian Chronicle,* October 2, 1818.

[37] Thomas Worthington to the General Assembly, December 5, 1815, Worthington Papers; "Poor House," *Liberty Hall,* November 20, 1815.

[38] George W. Knight, *History and Management of Land Grants for Education in the Northwest Territory* (New York, 1885), 114–36, 229–37; Rufus Putnam to Paul Fearing, November 20, 1800, Fearing Papers.

[39] Samuel Huntington, "Address to the Legislature," December 4, 1810, *Journal of the House, Ninth General Assembly,* 10; "Inaugural Address of Return Jonathan Meigs," December 4, 1810, ibid., 44.

[40] "Articles of Association of the Cincinnati Lancaster Seminary," *Liberty Hall,* March 8, 1814. See also Drake, *Natural and Statistical View, or Picture of Cincinnati and the Miami Country,* 154–60.

[41] "Articles of the Seminary," *Liberty Hall,* March 8, 1814.

[42] "Bacon," *Western Spy,* February 21, January 24, and January 31, 1817. See also Lawrence Cremin, *American Education: The National Experience, 1783–1816* (New York: Harper and Row, 1980); Carl F. Kaestle, *Pillars of the Republic: Common Schools and American Society, 1780–1860* (New York: Hill and Wang, 1983), esp. 3–61; and Michael B. Katz, *The Irony of Early School Reform: Educational Innovation in Mid-Nineteenth Century Massachusetts* (Cambridge: Harvard University Press, 1968).

[43] "For the Spy," *Western Spy,* June 6, 1817.

[44] "Q," *Western Spy,* June 13, 1817.

[45] Ibid.

[46] *Western Spy,* November 14, 1818; "Solon," ibid., August 15, 1818.

[47] "E," *Western Spy,* June 27, 1817; Edward D. Mansfield, *Memoirs of the Life and Services of Daniel Drake, M.D.* (Cincinnati, 1855), 106–7, 134–35.

[48] Worthington quoted in Sears, *Thomas Worthington,* 206–7.

[49] *Western Spy,* October 3, and August 22, 1818.

[50] "Thoughts on Education," *Western Spy,* July 17, 1819.

[51] "Robert Raikes," *Western Spy,* July 27, 1822.

[52] "A Public Dinner," *Western Spy,* August 31, 1822; J. P. Cutler, *Ephraim Cutler,* 114–15, 120; "Report of the House of Representative's Committee on School Lands," January 30, 1822, quoted in Atwater, *History of the State of Ohio,* 256.

[53] See note 4, chapter 5.

[54] Cutler to William Rufus Putnam, January 22, 1825, Hildreth Papers; J. P. Cutler, *Ephraim Cutler,* 171, 129, 135–43. See also Atwater, *Ohio,* 257–62; and Utter, *Frontier State,* 319–21.

[55] My discussion of the Ohio Canal movement is heavily indebted to the superb study of Harry N. Scheiber, *Ohio Canal Era.* The classic book on internal improvements in the early nineteenth century is George Rogers Taylor, *The Transportation Revolution, 1815–1860* (New York: Rinehart, 1951). See also Ronald E. Shaw, "Canals in the Early Republic: A Review of Recent Literature," *Journal of the Early Republic* 4 (1984): 117–42.

[56] "Navigation of the Ohio," *Liberty Hall,* September 4, 1815.

[57] Worthington to the General Assembly, December 5, 1815, Worthington Papers.

[58] "For the Spy," *Western Spy,* August 15, 1818, V; *Western Spy,* August 1, 1818.

[59] Message of Governor Ethan Allen Brown, January 8, 1819, John Kilbourn, comp., *Public Documents Concerning the Ohio Canals* (Columbus, 1832), 4.

[60] Message of Governor Ethan Allen Brown, December 7, 1819, ibid.

[61] William Steele to Brown, December 16, 1820, Brown Papers.

[62] Brown to Jonathan Dayton, February 4, 1821, Brown Papers; Report of Committee on

Canals, Ohio House of Representatives, January 3, 1822, Kilbourn, *Public Documents,* 22. See also Scheiber, *Ohio Canal Era.*

[63] Report of the Committee on Canals, Journal of the House of Representatives, January 3, 1822, Kilbourn, *Public Documents,* 26, 27.

[64] Report of Committee on Canals, January 21, 1824, ibid., 75.

[65] Alfred Kelley to Brown, February 23, 1824, Brown Papers.

[66] Atwater, *Ohio,* 263, 264.

Conclusion: "Ohio Has Behaved Nobly at Last"

[1] "Commencement of the Ohio Canal at the Licking Summit," *Ohio Archaeological and Historical Quarterly* 34 (1925): 66–99.

[2] Clinton quoted in "Press Notices of Governor Clinton's Visit to Ohio," *Ohio Archaeological and Historical Quarterly* 34 (1925): 107.

[3] Thomas Ewing quoted in "Commencement of the Ohio Canal," 87–88.

[4] *National Intelligencer,* February 15, 1825, quoted in Still, "Ethan Allen Brown and Ohio's Canal System," 41, 42; Clinton to Ethan Allen Brown, February 17, 1825, ibid., 42.

Essay on Sources

Since interested readers can find the sources I have consulted in writing this book in the extensive notes appended to the text, I intend this brief essay to be a selective rather than an exhaustive guide to the primary and secondary sources on the history of frontier Ohio.

Unpublished Sources

The best place for students of early Ohio to begin is in the manuscript collections of the Ohio Historical Society, located in the Ohio Historical Center in Columbus. The Arthur St. Clair Papers and the Winthrop Sargent Papers (as well as the Sargent Papers in the Massachusetts Historical Society in Boston) deal extensively with the territorial period. Also of primary importance are the Papers of Thomas Worthington, a goldmine of letters from correspondents throughout the state in the first two decades of the nineteenth century. Worthington's papers contain comments on a wide range of men and issues and would be of interest to anyone concerned with the organization of political power in the early American republic.

Not as extensive but of considerable value are the papers of several of Worthington's prominent allies and enemies. They include the Edward Tiffin Papers, the Samuel Huntington Papers, the Nathaniel Massie Papers, as well as the Records of the Chillicothe Wigwam of the Tammany Society. For the period after the War of 1812, the Ethan Allen Brown Papers, the Alfred Kelley Papers, the Duncan McArthur Papers, and the Micajah T. Williams Papers are especially valuable. Other collections of interest at the Ohio Historical Society are the Othniel Looker Papers, the Thomas Kirker Papers, the John Sloane Papers, the James Denny Papers, the John Fuller Papers, the Jeremiah Morrow Papers, the James Kilbourne Papers, the Jared Mansfield Papers, and the Edward D. Mansfield Papers. The Backus-Wood-bridge Papers contain the letters of an enterprising family from Connecticut; many of them focus on their efforts to establish a mercantile business in Marietta in the 1790s and the early 1800s.

In the 1970s, the Ohio Historical Society put the papers of thirteen early Ohio political leaders on microfilm, including those of St. Clair, Sargent, Worthington, Massie, and Tiffin. The extremely valuable guide to these collections is Linda Elise Kalette, *The Papers of Thirteen Early Ohio Political Leaders: An Inventory to the 1976–1977 Microfilm Editions* (Columbus: Ohio Historical Society, 1977).

The Dawes Memorial Library at Marietta College houses an extensive collection of works on the early history of Ohio, with special emphasis on Marietta. Students of politics will find much of interest regarding the statehood controversy in the Paul Fearing Papers; those concerned with the general history of the Ohio Company and the Marietta settlement will want to consult the Rufus Putnam Papers, the Cutler Collection, and the Samuel Prescott Hildreth Papers. Also of value regarding early Marietta are the Drowne Papers in the Rhode Island Historical Society, Providence.

At the Cincinnati Historical Society, the early collections are chiefly of use as points of entry into the society and progress of that settlement. Especially worthwhile are the Torrence Collection, the Jacob Burnet Papers, the William Hatch Papers (which contain an interesting memoir of life in early nineteenth-century Cincinnati), the John Smith Papers (which contain much of value regarding the Burr Conspiracy), the Greene-Roelker Papers (especially the letters of William Greene to his fiancée in Rhode Island in the late 1810s describing Ohio and the opportunities available to him), the Bates Family Papers, the Kemper Family Papers, and the David K. Este and Family Papers.

The Thomas Worthington Papers (largely a fascinating personal diary) and the Duncan McArthur Papers in the Manuscripts Division of the Library of Congress should also be consulted, as should the Caleb Emerson Family Papers, the John May Papers, and the Samuel Huntington Papers at the Western Reserve Historical Society Library in Cleveland.

Published Sources

Newspapers are invaluable sources. The only paper in the Northwest Territory in the 1790s was *The Centinel of the North-Western Territory;* published in Cincinnati, it was a strong opponent of the territorial government. After 1800, newspapers appeared in many of the major cities in the state. Among the most valuable are the *Chillicothe Scioto Gazette,* the *Chillicothe Supporter,* the *Chillicothe Fredonian,* the *Cincinnati Western Spy and Hamilton Gazette,* the *Cincinnati Liberty Hall,* the *Zanesville Muskingum Messenger,* the *Zanesville Express and Republican Standard,* the *St. Clairsville Ohio Federalist,* the *American Friend and Marietta Ga-*

zette, the *Chillicothe Independent Republican,* the *Chillicothe Ohio Herald,* and the *Marietta Western Spectator.*

The major theme of the historiography of frontier Ohio before the 1920s was a debate among descendants and admirers of the various early settlers. The question was who should receive the credit for shaping Ohio into a great state; the weapons were the papers (usually selectively edited) of the most controversial figures. The end result was a preoccupation with local and genealogical boosterism which begat parochialism. As Carl Wittke noted in 1941 in his "Editor's Introduction" to the six volume *History of the State of Ohio* (Ohio Historical Society), Ohio's historians had too often exalted "local pride at the sacrifice of impartial, scholarly judgment and method."

The first historians of early Ohio were intent upon emphasizing the influence of New Englanders and Federalists; consequently, they tended to discuss the Northwest Ordinance, the founding of Marietta, and the roots of antislavery, public education, and civil morality most fully. Their works included Jacob Burnet, *Notes on the Early Settlement of the North-Western Territory* (Cincinnati: D. Appleton, 1847), a semiautobiographical account by an early resident of Cincinnati who died a proud old-school Federalist; *Pioneer History* (Cincinnati: H. W. Derby, 1848) and *Biographical and Historical Memoirs of the Early Pioneer Settlers of Ohio* (Cincinnati: H. W. Derby, 1852) by Samuel Prescott Hildreth, a longtime resident of Marietta and an admirer of Rufus Putnam and his Ohio Company colleagues; Caleb Atwater, *A History of the State of Ohio, Natural and Civil* (Cincinnati: Glezen and Shepard, 1838), which is especially interesting on the public school and canal movements of the 1820s; William Smith, *The St. Clair Papers: The Life and Public Services of Arthur St. Clair,* 2 vols. (Cincinnati: Robert Clarke, 1882); and the works of the tireless descendants of Manasseh and Ephraim Cutler, William Parker Cutler and Julia Perkins Cutler, *Life, Journals, and Correspondence of the Rev. Manasseh Cutler, LL. D.* 2 vols. (Cincinnati: Robert Clarke, 1888), and Julia P. Cutler, *Life and Times of Ephraim Cutler* (Cincinnati: Robert Clarke, 1890). Since most of these works were largely compilations of letters and speeches, they tended to echo the positions and attitudes of their subjects.

Southern-born immigrants and the opponents of the territorial government were not without their admirers, however. They included the Rev. Dr. Joseph Doddridge, "Notes on the Settlement and Indian Wars of the Western Parts of Virginia and Pennsylvania, From the year 1763 until the year 1783 inclusive," in Samuel Kercheval, *A History of the Valley of Virginia* (Woodstock, Va.: John Gatewood, 1850), 164–263; W. H. Hunter, "The Pathfinders of Jefferson County," *Ohio Archaeological and Historical Society Publications* 6 (1898): 96–313; John McDonald, *Biographical Sketches of General Nathaniel Massie, General Duncan McArthur, Captain William Wells, and General Simon Kenton* (Dayton: D. Osborn and Son, 1852); John A. McClung, *Sketches of Western Adventure* (Louisville: Richard H. Collins, 1879); *Autobiography of Rev. James B. Finley: or Pioneer Life in the West,* ed. W. P. Strickland (Cincinnati: Methodist Book Concern, 1854); James B. Finley, *Sketches of Western Methodism,* ed. W. P. Strickland (Cincinnati:

Essay on Sources

Methodist Book Concern, 1854); William E. Gilmore, *The Life of Edward Tiffin, First Governor of Ohio* (Chillicothe: Horney and Son, 1897); and David Meade Massie, *Nathaniel Massie, a Pioneer of Ohio* (Cincinnati: Robert Clarke, 1896). The most scholarly corrective to the emphasis on New England influence in the settlement of Ohio was Robert E. Chaddock, *Ohio Before 1850: A Study of the Early Influence of Pennsylvania and Southern Populations in Ohio* (New York: Columbia University Press, 1908).

In the first half of the twentieth century, a number of professional historians produced fine studies of frontier Ohio. One of the first was Archer Butler Hulbert, a professor of history at Marietta College, who provided the most accurate and thorough account of the Ohio Company in his introduction to *The Records of the Original Proceedings of the Ohio Company,* ed. Archer Butler Hulbert, 2 vols. (Marietta: Marietta Historical Commission, 1917). Even more important in bringing balance and scholarly standards to the history of early Ohio was Beverley W. Bond, Jr., a Virginia-born professor of history at the University of Cincinnati. Bond's most important works are *The Civilization of the Old Northwest: A Study of Political, Social, and Economic Development, 1788–1812* (New York: Macmillan, 1934); *The Foundations of Ohio* (Columbus: Ohio State Archaeological and Historical Society, 1941); *The Correspondence of John Cleves Symmes, Founder of the Miami Purchase,* ed. Beverley W. Bond, Jr. (New York: Macmillan for the Historical and Philosophical Society of Ohio, 1926); and *The Intimate Letters of John Cleves Symmes and His Family,* ed. Beverley W. Bond, Jr. (Cincinnati: Historical and Philosophical Society of Ohio, 1956). Bond's studies are long on detail and short on interpretation. Nonetheless, they are reliable accounts that sought to put the history of the Ohio Country into the larger context of American development. Another valuable collection of papers published in this period is Clarence E. Carter, ed., *The Territorial Papers of the United States,* 26 vols. (Washington, D.C.: Government Printing Office, 1934).

Other historians working between 1920 and the 1950s wrote important monographs, most of them developing, to one degree or another, the frontier thesis of Frederick Jackson Turner. The best of these is Randolph Downes, *Frontier Ohio, 1788–1803* (Columbus: Ohio State Archaeological and Historical Society, 1935), a lively and insightful narrative. Also valuable are the works of William T. Utter, especially *The Frontier State, 1803–1825* (Columbus: Ohio State Archaeological and Historical Society, 1942); James M. Miller, *The Genesis of Western Culture: The Upper Ohio Valley, 1800–1825* (Columbus: Ohio State Archaeological and Historical Society, 1938); and William T. Hutchinson, "The Bounty Lands of the American Revolution in Ohio" (Ph.D. diss., University of Chicago, 1927). The capstones to thirty years of significant work were R. Carlyle Buley's masterful and encyclopedic *The Old Northwest: Pioneer Period, 1815–1840* (Bloomington: Indiana University Press, 1950); the straightforward Turnerian overview of John D. Barnhart, *Valley of Democracy: The Frontier versus the Plantation in the Ohio Valley, 1775–1818* (Lincoln: University of Nebraska Press, 1953); and Stanley Elkins and Eric McKitrick, "A Meaning for Turner's Frontier: Democracy in the Old Northwest," *Political Science Quarterly* 69 (1954): 321–53. Elkins and McKitrick's article is highly theoretical; but it is more suggestive than any other work I know on the Old Northwest.

These works brought the Turnerian period of frontier Ohio historiography to a climax—and a cul-de-sac. Significant works have appeared in the last three decades, but no overall interpretative framework has displaced that of Turner. The best evidence of this is the fact that the studies of Buley, Bond, Barnhart, and Downes remain the standard works on the period. Readers interested in early Ohio will find much of value in two collections of articles: *The Old Northwest in the American Revolution: An Anthology*, ed. David Curtis Skaggs (Madison: State Historical Society of Wisconsin, 1977) and *The American Territorial System*, ed. John Porter Bloom (Athens: Ohio University Press, 1973). Other works of interest include, Mary Lou Conlin, *Simon Perkins of the Western Reserve* (Cleveland: Western Reserve Historical Society, 1968); Alfred Byron Sears's sound biography of *Thomas Worthington: Father of Ohio Statehood* (Columbus: Ohio Historical Society, 1958); Harry R. Stevens, *The Early Jackson Party in Ohio* (Durham, N.C.: Duke University Press, 1957); John Theodore Grupenhoff, "Politics and the Rise of Political Parties in the Northwest Territory and Early Ohio to 1812, with an Emphasis on Cincinnati and Hamilton County" (Ph.D. diss., University of Texas-Austin, 1962); Stephen Carey Fox, "The Group Bases of Ohio Political Behavior, 1804–1848" (Ph.D. diss., University of Cincinnati, 1973); Ellen S. Wilson, "Speculators and Land Development in the Virginia Military Tract: The Territorial Period" (Ph.D. diss., Miami University, 1982); and Malcolm Rohrbough's excellent survey of *The Trans-Appalachian Frontier: People, Societies, and Institutions, 1775–1850* (New York: Oxford University Press, 1978). Jeffrey P. Brown's article, "The Ohio Federalists, 1803–1815," *Journal of the Early Republic* 2 (1982): 261–82, based on his thorough and extremely useful reconstruction of early Ohio politics in his dissertation, "Frontier Politics: The Evolution of a Political Society in Ohio, 1788–1814" (Ph.D. diss., University of Illinois at Urbana, 1979), should also be consulted.

The most stimulating and influential books published in the last three decades are Richard Wade, *The Urban Frontier: Pioneer Life in Early Pittsburgh, Cincinnati, Lexington, Louisville, and St. Louis* (Cambridge: Harvard University Press, 1959), and Harry N. Scheiber's *Ohio Canal Era: A Case Study of Government and the Economy, 1820–1861* (Athens: Ohio University Press, 1969). An article more directly concerned with the issues discussed in this book is Donald Ratcliffe, "The Experience of Revolution and the Beginnings of Party Politics in Ohio, 1776–1816," *Ohio History* 85 (1976): 186–230; this piece is a pioneering effort to reintegrate the history of frontier Ohio politics with larger trends in American historiography, particularly the revisionist interpretation of the political culture of the Early Republic prompted by the discovery of republicanism in Bernard Bailyn, *The Ideological Origins of the American Revolution* (Cambridge: Belknap Press, 1967) and Gordon S. Wood, *The Creation of the American Republic, 1776–1787* (Chapel Hill: University of North Carolina Press for the Institute of Early American History, 1969). (The literature on republicanism which mushroomed in the 1970s is reviewed in two articles by Robert Shalhope, "Toward a Republican Synthesis: The Emergence of an Understanding of Republicanism in American Historiography," *William and Mary Quarterly*, 3d ser., 29 (1972): 48–80, and "Republicanism and Early American Historiography," *William and Mary Quarterly*, 3d ser., 39 (1982): 334–56.)

Implicitly, Ratcliffe was pointing historians of early Ohio toward a revitalization and reexamination of frontier politics in the light of developments in the intellectual and political history of the United States as a whole. Too often, Ohio historians have treated their subject in isolation from both the cultures in which frontier settlers were born and raised and the larger issues in the historiography of the early American republic. It is worth remembering that the entire nation in the 1780s and 1790s was a frontier in the sense that there was no clear consensus about legitimate behavior or values. From this perspective, the ideological controversies in early Ohio become "hothouse" versions of the general confusion and conflict in America after the Revolution.

One cannot, for example, fully appreciate the actions and rhetoric of the territorial hierarchy in the 1790s without understanding the larger goals of the men who created and put in motion the federal government at the same time. Basic studies of the Federalist persuasion can be found in Wood, *Creation of the American Republic;* Gerald Stourzh, *Alexander Hamilton and the Idea of Republican Government* (Stanford: Stanford University Press, 1970); John R. Murrin, "The Great Inversion, or Court versus Country: A Comparison of the Revolution Settlements in England (1688–1721) and America (1776–1816)," in *Three British Revolutions: 1641, 1688, 1776*, ed. J. G. A. Pocock (Princeton: Princeton University Press, 1980), 368–453; Richard H. Kohn, *Eagle and Sword: The Federalists and the Creation of the Military Establishment in America, 1783–1802* (New York: Free Press, 1975); Linda Kerber, *Federalists in Dissent: Imagery and Ideology in Jeffersonian America* (Ithaca, N.Y.: Cornell University Press, 1970); and David Hackett Fischer, *The Revolution of American Conservatism: The Federalist Party in the Era of Jeffersonian Democracy* (New York: Harper and Row, 1965). Along similar lines, the forthcoming work by Peter S. Onuf on the Northwest Ordinance will add greatly to our understanding of the evolution of a national policy regarding the West in the 1780s and the 1790s.

The ideology of Ohio's Jeffersonian Republicans takes on greater significance and clarity when analyzed in the larger context of Jeffersonian Republicanism developed by Lance Banning, *The Jeffersonian Persuasion: Evolution of a Party Ideology* (Ithaca, N.Y.: Cornell University Press, 1978); Drew R. McCoy, *The Elusive Republic: Political Economy in Jeffersonian America* (Chapel Hill: University of North Carolina Press for the Institute of Early American History, 1980); and Forrest McDonald, *The Presidency of Thomas Jefferson* (Lawrence, Kansas: University of Kansas Press, 1976).

The ongoing work of Joyce Appleby into the origins of a "liberal" counterpart to republicanism is especially valuable in interpreting the rhetoric of Ohio's Jeffersonian gentry. See, Appleby, *Capitalism and a New Social Order: The Republican Vision of the 1790s* (New York: New York University Press, 1984); Isaac Kramnick, "Republican Revisions Revisted," *American Historical Review* 87 (1982): 629–64; and John P. Diggins's idiosyncratic but provocative critique of the republican paradigm, *The Lost Soul of American Politics: Virtue, Self-Interest, and the Foundations of Liberalism* (New York: Basic Books, 1985).

On the Jeffersonian Republicans in power, Richard E. Ellis, *The Jeffersonian Crisis: Courts and Politics in the Young Republic* (New York: Oxford University Press, 1971); Fischer, *Revolution in American Conservatism;* and Ronald P. Formisano, "Deferential-Participant Politics: The Early Republic's Political Culture, 1789-1840," *American Political Science Review* 68 (1974): 473–87, are indispensable.

Of the states adjacent to Ohio, Kentucky had been the one most blessed with enterprising political historians in recent years. See the excellent studies by Patricia Watlington, *The Partisan Spirit: Kentucky Politics, 1774–1792* (New York: Atheneum for the Institute of Early American History, 1972); Mary K. Bonsteel Tachau, *Federal Courts in the Early Republic: Kentucky, 1789–1816* (Princeton: Princeton University Press, 1978); Tachau, "The Whiskey Rebellion in Kentucky: Forgotten Episode of Civil Disobedience," *Journal of the Early Republic* 2 (1982): 239–59; and Joan Wells Coward, *Politics in the New Republic: The Process of Constitution Making* (Lexington: University Press of Kentucky, 1979).

While this book could hardly be described as a work of social history, I have benefitted from reading several studies of other frontier areas in the Early Republic. Historians of frontier Ohio have only begun to investigate the history of women, blacks, Indian-white relationships (other than military), and ordinary farmers and hunters; any one of the studies listed below would serve as an excellent model for similar work on the Ohio Country. They include (from west to north to south of Ohio): Don Harrison Doyle, *The Social Order of a Frontier Community: Jacksonville, Illinois, 1825–1870* (Urbana: University of Illinois Press, 1978); Paul Johnson, *A Shopkeeper's Millenium: Society and Revivals in Rochester, New York, 1815–1837* (New York: Hill and Wang, 1978); Mary P. Ryan, *Cradle of the Middle Class: The Family in Oneida County, New York, 1790–1865* (Cambridge: Cambridge University Press, 1981); Stephen A. Marini, *Radical Sects of Revolutionary New England* (Cambridge: Harvard University Press, 1982); Richard R. Beeman, *The Evolution of the Southern Backcountry: A Case Study of Lunenburg County, Virginia, 1764–1832* (Philadelphia: University of Pennsylvania Press, 1984); *An Uncivil War: The Southern Backcountry during the American Revolution,* ed. Ronald Hoffman, Thad W. Tate, and Peter J. Albert (Charlottesville: University Press of Virginia, 1985); Robert Mitchell, *Commercialism and Frontier: Perspectives on the Early Shenandoah Valley* (Charlottesville: University Press of Virginia, 1977); Juliet E. K. Walker, *Free Frank: A Black Pioneer on the Antebellum Frontier* (Lexington: University Press of Kentucky, 1983); and Daniel H. Usner, Jr., "American Indians on the Cotton Frontier: Changing Economic Relations with Citizens and Slaves in the Mississippi Territory," *Journal of American History* 72 (1985): 297–317.

Finally, general studies of significance for historians of frontier Ohio include Alfred F. Young, ed., *The American Revolution: Explorations in the History of American Radicalism* (DeKalb: Northern Illinois University Press, 1976); W. J. Rorabaugh, *The Alcoholic Republic: An American Tradition* (New York: Oxford University Press, 1979); Robert Wiebe, *The Opening of American Society: From the Adoption of the Constitution to the Eve of Disunion* (New York: Alfred A. Knopf, 1984); James Henretta, "Families and Farms: *Mentalité* in Pre-Industrial America," *William and Mary Quarterly* 3d ser., 35 (1978): 3–32; David Brion Davis, *The Problem of Slavery in the Age of Revolution, 1770–1823* (Ithaca, N.Y.: Cornell University Press, 1975); Howard Lamar and Leonard Thompson, eds., *The Frontier in History: North America and Southern Africa Compared* (New Haven: Yale University Press, 1981); Gordon S. Wood, "Evangelical America and Early Mormonism," *New York History* 61 (1980): 359–86; Nathan O. Hatch, "The Christian Movement and the Demand for a Theology of the People," *Journal of American History* 67 (1980): 545–67; Gordon S. Wood, "Conspiracy and the Paranoid Style: Causality and Deceit in the Eighteenth Century," *William and Mary Quarterly,* 3d ser., 39 (1982): 401–41; Thomas P. Slaughter, *The Whiskey Rebellion: Frontier Epilogue to the American Revolution* (New York: Oxford University Press, 1986); and Elliott J. Gorn, " 'Gouge and Bite, Pull Hair and Scratch': The Social Significance of Fighting in the Southern Backcountry," *American Historical Review* 90 (1985): 18–43.

Index

Index